Flower Chronicles

The University of Chicago Press

Chicago & London

FLOWER
CHRONICLES

by E. BUCKNER HOLLINGSWORTH

With a new Foreword by
PETER BERNHARDT

Portions of this book have appeared in the following periodicals and are used with the permission of the copyright owners:

The National Horticultural Magazine: "Nasturtium," October, 1952; "Iris," April, 1953; "Peony," April, 1954; "Lily," April, 1955.
Horticulture: "Prehistoric Flowers," September, 1952.
The Home Garden (now incorporated with *Flower Grower,* the Home Garden Magazine, Literary Guild of America, Inc.): sections of "Lily," July, 1953.
The Bulletin of the Garden Club of America: "Peony, the Food of Kings," March, 1954.
The ten lines from "The Blue in a Bog" on pages 72–73 are taken from *Collected Poems* by Edna St. Vincent Millay, published by Harper & Brothers, Copyright, 1921, 1949.

The University of Chicago Press, Chicago 60637
The University of Chicago Press, Ltd., London
Copyright © 1958, renewed 1986 by Kirk Hollingsworth
Foreword © 2004 by Peter Bernhardt
All rights reserved.
First published in 1958 by Rutgers University Press
University of Chicago Press edition 2004
Printed in the United States of America
11 10 09 08 07 06 05 04   1 2 3 4 5

ISBN: 0-226-34980-2

Library of Congress Cataloging-in-Publication Data

Hollingsworth, Buckner.
    Flower chronicles / by Buckner Hollingsworth ; with a new foreword by Peter Bernhardt. — University of Chicago Press ed.
    p. cm.
    Originally published: New Brunswick, N.J. : Rutgers University Press, c1958.
    Includes bibliographical references.
    ISBN 0-226-34980-2 (pbk. : alk. paper)
    1. Flowers—History. I. Title.

GT5160.H6 2004
582.13—dc22

                                                            2004047896

♾ The Paper used in this publication meets the minimum requirements of the American National Standard for Information Sciences—Permanence of Paper for Printed Library Materials, ANSI Z39.48-1992

For
THREE HOLLINGSWORTHS
WILL
KIRK
JOHN

CONTENTS

ACKNOWLEDGMENTS

The author would like to acknowledge her indebtedness and express her gratitude to:

The Library of Congress; the New York Public Library with special reference to the staffs of the Rare Book Room and the Research Department; the libraries of the Metropolitan Museum of Art; the Wilbour Library of the Brooklyn Museum; the library at the New York Academy of Medicine; the Pierpont Morgan Library; the libraries of both the Horticultural Society of New York and the Massachusetts Horticultural Society, particularly the latter, whose librarian, Miss Dorothy S. Manks, has kept the author supplied with a steady stream of books by mail and has helped with many details of research; the New York State Library at Albany; Baker Library at Dartmouth College, where everyone from the staff at the circulation desk to the research department and administrative officials has been unfailingly generous with help; and to two small village libraries—one at Nyack, New York, and the other at Windsor, Vermont, who have given every facility they had to offer.

Finally, the interest which Mr. James R. Harlow, managing editor of the *National Horticultural Magazine,* the Journal of the American Horticultural Society, has taken in this research has been a steady source of inspiration and encouragement.

The publishers acknowledge with appreciation the assistance of Mrs. E. Enid Grote, librarian of the Horticultural Society of New York, in collecting a number of the illustrations in this book.

FOREWORD

A Garden of Paper and Ink

And don't throw the past away
You might need it some rainy day
Dreams can come true again
When ev'rything old is new again
—Peter Allen & Carole Bayer Sager,
"Everything Old Is New Again"

An older, gentler generation of readers could have complained that
Edith Buckner Hollingsworth (1892–1979) led them down the garden path. There are whole chapters in *Flower Chronicles* (first published by Rutgers University in 1958) that read like elaborate exercises in irony. It was as if the author conducted a tour of a formal
garden and paused to announce, "Oh, isn't this a lovely bed of flowering cosmetics, laundry products, ineffective medicines, obscure
verse, religious artifacts, and puddings?"

We are used to the hypocrisy of politicians, publicists, and public
moralists, so why not expect duplicity in the garden? Most of us are
familiar with the double lives lead by annual poppies (*Papaver som-
niferum*), sprinkling their seeds on bagels while pushing heroin on
street corners. Hollingsworth exposed the romantic rose (*Rosa*) as a
quack pedaling a fake cure for rabies. The iris (*Iris*) was a French
hairdresser catering to such a spendthrift clientele that the coiffures
it helped scent may have contributed to the revolutionary rage of
the poor. Should we regard peonies (*Paeonia*) as forgotten nurse-
maids of teething babies or as doomed Chinese concubines? Hollingsworth offers you a unique image of your own garden. It's really

Foreword

a wealthy retirement community in which the residents conceal their old scandals by supporting popular taste and fashion.

For this reason I have treasured my first edition of *Flower Chronicles* since the late 1960s. It was one of the first "prizes" I found as a teenager one Saturday afternoon in Manhattan while pillaging secondhand bookshops in Greenwich Village. Plenty of copies were available—the sickly yellow, easily crumpled dust jacket featured a crude woodcut that must have deterred impulsive purchases. Who knew that this book would serve me one day as a professor of botany? I even took it to Sydney, Australia, from 1990 to 1992, and it proved invaluable during that time when I was a resident author for the Royal Botanic Gardens and a columnist for *The Sydney Review.* The then director of the Royal Botanic Gardens offered to purchase my copy (fat chance!). Two of my own natural history books published between 1993–2000 used references from *Flower Chronicles* to give historical texture to humanity's long-term exploitation of plants.

Exaggeration is a useful tool in education because people always relate to examples of excess. My students still get to hear Hollingsworth's long list (p. 125) of what one man traded for a single tulip bulb. Drying the tips of the female organs of more than four thousand flowers of *Crocus sativuus* still makes only one ounce of the spice and dyestuff we call saffron (p. 135). Our modern skin-care industry makes such impossible claims that it is easy to understand why people once believed that primrose (*Primula*) ointments could ban wrinkles, freckles, sunburn, and even stop bashful men from blushing (pp. 198–99).

How can a book of "unnatural" history remain so informative? Look at the acknowledgements. Born in Maryland, E. B. Hollingsworth (née Kirk) attended Bryn Mawr College and majored in art history. Her professors' emphasis on the value of scholarly research helped her become the art editor for *Century Magazine,* and also prepared her to write this book. Some sections of *Flower Chronicles*

Foreword

were published separately as magazine articles from 1952 to 1955, which indicates that she spent a minimum of seven years using the services of many of the great libraries on the East Coast. In particular, she understood the value of specialized collections available through the Metropolitan Museum of Art, the Massachusetts Horticultural Society, and even the New York Academy of Medicine, which, at the time, gave her access to thousands of old cookbooks (p. 110).

While I can match her energy and enthusiasm, it has taken me decades to develop the intellectual courage she showed in *Flower Chronicles*. As a research associate of the Missouri Botanical Garden here in St. Louis, I have access to rare books that go back to 1474 and have examined several of the volumes that Hollingsworth listed in her bibliography. Until rather recently, though, these same tomes intimidated me. Have you ever read any of the herbals published between the sixteenth and early-eighteenth centuries? Some are four or five inches thick, heavy as bricks, and so oversized that they must be stored flat. Once opened it's hard to find what you need, as almost all classic herbals are devoid of indices and were published long before modern plant classification made it possible to cluster similar plants together into easily recognizable families.

In the first chapter Hollingsworth mentions how she had to limit herself to works that first appeared in English or early English translations. This may sound like laziness, but remember that our concepts of grammar and spelling have altered significantly since 1525. That's the year of the first edition of *Banckes's Herbal,* the oldest compendium on useful plants listed in her bibliography. Reading long passages in old books is frustrating because the calligraphy can cause eyestrain (e.g., pp. 64, 82, 96) and one loses time discriminating between the letters (*s* and *f,* for example). Each line may have more than one interpretation depending on how you unscramble sentences and define words. Hollingsworth was clearly an author who understood how to set reasonable parameters to finish a complicated project.

Foreword

The science historian Stephen Jay Gould (1941–2002) gave a number of public lectures and wrote several articles on the danger of dismissing everything written by naturalists, geologists, and early biologists who committed the unpardonable sin of dying before the age of Charles Darwin. Gould argued that to understand the development of any branch of science you needed firsthand experience reading original works, instead of relying on the comments of another historian who may have only skimmed the text or sneered at the illustrations. Hollingsworth had the same philosophy. Her writing style indicates she developed a comfortable familiarity with many classic publications before she decided which one to quote and discuss. She was able to empathize with long-dead authors, recognizing them as fellow gardeners. Having read sections of Gerard's *The Herball, or Generall Historie of Plantes* (1597), I understand her affection. Gerard was one of the few Renaissance herbalists to offer details on his living collection (he even grew his own mandrakes).

No wonder *Flower Chronicles* continues to surpass most of the more recent books on the history of domesticated plants. Hollingsworth enjoyed flower myths and legends but she knew that American literature didn't need another book on the subject. *Flower Chronicles* wasn't padded with color photos and plates either. Fifteen major plant groups representing sixteen genera of flowering plants (*Bellis* and *Chrysanthemum* share the same daisy chapter) received their own essays. This diversity distinguishes *Flower Chronicles* from more recent books devoted entirely to *the* orange (*Citrus aurantifolia*) or *the* chili pepper (*Capsicum annum*) or *the* rose. In the introductory chapter Hollingsworth warned that she wouldn't discuss plant care. In the absence of gardening tips she gave herself adequate time and space to defend her deceptively simple hypothesis that the long-term use of many different flowers meant one thing: gardening represented serious attempts by most traditional cultures to make life bearable.

Foreword

It is worth noting that there are brief moments in this book when the author followed the methodology of scientists in the field of ethnobotany. This is a discipline in which the botanist must employ the same "learn-by-doing techniques" used by anthropologists. A modern ethnobotanist is still expected to learn the procedures employed by nontechnological societies for making and taking drugs derived from plants. For example, Richard Evans Schultes (1915–2001) of Harvard University was known to have sampled every psychotropic species introduced to him by tribes living in South American rainforests. We may speculate that while Schultes was snorting different preparations for ebena snuff and recording his responses, Hollingsworth was cooking and eating tulip pistils (she thought they tasted like asparagus) or the roasted roots of peonies (acrid but not unpleasant).

I have three professional concerns for anyone prepared to discover or rediscover *Flower Chronicles*. First, *none* of the recipes or remedies reproduced in this book should be regarded as effective or safe. At best Hollingsworth treated these potions as jokes of history. Her son, Kirk Hollingsworth, told me she enjoyed regaling ill friends with medieval prescriptions that usually involved "essence of a particular flower plus something like frog's urine." Yes, she was attracted to edible flowers but her book was published before the scientific community understood how plant cells could accumulate manmade poisons. A sauce for lamb made of carnation (*Dianthus*) petals (p. 264) does sound like a nice alternative to mint jelly but do you know what sprays were used on those flowers before they entered your kitchen? More importantly, some people experience severe allergic responses to entirely natural molecules found in floral glands, pollen, and scents.

Second, misidentifications were common in the early herbals. These authors lacked the hand lenses and microscopes we now take for granted, had different names for the same plant, and often lacked living or preserved specimens needed to produce dependable illus-

Foreword

trations. A universally acceptable procedure for prioritizing, standardizing, and publishing the scientific names of plants began with the Swedish botanist Carolus Linnaeus (1707–1778) and his students. Hollingsworth was obviously intrigued by early illustrations that look nothing like the plants in her garden or in a seed catalogue. Her captions did not offer an alternative explanation for monstrously different forms, and it's time to inform the reader that we are not looking at an artistic flight of fancy or a major mutation:

> *p. 64.* The so-called "iris" is obviously a member of the philodendron family (*Araceae*). The cob-like flowering stalk (known as the spadix) is hooded by a leafy organ called the spathe. The turnip-shaped tuber (producing smaller roots) and the two stalky leaves suggest it's one of several European species the English call lords and ladies (*Arum*). I wonder if the confusion is based on ecology or home economics? Both *Iris germanica* and some *Arum* species prefer damp, marshy conditions. Europeans used the underground parts of both plants to launder clothing. Hollingsworth (p. 68) noted that iris root "sweetened" linen. Mabberley (1990) listed *Arum maculatum* as a whitening starch under its old name of Portland arrowroot.

> *p. 89.* Most *true* lilies (members of the genus *Lilium*) have a scaly bulb and the foliage leaves are attached directly to the lower half of the flowering stalk. This drawing shows a mass of fibrous roots instead of a bulb, and ribbons of leaves grow around the base of a nearly naked flowering stalk. Here we have one of the first anatomically correct illustrations of an Asian day lily (*Hemerocallis*) in a European herbal.

> *p. 141.* Neither illustration depicts a saffron crocus (*C. sativus*), which isn't surprising. Real saffron is so costly that many unrelated species have been substituted for centuries. Plant hunters

Foreword

exploring Europe, India, South America, and southern Africa (Bernhardt, 1993) looked for spice plants that would also yield a yellow dye. The curious drawing on the left resembles woodruff (*Galium odoratum*) but its dried foliage was used to flavor May wine, not paella. Its relative Lady's bedstraw (*G. verum*) has yellow flowers but they smell like urine and the herb was once used to curdle milk, not dye gowns. As for the plant on the right, the buds are closed so they could be anything. They might represent closed flowering heads in the daisy family (*Asteraceae*) since petals of *Calendula* and leopard's bane (*Arnica montana*) are old but poor alternatives to saffron.

Finally, garden flower history marches on. Some recent books present important and fresh information on underdeveloped topics in *Flower Chronicles*. Since Hollingsworth could not read works written in classical Persian she was unable to answer where and when tulips (*Tulipa*) were first domesticated (p. 116). We now understand that the *tulipan* bulbs that Ogier Ghiselin de Busbecq found in Turkey and sent to the Holy Roman Empire in the 1550s were not wild plants at all but pampered breeds. I think that Hollingsworth would have welcomed the most recent flower historians. Considering her own interest in Egyptian archaeology she would have been especially delighted by the work of Manniche (1989). If *Flower Chronicles* whets your interest in the history of ornamental plants, the following references also bridge the gap between general publications and technical treatments:

Baumann, H. 1993. *The Greek plant world in myth, art, and literature.* Portland: Timber Press, 1993.

Bernhardt, P. 1993. *Natural affairs: A botanist looks at the attachments between plants and people.* New York: Villard Books, 1993.

Foreword

Goody, J. 1993. *The culture of flowers.* Cambridge, UK: Cambridge University Press, 1993.

Le Rougetel, H. 1988. *A heritage of roses.* Owings Mills, MD: Stemmer House Publishers, 1988.

Mabberley, D. J. 1990. *The plant book: A portable dictionary of the higher plants.* Cambridge, UK: Cambridge University Press, 1990.

Manniche, L. 1989. *An ancient Egyptian herbal.* Austin, TX: University of Texas Press, 1989.

Pavord, A. 1999. *The tulip.* London: Bloomsbury Publishing, 1999.

Segal, S. 1990. *Flowers and nature: Netherlandish flower painting of four centuries.* Amstelveen, Neth.: Hijink International, 1990.

Flower Chronicles

From the garden to the stillroom and thence to the sickroom the medicinal use of flowers is traced. Title-page decoration from Adam Lanitzer's *Kreuterbuch Künstlichercoute*, printed at Frankfurt in 1609. (*Horticultural Society of New York*)

Books and Flowers

AN AMATEUR'S ADVENTURE IN RESEARCH

All gardening is a labor of love. Professionals who earn their living at it are rarely less enthusiastic than are the amateurs who dig and sweat and weed and mulch with so much fervor.

For most of us this enthusiasm stems out of our own past. Few people fail to carry in their memories pictures of a child gathering spring beauties or windflowers in the thin April sunshine; combing a hillside for violets; or squatting in a wood inarticulate but happy at the sight of some rare flower—a painted trillium or a showy orchis.

Out of such memories come botanists, horticulturists, plain dirt gardeners, and flower lovers of all kinds. Out of such memories grew my own lifelong interest in flowers that blossomed eventually into an acute curiosity about flowers in the past. What roles have flowers played throughout history? What relationships have they had with man over all the thousands of years that he has known and loved and used them?

The story of flowers is, in however minor a sense, part of the story of mankind. This book gives the histories of some of our most familiar garden flowers set against the backdrop of human history.

Long before there were gardens, flowers had so stirred the imagination and affection of man that he found ways to use

3

them—ways that ranged from such grave matters as religious symbols to such gay ones as perfumes and powders.

Some flowers have served man as food, and practically all flowers have gone into his medicines. They have been beloved and familiar themes in folklore. There are really a surprising number of ways in which flowers have shared men's lives outside of gardens.

That phrase "outside of gardens" has a special meaning here. A flower has three stories, the botanical, the horticultural and the historical. This book has no concern whatsoever with botany or horticulture. Flowers have had closer connection with man than as a science or as an ornament. They have been part, even though a very small part, of his everyday life in many ways. It is these intimate connections that flowers have had with man that I would like to trace here, describing them as well and as clearly as I can.

When my curiosity about flowers in the past had prodded me sufficiently I turned to some of those fine books on flowers and flower lore that were published toward the end of the nineteenth century. In them I read descriptions of flowers in folklore, flowers in medicine, flowers in heraldry, flowers, in fact, in practically everything! But as I read I was surprised to discover that I was not really interested in "flowers." Unconsciously I had been looking for something I had failed to find—the personal histories of some very old friends, roses, irises, lilies, daisies, cornflowers and various others. Nor did I feel any great enthusiasm for "lore." History was what I was after.

The word "history" brought me up short. It emphasized the fact that I was in search of individual histories—by genus, of course—of certain flowers and that I wanted those histories related to the history of man. Everyone knows, for instance, that the lily has served for almost two thousand years as a

4

symbol of the Virgin Mary. But how many people realize that peony roots were once the food of kings? The poppy is brought to our attention on Memorial Day as the symbol of one war, but not many of us remember that it was the cause of another.

However interesting the idea may be that flowers have histories of their own, I doubt that I would have pursued the matter if circumstances had not snatched me out of my own garden. Some years ago my husband and I accepted the pleasant job of running a small museum in New England during the summer months. This meant that the garden I had made in Rockland County, New York, and which I had tended for fifteen years was turned over to the tender mercies of summer tenants.

There was little time for gardening in New Hampshire. Nor did I want to start afresh on land that was not my own. So, since I was not working with flowers, I found myself thinking about them and reading about them rather more than I would ordinarily have done. Once the idea of individual flower histories had occurred to me I set out to find a book that contained them. But the book failed to materialize. At that time the fine and comprehensive work by Alice M. Coats had not been published. This was fortunate for me as there was nothing then to discourage me when I began to think it might be fun to look up some flower histories myself. It was.

Before I knew it I had embarked upon a search that was to carry me back to the tombs and palaces of kings dead for thousands of years, back to medieval kitchens and eighteenth-century boudoirs. It led me to the myths and legends that show us something of how men thought and felt before they learned to write. It both amused and horrified me to discover the fantastic and sometimes dangerous ways that flowers were used in medicine. It rewarded me with a whole series of introductions to men and women whose lives touch mine across centuries because they, too, have enjoyed or used the flowers I love—a petty tradesman of Bronze Age Crete; Tutankhamen's queen; a Greek botanist; an Anglo-Saxon leech; a thirteenth-century monk; a scholarly gentleman of the Renaissance; two great Elizabethan gardeners; a Restoration housewife; a Quaker merchant of eighteenth-century London; and America's first botanist, among many others.

No one ever entered so vast a field more wide-eyed and innocent than I. I did not anticipate any great difficulty. This would be, I thought, the rather ladylike job of assembling material that was easily available and then editing it into the form I wanted. But it turned out not to be so simple as all that. I found that I had to dig for some of the facts. But by that time I was committed—far too interested to turn back. Then, too, a minor triumph—very minor, but still a triumph— gave me some much-needed self-confidence at the very beginning of my research.

The history of any flower starts with the first men who noticed that flower enough to draw or carve its picture. Or, failing any visual representation, what people have cared enough about that flower to embody it in their myths?

Many a gardener has speculated about who might have been the first man—or was it a woman?—who snatched a common flower, a wild rose or a lily, and stuck it in his or her shaggy hair because it was pretty. It is the idlest of speculations, since we can never know the answer. But archaeology shows us that all along that dim road that man has traveled out of savagery into civilization some men have looked at flowers and loved them. We know because many shards of ancient pottery are decorated with flower designs. Varying in its temper but there for all to see on the cooking utensils of a vanished race is the same emotion that drives a modern gardener out of bed into wind and rain to make sure that the stakes still hold up the tall blue spires of delphinium. Man does not live by bread alone.

The common garden flowers "beloved by our grandmothers," according to many of the garden books, date far beyond our grandmothers to ancestors too remote to be included in any family tree. But there are scraps of evidence to be picked up over more than four thousand years that show us in painting, sculpture and architecture, or by the written word, how man first used the flowers that now adorn our gardens.

Most of the archaeological discoveries and reports that contain references to flowers in the remote past have appeared during the past half century. Hilderic Friend, T. F. Thiselton-Dyer, Angelo de Gubernatis, and other nineteenth-century scholars who wrote on flowers and flower lore were unable to carry their flowers further back in time than ancient Greece and Rome. Such work as had then been done in Egypt and Assyria was not widely known among laymen. The wealth of material from Crete, southern Mesopotamia, and various other parts of the Middle East was still in the future. It is easily accessible to any of us today, but so far no one seems to have made use of it in relation to flowers.

I happen to be one of those avid readers of books on archaeology for the layman, and my interest stood me in good stead when I began to look for flowers in the remote past. In W. R. Dykes's great monograph on the iris I read that the earliest known representation of an iris was in a carving on the wall of the temple at Karnak. Thutmosis III had had it placed there along with other plants he brought home to Egypt after his conquest of Syria in 1479 B.C. That date should have been early enough to satisfy anyone, but as I noted it down I was nagged by a dim memory of some Bronze Age pictures in Crete. That sent me eventually to Sir Arthur Evans' *The Palace of Minos at Knossos,* and there, to my boundless delight, were flowers—

many flowers. Here are "firsts" in abundance. Most of them date from the period known as Middle Minoan III, which runs from about 2100 to 1600 B.C. Lilies, crocus and iris all were beautifully painted in this period, sometimes on frescoed walls, sometimes on pottery jars. On one of the wall frescoes of this time there appears the earliest picture of a rose we know, and there are tulips on a pottery jar that are of special interest. The iris on Minoan walls were old before Thutmosis' sculptor lifted his chisel.

To have bettered a date given by so distinguished an authority as Dykes was a small triumph that at the beginning of my work was heartening. I could even go forward with an elderly approximation of a swagger!

Here and there in remote antiquity we come upon traces of or references to other flowers. But only on the island of Crete can we find so many actually portrayed, done so long ago and with such loving care that we recognize not only the genus but sometimes even the species.

Before we leave the flowers of the remote past there is one which everyone who is interested in this subject should bear in mind. The flower that appears on the headdress of the Sumerian queen, Shub-ad, is almost certainly the oldest representation of a specific flower in the world—somewhere between forty-five hundred and forty-eight hundred years old.

The queen's headdress is an intricate affair of gold ribbon and ornaments with a sort of "Spanish comb" arrangement rising at the back into five points, each tipped with the same slightly conventionalized flower. The queen's court ladies wore much the same headdress except that their combs carried only three flowers. Each of these gold flowers is about two inches wide and has eight petals. There is a circle of lapis in the center.

When some hard-working scholar has given Shub-ad's flower its familiar name, the queen will step a little closer to us out of

the shadows of those four thousand-odd years. But it is never
easy to give a name to a flower of great antiquity, even when
one has a gold one like this to go on. A great deal of highly
specialized knowledge is brought into play before any botanist
dares to make a specific identification.

The whole question of identifications in the past is too complicated to discuss here, but I would like to express my indebtedness to various scholars who have labored mightily at this thank-
less task. Not long ago I came across a remark to the effect that
three-fourths of the identifications of plants that T. O. Cockayne
had made in Anglo-Saxon leech-books were incorrect. Since
no clue was offered me as to where I could find better ones,
Cockayne stands firm in the flower histories that follow. Two
modern scholars in this field are the late R. Campbell Thompson,
who died in 1949, and P. E. Newberry, who identified the
plants found in Tutankhamen's tomb. But the bulk of this
sort of work was done in the nineteenth century. In addition to
Cockayne, there is the French botanist, Antoine Fée, who identified the plants in the edition of Pliny that I have read. Fée's
Flore de Virgil was published in 1822. The identifications in
the English edition of Dioscorides, published in 1934, were based
on the work of Charles Daubeny, who lectured on Roman husbandry at Oxford University in 1857.

The mention of Dioscorides brings us neatly and very appropriately to the most fascinating of all the subjects that are
a part of my flower histories—herbals. Dioscorides was the
author of the most influential herbal ever written. In due course
we shall come back to him, but for the moment I would like
to turn to herbals in general.

When herbals began to crop up in my reading about flowers
I was very vague as to what they were. It was cheering to come
upon Charles Singer's precise definition: *An herbal is a collec-*
tion of descriptions of plants put together for medical purposes.

It will be abundantly clear, I trust, in the following pages that herbals not only offer endlessly interesting detail about the uses to which flowers have been put in medicine, but herbals also give us much folklore, as well as botany and horticulture of the past.

I do not mean for a moment to imply that any herbalist ever deliberately set out to include folklore, botany or horticulture in his work. On the contrary, such men as John Gerard and John Parkinson, who were the authors of famous herbals in the seventeenth century, considered themselves herbalists first and foremost, even while going into the most minute horticultural details. William Turner, who preceded Gerard and Parkinson by a generation, was pre-eminently a physician, although every word he wrote betrayed the botanist the times did not permit him to become.

Anthropology also slipped into the herbals, unbeknownst to the herbalists. Someday, I like to think—although this may be only the wild guess of a layman—anthropologists who set out to study our remote European ancestors may find valuable clues to our primitive past embedded in herbals. Childhood is often hagridden with nameless fears, and some of the fears that darkened the childhood of man can be found in his early medicine. Demons and evil spirits harassed him. Only the magic of the medicine man could cure one possessed by an evil spirit. So it is out of a very dim, distant past indeed that we get such bits of magic as those involving artemisia, peony, mandrake and many other plants. Primitive magic is of great interest to anthropologists, but one does not have to be an anthropologist to enjoy the scraps of folklore scattered through the earliest herbals.

When it comes to the contribution that herbals have made to botany even an amateur can be on firm ground. Theophrastus, a pupil of Aristotle, conducted his *Enquiry into Plants* during the great days of Athens. This extraordinary man, working in the fourth century B.C., recognized that fungi, algae and lichen were plants; noted the distinction among annuals, biennials and perennials; dealt with organs in the order of their development and, among other notable intellectual achievements, recognized many groups of plants as such. Over a hundred of our genuses bear the names Theophrastus gave them although these names were rebestowed by Linnaeus in the eighteenth century. For, however justly Theophrastus may be called the father of botany, his progeny did not come of age for many centuries. His work, like so much else of value, was lost to sight during the crumbling of civilization that we know as the decline and fall of Rome. Happily it was rediscovered not long after printing had been invented and it exercised an enormous influence upon the sixteenth-century group of men who were to become the first of modern botanists.

Between these men and Theophrastus lay something close to eighteen hundred years, all, or practically all, of them barren of botanical writing. Any other Greek work along those lines had disappeared and Roman talents lay in other directions. In our own era herbals present almost the only writing that was done about plants; any other was scant and negligible. The descriptions of plants that appear in herbals from about A.D. 50 to about 1550 vary enormously, of course, from herbalist to herbalist and from period to period. But with rare exceptions the standard was never very high, from the point of view of either plant descriptions or medical utility. Modern botanists who do research on plants of the Middle Ages must lead lives of great frustration. Think of trying to identify plants back in a time when a whole chapter in a serious medical work could be devoted to the following description of an herb and its medical virtues:

Flower Chronicles

Herba Petri
This is called the Cousloppe (cowslip)

Since herbals had sunk to such depths during the period of intellectual stagnation preceding the Renaissance, it might be a good idea at this point to turn back to their bright beginnings and introduce Dioscorides, whose herbal is the earliest complete one we have.

Dioscorides was born in one of the Roman provinces in what is now Turkey. He was Cilician by birth, Greek by education, and presumably Roman by citizenship. Since there is every indication that he traveled widely around the Mediterranean, it is thought that he may have been an army doctor serving with Nero's legions. About A.D. 50 he produced his great work, *De Materia Medica*, an herbal that was to influence all medicine in Europe for, incredible as it may seem, close to eighteen hundred years.

There were Greek herbalists before Dioscorides, and we know their names from his contemporary, Pliny. At the end of each chapter in his monumental *Natural History*, Pliny put bibliographies, and those that follow the section on medical plants list Greek herbalists whose work is now lost to us. But from these earlier works Dioscorides derives. Herbalists were not creative writers. They recorded, in addition to whatever they had observed for themselves, all that they had learned from their predecessors. Their predecessors had done likewise, and so on back until we come to that unknown man at that unknown time who first gathered together the herbal lore of his people and used the new invention of writing to preserve it for the future. All herbals evolved, however remotely, from the medicine of the prehistoric past. A large part of their fascination hinges precisely on that fact.

Dioscorides, then, was not only the great doctor and herbalist of his time, but he is also the one remaining link with earlier herbal medicine. Logical and rational though he was himself, bits and pieces of a far-off magic can be found in his work.

When Rome fell a number of copies of *De Materia Medica* survived. The same holds true for the works of Galen, who came along a century after Dioscorides. His general medical

Dioscorides receiving a root of the mandrake from the Goddess of Discovery. Goodyer's translation of *The Greek Herbal of Dioscorides*, edited by R. T. Gunther. (*Used by permission of the estate of Dr. R. T. Gunther and of the publisher, The University Press, Oxford*)

writings and Dioscorides' herbal were cherished in the monasteries, the only places where learning was valued and respected
during the Middle Ages. The Church set her seal of approval
on both the herbalist and the doctor, and they were held for
centuries to be practically infallible. Even after the advance of
scientific knowledge brought their conclusions into question,
their influence continued to be potent right down into comparatively modern times.

Naturally, many other herbals were written between the
fall of Rome and the Renaissance. Some of them will be mentioned in this book because the Anglo-Saxon leech Bald, for
instance, and the French herbalist Odo of Meune presented
me with some irresistible items related to my flowers. But such
men had little to offer except bits of local lore that added color
to the traditional medicine on which their herbals were based.

The Renaissance, however, came with a great awakening light
to Europe. The liberating influences of the Reformation, the
revival of learning, and the rapidly growing number of printed
books stimulated men to look at the world about them with
fresh eyes and with open minds.

In the sixteenth century a group of scientifically minded
men began to look closely at plants. These men were herbalists
who were scattered all the way from England across the Low
Countries, France, Germany and Switzerland into Italy. The
roster includes Mattioli, Fuchs, Turner, Gesner, Clusius,
Dodoens, Lobel, Gerard and Parkinson, to mention only a few.
These men and others like them at long last proposed to give
the local flora a careful examination and compare it with what
they found in Dioscorides' herbal. Since they were Protestants,
practically to a man, they were untroubled by the ban which
had hitherto prevented anyone from solving the riddle posed
by Dioscorides' descriptions of plants.

The man who wrote *De Materia Medica* knew the Mediterranean flora. He described many plants that did not even exist in the north of Europe. In other cases, the species he described were unfamiliar. But during the period when copies of this Greek herbal did make their way into Northern Europe, life was too grim a business for anyone to bother about botanical discrepancies. By the time someone had the wit to realize the difficulties involved in accepting Dioscorides without question, his work had become sacrosanct and it was safer to let it alone. The herbalists of the Renaissance did not, of course, all arrive simultaneously at a decision to subject Dioscorides to critical analysis, but the problem of identification that had troubled so many of them served as a starting point. From a critical comparison of plant descriptions it was only a step to original descriptive work.

A strange footnote to the story of Dioscorides is the fact that no English edition of his herbal was published until our own time. It was "Englished" between 1652 and 1655 by John Goodyer, the great botanist of Petersfield, who wrote out the entire Greek text with an interlinear translation. Goodyer was unable to get a patron to subsidize the publication of his manuscript, which ran to 4,540 quarto pages, so it languished in the library of Magdalen College at Oxford for almost three hundred years. When it was finally found and edited by Robert T. Gunther in 1934 its value was entirely academic—a delight to the scholar and to the connoisseur of horticultural oddities— but no longer of any practical use to medicine.

Now, to get back to our Renaissance herbalists, it was only a step from a critical comparison of Dioscorides' plant descriptions to original observations. Once this step had been taken, the herbalists reached out into a new world and their descriptive work gives them away. The delight with which a man like William Turner describes a primrose has nothing whatever to do with medicine, although Turner believed in all sincerity that he was writing a medical work. The exact details he enumerated are those that any botanist wants to know. Turner and his contemporaries were founding a science that was not even to have a name until a hundred years after his death, but they founded it well and truly and joyfully. Botany began with the Renaissance herbalists.

Two other herbalists of the time branched off in a different direction. Since herbals have always been concerned with the physick garden, they naturally hold a place in the history of gardening, but it is with John Gerard and John Parkinson that they enter garden literature. Few gardeners who have read anything about the history of their art have failed to be enchanted when they dipped into the books of these two herbalists. For though, like Turner, Gerard and Parkinson considered themselves medical men, they were pre-eminently gardeners. This naturally makes for a certain confusion of mind which one can find in Parkinson's great book published in 1629, to which he had given the punning title,

> Paradisi in sole (Park in Sun's)
> Paradisus terrestris (Earthly Paradise)

Parkinson's paradise begins with a description of how to lay out a garden—the "forme or frame of a garden of delight . . . with its knots, arbours and allies." He then goes on to list the flowers needed for this garden, ending each description with its medical "vertues." Botanists find valuable data in this book as well as in Gerard's *Herball*, but these two herbalists added to botanical details the most careful and minute horticultural information they could gather. They tell how they cultivated plants themselves and how their friends and correspondents cultivated them. Herbalist and gardener are hopelessly intertwined.

Gerard's book betrays the same confusion in its title: *The*

Books and Flowers

Herball or a *General Historie of Plants.* A general history of plants has nothing to do with herbal medicine, but in the seventeenth century no one was too particular about such matters and certainly we have no cause for complaint when we read a book filled with lyrical descriptions of flowers and the joy of growing them.

Gerard has been criticized, not only in our time but in his own, because he incorporated the work of another man in his book without giving credit to his source. A translation of *Pemptades* by the Dutch botanist Rembert Dodoens, published twenty years earlier, fell into Gerard's hands and there is no reason to doubt that he took advantage of his windfall. Eleanour Sinclair Rohde, one of the great authorities on herbals, has, however, a comment to make about Gerard's iniquity for which everyone who cares about his herbal should be grateful: "One reads his critics with the respect due to their superior learning and then returns to Gerard's *Herball* with the comfortable sensation of slipping away from a boring sermon into the pleasant spaciousness of an old-fashioned fairy tale. For the majority of us are not scientists, nor do we care very much about being instructed. What we like is to read about daffodils and violets and gilliflowers . . . and all the other delicious old-fashioned English flowers. And when we read about them in matchless Elizabethan English we ask nothing more."

Plagiarism was a word which had not yet come into use in Gerard's day, but its practice seems to have been fairly common. Parkinson, for instance, was known to have bought the papers of Lobel,⸙ the Flemish botanist and physician to King James I of England, after Lobel's death in 1616. There is good reason to believe that a great deal of Lobel's work went into Parkinson's *Theatrum Botanicum,* which he considered his major work.

At any rate, Parkinson succeeded Lobel as apothecary to King James and also held this position in the reign of Charles I,

Frontispiece from *Giardino di Agricoltura* by Marco de Busato da Ravenna. Printed at Venice in 1593. (*Horticultural Society of New York*)

18

so he must have been especially successful in his profession. One suspects that he felt a little apologetic about his first book, the *Paradisi,* because it may have seemed to him frivolous—not close enough to the good medical tradition in which he believed. For when Parkinson was seventy-three he brought out in the *Theatrum Botanicum,* a straight herbal, in which some thirty-eight hundred plants are described. Its very weight and bulk, not to mention its heavy pedantic title, were against it. It never attained the popularity of Gerard's herbal—which was no featherweight, either—and unhappily Parkinson lived long enough to have this bitter truth brought home to him. It was the harder to bear because the lonely, childless old man had sent his lifework out into the world with the clumsy but pathetic admonition: "Goe forth now therefore thou issue artificial of mine, and supply the defect of a Naturall, to beare up thy father's name and memory to succeeding ages." Parkinson never attained the flexible and beautiful English that Gerard wrote so fluently, but one feels sorry that he could not have known that his name and memory would stay bright as long as people continued to love flowers. The book that seemed unimportant to him is important to the history of horticulture and lives happily in the affection of every gardener who has ever wandered in Parkinson's "Earthly Paradise."

Gerard's *Herball* was his only book, but, like Parkinson, he was a busy man. He was a member of the Barber-Surgeons' Company and seems to have practiced his profession, although somehow one does not think he did much haircutting. In addition to any professional practice he may have had he kept a large garden of his own and supervised the gardens of Elizabeth's great chancellor, Burghley—one at Burghley's town house in the Strand, the other at his country estate in Hertfordshire.

Gerard's garden was in Fetter Lane, Holburn. He was certainly a nobody when he came to London in his youth, but he had made a place of modest prominence there by the time his *Herball* appeared in 1597. A year later another man from the provinces who had made his way to London took up residence in Holburn, not far from where Gerard lived. Miss Rohde thinks it probable that Shakespeare visited Gerard's famous garden and that the two men knew each other, if only slightly. The temptation to speculate about the possibilities inherent in such an acquaintance is very great, but there is not a shred of evidence to show that they ever met.

After Gerard and Parkinson, herbals reverted to their proper sphere of medicine. The exciting excursions their authors had made into botany and horticulture had been carried out by exceptional men working during a time of great intellectual stimulation. As the glow of the Renaissance faded, herbals went back to a humdrum medical existence which was to last for another two hundred years, but their great days were behind them.

Herbals were, however, only one of the new worlds that I enjoyed exploring while I was at work on this book. Another and more personal one was the stillroom. No modern woman can step from her own streamlined kitchen into the seventeenth- or eighteenth-century stillroom without being moved by both sympathy and respect for the hard-working woman who had ruled there. Her portrait has been drawn in ruthless detail by Gervase Markham in the title of one of the earliest stillroom books published in England:

The English House-Wife
Containing
The inward and outward Vertues which ought to be in a
Compleat Woman
as her skill in Physicke, Chirurgery, Cookery, Extraction
of Oyles
Banqueting stuff, Ordering of Great Feasts

Books and Flowers

He goes on into brewing and baking and other things "belonging to a household," together with his intention to publish all this for "the generall good of this Kingdome."

The stillroom itself was, of course, originally the distillery where stills were kept for making cordials and perfumes. Here, too, were those clumsy alembics and awkward bains-marie which were the ancestors of our shining laboratory equipment. But at some very early date the stillroom was expanded to take in many more activities than just distilling. All medicines, distilled or not, came to be made there, as were cosmetics, ointments and powders. A number of conserves, jellies and candies were used medicinally as well as for sweetmeats, so gradually certain specialized forms of cooking also invaded the stillroom.

The heart of the stillroom lay in its stillroom book. Some of these date back to a time when they were written on parchment scrolls. Others are in less archaic manuscript form. Then, toward the end of the sixteenth century, books containing prescriptions, receipts and household hints began to be published. Today these books are classified as cookbooks but actually they often contain as many prescriptions for medicines as they do receipts for the preparation of food. Directions for making perfumes and cosmetics of all kinds are included as a matter of course, as are a wide variety of instructions ranging from how to clean gold and silver lace to how to keep flies away from "oyle" paintings!

A few of the later manuscript stillroom books have been published, and one of these serves as an especially fine example of the species. In 1908 H. W. Lewer transcribed, edited and published *A Book of Simples*.

No one knows the name of the family who owned this book, but the evidence of the handwriting shows that it was used by three different mistresses of the house. Early in the eighteenth century some unknown lady of the manor wrote out with pride "a receipt for making The Wood-Street Cake" on the first of the fine vellum leaves of her new stillroom book. It was a handsome volume, bound in dark-green morocco and beautifully tooled.

The contents came to the owner much as the card catalogues of receipts come to us today. Some we have copied down from our grandmother's cookbook, some come from contemporary publications, and a number have been given us by or been begged from friends and neighbors. "Lady Button's Melancholy Water" and "Mrs. Skillet's Receipt for the Black Jaundice" still intrigue us, though they have outlived their usefulness by two hundred years.

The stillroom books bear eloquent testimony to the weight of the medical responsibility that women used to carry. Housewives were expected to diagnose, treat and nurse everything from a sprained ankle to plague or hydrophobia. Prescriptions for the latter are numerous and heartbreaking, each so desperately hopeful, each so futile. It was taken entirely for granted that the housewife could cope at a moment's notice with the kind of accident or emergency that would send any modern woman to the telephone to summon an ambulance. Neither telephone nor ambulance being handy, the housewife of that earlier day turned to her stillroom. From its shelves she would take down the ointment, cordial, "electuary," or whatever she judged she needed. Professional medical help, if available at all, would be many hours and many miles away. She was on her own.

So, due to its basic importance, the stillroom was one of the busiest places in any household, large or small. It required no mean organizing ability to keep it functioning properly. The housewife usually had plenty of help, but it was ignorant help, often so careless and slovenly that her constant supervision was necessary. Who but the mistress of the house could oversee such a delicate operation as the gathering and clarifying of May dew? And who else could be trusted to time something on the stove by reciting the *Miserere* "very leisurely"? Only her forethought could so arrange matters that the work went forward in an orderly way.

Doctor treating a patient. Woodcut from *The Grete Herball*, 1526. (*The Pierpont Morgan Library*)

Behind the stillroom lay the garden. Gardens themselves have occupied men's attention ever since God planted a garden eastward in Eden and man tried to follow His example. Flowers belong in gardens. A book about flowers cannot ignore gardens however firmly one plans to eschew horticulture.

When I looked into the history of gardening I was exceedingly surprised to learn that the gardens of our Western world are not much more than four hundred years old. The Hundred Years' War in Europe and the Wars of the Roses in England put an end to the feudal era. Only after those two great struggles were over did ornamental gardens as we know them begin. A new type of architecture fathered our gardens.

Gradually and gratefully men of substance began to realize that they no longer needed fortified dwellings with moats and drawbridges, watchtowers and crenelated walls. Daringly at first, more as a matter of course as time went by, men built themselves houses of wood or brick set out in open fields or on hillsides. The Tudor manor of England was typical of such houses. As they came into use the land around them cried aloud for order and ornament. Gardens began.

But what of flowers before that? No one who cares about them can quite believe that they were entirely ignored even in the far past or during periods when life was so hard that men had no time or leisure for gardening.

Just such a period had preceded that Tudor manor—preceded it over a span of close to a thousand years. For between the fall of Rome and the end of the feudal system the times had mostly been too grim for gardening. Little gardens were sometimes made within the walls of a castle, usually for the ladies. The sacristans of great churches often maintained gardens in which to grow flowers for church decoration on feast days and holidays. But by and large the only gardens worthy the name during all this time were the physick gardens.

The physick garden is a fascinating theme in itself but the only aspect of it that concerns us here is the fact that a very large number of plants we now count as purely ornamental were then grown in the physick garden as medicinal herbs.

What a comfort they must have been, those utilitarian gardens, to men and women hungry for the kind of beauty only flowers have to offer! There was, we can feel very sure, a physick garden in that monastery in Paris where a famous lecturer on theology, who was also a philosopher, lived about 1250.

Books and Flowers

When he came to write his encyclopedia, Bartholomaeus Anglicus naturally included a section on medicinal plants. As we
read we can see him in his Franciscan gray happily pacing the
paths between the beds of herbs in the monastery physick
garden. It is our good fortune that roses and violets, iris and
lilies were herbs and that this thirteenth-century monk was as
much poet as scholar. For what other encyclopedist has ever
described the rose as a flower that "wrayeth her thorn with
fayr colour and good smell" or the violet as a "a lytyll herbe"
whose ". . . lytylnes . . . in substance is nobly rewarded in
gretnesse of savour and of vertue."

Before the physick gardens of the Middle Ages there were,
of course, gardens in classical times and in antiquity but we
really know very little about them and almost nothing about
the flowers they contained.

If the above attempt at an outline of gardening seems deplorably superficial, no one is more aware of the fact than I.
Anyone, however, who has ever tried to condense the history of
gardening into a few hundred words will not be willing to
cast the first stone! But, feeble as it is, it is included here because
certain points in it are needed as background in the stories of
some of the flowers that follow.

As histories of gardening, herbals and stillroom books opened
new and interesting prospects before me I began to take a wary
look at what I had so lightheartedly set out to do. There were
flowers to be found in regular medicine as well as in herbal
medicine; there was cooking outside the stillrooms. Also there
were cosmetics and perfumes, heraldry, odd bits of history that
would all have to be investigated. Obviously my original idea
of covering most of the garden was out of the question. No
one lifetime would be long enough for that. So I faced the
alternatives. Either I could spend years at a workmanlike and
scholarly account of a single flower or I could do a rough sketch

of many—each story as careful and exact as I could make it, but without any pretense of covering all the material, tracing down all the sources or even assembling any but the main facts. It is this latter course that I have chosen, partly because I am not scholar and linguist enough to achieve the former and partly because there is no single flower in the garden so preeminently interesting and beloved as to occupy my whole attention.

Others, I hope, will pick up the job where I have left it. There are still dozens of flowers whose histories it will be fascinating to explore. And may anyone else who travels this road in search of flowers have as much fun on the way as I have had.

Even though I accepted a more modest aim than my original one I have had to impose certain limitations on myself. For obvious reasons I chose to follow my flowers through history in English with only an occasional side excursion into French. But even if I were familiar with all the languages of Europe, with classical Greek and Latin thrown in, the field is too wide for any one person to cover. So I have told my stories as I have found them in English sources, which is after all appropriate since so many of our flowers have come to us from English gardens.

In the interest of brevity and smooth reading I have dealt sparingly with qualifications. "So far as I know," "perhaps," "it is thought," "almost certainly," and other such phrases have been eliminated. I would like my readers to bear in mind that in all modesty I herewith qualify everything that cannot be absolutely nailed down. But it is tiresome to the reader to be constantly reminded of this in the text. So, "so far as I know" and "so far as I have been able to find out," everything I have written is the truth although, like everyone else, I have certainly made mistakes.

Apologies are tedious and I have none to offer for the interest and enthusiasm that set me to work. But in self-defense I have pointed out the magnitude of the problem lest anyone lay too much stress on the sins of commission and omission with which this book must be replete, try as I will. Like Gerard, I confess that mine is a task "for greater Clarkes to undertake." Yet I have so enjoyed the doing of it that if other people who care about flowers find one-tenth of the pleasure in reading these flower histories that I do in reading the work of that great Elizabethan gardener, then I shall, like him, "thinke my selfe well rewarded."

"Discourse on the Virtues of the Rose" from Symphorianus Champerius'
Rosa Gallica printed at Paris in 1518. (*Mallock Room, New York Academy of Medicine*)

Rose

Go, lovely Rose—
Tell her that wastes her time and me

* * *

How small a part of time they share
That are so wondrous sweet and fair!

Only a poet can find the proper words with which to describe a rose. Three hundred years ago Waller's young lover linked it with all beauty and all tenderness and to the poignant brevity of these in our individual lives.

The rose has not always inspired such sentiments. The early Church Fathers looked upon the flower with abhorrence and refused to let it symbolize the Virgin or any other Christian personage. To them the rose was closely associated with the debauchery of the Roman Empire during the first century of the Christian era.

Like the Greeks before them, the Romans had dedicated the rose to the goddess of love and the god of wine. Wine, women and roses went naturally together in Roman minds and the early Church did not approve of the combination. There was good reason for loathing it. That drunken Roman aristocrat, weaving his way to his place at a banquet, his chaplet of roses askew, cut merely a foolish figure in some eyes. To a watching Christian slave he was sinister. He and his kind cheered when the great gates of the Colosseum were flung open and lions roared into the arena where unarmed human beings met them with only faith as a weapon. It is always hard to realize that this

29

now hackneyed piece of melodrama actually happened. But the Church remembered and centuries had to pass before anyone would have dared to refer to the Virgin Mary as the Rose of Heaven.

Nero is said to have spent four million sesterces for roses at a single banquet. (A sesterce was a brass coin equal in value to four donkeys.) The couches on which Roman banqueters reclined were often strewn with rose petals and occasionally supplied with pillows stuffed with them. A literal bed of roses was by no means unknown. Tables and floors, even streets and lakes, had rose petals scattered over them. Rose petals floated on the surface of wine. Garlands of roses decorated halls and dining rooms. But, above all, roses adorned the person. Garlands were worn around the neck and chaplets on the head. Violets and narcissus also were used for chaplets but the rose was the most popular.

In addition to all its charms of scent and color and texture the rose had a special meaning for Roman revelers. The wearing of a rose chaplet or a garland of roses hung over a dining table meant that every word uttered there was said "sub rosa"—under the rose. According to the Roman code, no gossip, information or confidence made under the rose could honorably be repeated outside. Out of this long-ago convention came not only our saying "under the rose" but an actual rose. For the central ornament on many a dining-room ceiling is nothing more than a conventionalized rose set there originally to remind the guests not to abuse the hospitality they enjoyed.

The Romans took their association of the rose with a discreet silence from a Greek myth. The rose was dedicated to Aphrodite, goddess of love. So it was with a rose that her son, Eros, bribed Harpocrates, god of silence, not to gossip about his mother's amorous indiscretions—surely an extraordinarily tolerant attitude for a son to take. Be that as it may, the Romans transposed this myth into their own terminology and thus associated the rose with Venus and Cupid.

The demand for roses grew to such extravagant proportions during the days of Roman decadence that various colonies began growing them on a vast scale for export. Egypt was one of the colonial possessions that took to rose culture and it is known that she shipped great quantities to the capital. How they were kept fresh on the long voyage is still unknown.

The trip in Nero's day was not, however, considered a long one. It was rather one of those modern miracles about which we ourselves are hearing so constantly. For the Romans, it seems, had learned to rig a ship with sails—plural, not singular—and, furthermore, sails of linen. "What audacity in man! . . . to sow a thing in the ground for the purpose of catching the winds and the tempests, it being not enough for them, forsooth, to be borne upon the waves alone!" Like our modern equivalents, jets and rockets, this first-century miracle produced extraordinary speeds. "To think," Pliny continues, still writing about flax, "that here is a plant which brings Egypt into close proximity to Italy! So much so, in fact, that Galerius and Balbillus, both of them prefects of Egypt, made the passage to Alexandria from the Straits of Sicily, the one in six days, the other in five!" Even if roses had been shipped from Egypt on the Roman version of the *Queen Elizabeth* or the *United States,* it is difficult to figure out how they arrived fresh enough to be useful.

So far we have followed the rose into classical antiquity but we can trace it much further back than that. The fact that it appears in Greek mythology takes it back to an unknown but very early date in that country. But in Crete we can be more specific. There we can place it at not less than three thousand five hundred years ago. At a time when still primitive tribesmen were roaming the mountains of Greece men not very far out in the Mediterranean had developed a high degree of culture. They not only knew and admired the rose but one of their artists had drawn it.

On the island of Crete a Bronze Age people whom we call Minoans had reached an advanced state of culture at an astonishingly early period. By the middle of the sixteenth century B.C. they had among other amenities an elaborate architecture, a linear script, and a number of highly developed skills, notably in pottery. Also, as a pleasant surprise, in plumbing! The sanitary arrangements in the palace of Minos are amazingly modern and efficient. Here and there on the island there are parts of a 4,000-year-old system still in working order.

Around the palace of Minos there grew up the great city of Knossos. On a narrow street in a crowded district of the city was a small house that was set apart by an odd circumstance. When Sir Arthur Evans, the great archaeologist who discovered and excavated Knossos, came to dig at this site he and his men found a curious pile of blocks—thin, crumbly, but obviously stacked by human hands. The smooth face of each block showed a painted surface and these, eventually pieced together, produced several frescoes belonging in a room of the house in whose ruins they were found. No one knows why, when or by whom they were stacked as they were, nor how they survived for centuries the condition they were in.

Sir Arthur believed that the owner of the House of the Frescoes was a skilled craftsman or minor tradesman. But, however modest may have been the social or economic status of that householder, he was a man of cultivated taste and had the means to gratify it.

In one of the frescoes a blue monkey is the central figure, in another a blue bird, both creatures set in a rocky landscape gay with flowers. There is a vetch or pea-like plant of some sort, a spray of ivy, pancratic lilies, papyrus, crocus, iris—and roses.

Rose

It does not matter in the least that the artist drew those roses with six petals and their leaves in groups of three like those of a strawberry plant. They are unmistakably roses—the oldest roses in the world.

In addition to the roses on the walls of a Minoan house there is the name of a neighboring island to suggest that in prehistoric times the islands in this part of the Mediterranean may have been covered with wild roses. Nowhere in the myths that tell the story of the origin of the island of Rhodes are roses mentioned. But the root for the Greek word for rose and for the name of the island is the same. Back beyond myths, matter-of-fact because so literally true, a Neolithic people may originally have called their home the Island of Roses.

Given the name of Rhodes, this is a very natural deduction but there is no evidence to back it up until we come well down into historic times. When Rhodus, the capital of the country, was built in 408 B.C. the new coins struck at the time carried the head of Helios on one side and a wild rose on the other.

The people of Rhodes were, like those of Crete, a seafaring folk with a lively overseas trade. They exported a great deal of wine, chiefly to Egypt and Sicily. In both of those countries numerous handles of Rhodian wine jars have been found, stamped, like the coins, with the head of Helios and the wild rose.

For all that the evidence is so slight, it seems by no means beyond the bounds of probability that roses were recognized and admired in prehistoric times, long before even the Minoan rose bloomed on the walls of a house in Knossos.

Roses took their place in medicine on the very best authority. Not only were they mentioned among the herbs used by Hippocrates and Galen—the most revered names in classical medicine—but they also received the blessing of the earliest and most

eminent herbalists. Both Pliny and Dioscorides agreed that the
rose was a valuable medical herb. Between them they recommended roses for curing irritations of the eyes, ears, mouth,
stomach, intestines and rectum; for headache and toothache;
for diseases of the lungs, stomach and intestinal tract; for female
disorders; for wounds, boils and tumors; for hemorrhoids ("ye
paine of ye seat"?) and hemorrhages; for erysipelas, sleepless-
ness, clearing of the brain, checking excessive perspiration and
curing hydrophobia.

We might pause for a moment over that last and most dreadful disease. Pliny tells the story of a young soldier, serving with
Roman troops on the Spanish border, who was bitten by a
mad dog. The soldier's mother was warned in a dream of what
had happened to her son, so she immediately sent him a dog rose
with directions as to how to use it. It reached the young man
at precisely that critical moment when he had developed an
aversion to water. He followed his mother's instructions, made
a tincture of the plant, drank it, and "against all hope and
expectation his life was saved."

The tincture the Roman matron recommended was only one
way of getting the virtue of the rose off the bush and inside the
patient. Oil of roses was not the fabulously expensive essential
oil called "attar," but many rose petals were macerated in olive
or sesame oil to give the oil the flavor and scent of the flower.
"Mell roset" was honey of roses and "could be given compe-
tently [suitably] to the feeble, sick, phlegmatic, melancholy
and choloric people." Fresh or dried rose petals were steeped in
water or wine to make tinctures and infusions. The water or
wine might or might not be boiling. Rose syrups, conserves and
jellies were all originally used as medicines, but when the Arabs
brought the art of distilling to Europe rose water exceeded all
other medical products of the rose in importance.

The medical history of the rose does not, however, rest on

the limited number of diseases for which Pliny and Dioscorides recommended it. Nor was the rose confined to medicines in which it was the chief ingredient as it was in rose water and rose oil. As time went by and medicines became more and more complicated, roses went into almost anything along with almost anything to cure almost anything.

In despair of ever finding a systematic way of presenting a brief picture of the rose in medicine I jotted down a list of particularly interesting prescriptions that use roses. Strangely enough, these prescriptions turned out to be almost exactly two hundred years apart. Arbitrary, illogical, inconsistent, even ridiculous, the list is not entirely inappropriate to the story of the rose in medicine.

Taking a long stride across history after Pliny and Dioscorides and skipping nothing more than the decline and fall of Rome and a good part of the ensuing Dark Ages, we begin with a prescription by an Anglo-Saxon leech named Bald who lived between A.D. 900 and 950.

One cannot help being entertained by much of Bald's medicine. But it should be a gentle amusement without malice because Bald was by no means a fool. He may have been far in advance of his time. Any modern doctor would nod agreement to Bald's instructions about taking into account the general "nature of the body of the patient, whether it be strong and hardy . . . or whether it be nice and tender and thin. . . . For a mickle difference is there in the bodies of a man, a woman and a child . . . of a laborer and of the idle, of the old and of the young." Now, this has something of the soundness and sanity of Greek medicine. It is conceivable that Bald may have read something of the sort in such fragments of Hippocrates as might have come his way. If so, he deserves high praise for remembering this bit. If it was entirely his own idea, he was a brilliant man.

However high his intelligence, Bald could not escape his time, and much of his medicine is no more advanced than one would expect of the tenth century. Take, for example, his treatment for "a sore maw: leaves [petals] of rose, five or seven or nine and of pepper corns as many, rub them small and administer in hot water to be drunk." A useful adjunct to this rose-and-pepper cure was Bald's suggestion for a tenth-century equivalent of our hot-water bottle or electric heating pad. "It is also helpful to him that a fat child should sleep by him, and that he should put it always near his wamb [stomach]."

Two hundred years later the rose was listed in *Macer's Herbal* for such run-of-the-mill ailments as bowel troubles, heartburn and eye irritations. But along with this conventional medicine went a couple of receipts that are pure magic. They probably date back to a time long before the Christian era. It does not seem to have bothered anyone during medieval times that a little black magic should be mixed up with medicine. Here, then, in case you are feeling malicious, is a simple method of blighting your neighbor's fruit trees. (It sounds oddly like a little modern magic to àttract the birds in winter.) Take a grain of powdered rose petals and a grain of mustard seed and mix them with the fat of a green woodpecker:

> And yane hang yt in a tre
> In what place so yt it be
> And never schall ye tre fruyt bere
> Whyl yt con feccyon hangyt yere.

A truly sinister confection!

By the fourteenth century medical prescriptions had become so complicated that one never feels that the rose or any other single ingredient had any importance. Prescriptions called for so many herbs, often twenty or thirty, that no one of them was more effective than the rest. But, for the record, the rose was there. It usually is to be found in the prescriptions for making the many versions of a medicine called "A Drynke of Antioch." This was used as a cure for wounds and that, plus its name, suggests that it may have originated during the crusades.

Rose from *The Grete Herball*. (*The Pierpont Morgan Library*)

To make one version of this drink you "take erbis [twenty-eight of them including rose] and frye hem in fresche botter and wryng hem throw [through] a cloth . . ." presumably into beer or ale. "A precious water to clere a mannys sight . . ." begins "Take the rede rose . . ." but adds twenty-three more herbs. These are steeped in white wine for twenty-four hours and then distilled three times. The first water "schal seme colour of golde" and the second silver, indicating their respective strengths.

Flower Chronicles

BULLEINS/*Bulwarke of defence/againste all Sickness, Sores and woundes that dooe/daily assaulte mankinde . . . Doen/by Williyam Bulleyn . . .* 1562 is the work of a man who was supposed to have been a relative of the unhappy Anne, although her name is usually spelled "Boleyn."

"Williym" must have been a successful physician, as only a practitioner with well-to-do patients would have dared to prescribe so expensive a remedy as he did for the common cold, though it must be admitted that this was also recommended for a number of other ailments. It was called an Electuary of Gems.

An electuary was a medicine made of a powder or powders incorporated in honey, syrup or conserve. Bulleyn's sweet was honey of roses and his powders consisted of "Pearls, two little pieces of sapphire, jacinthe, canelian, emeraldes, garnettes, of each one ounce; with mace, basil-seeds, ginger, cinnamon, spikenard, gold and silver leaves, redde coral, amber and shavings of ivory . . ." In spite of the honey of roses it sounds frighteningly like a good dose of ground glass!

In the eighteenth century roses continued to be used copiously and still in vastly complicated prescriptions. One medicine called "Balsame," taken from a stillroom book, is described as being good to cure plague, deafness, wounds, scalds and burns, sciatica, any poison, any swelling, the stings of adders, snakes and other venomous creatures, measles, sore breasts, "the wind collicke," piles, and reaches a fine anticlimax with a stitch in the side!

In the same stillroom book there is a prescription labeled "Mr. George Horseyes green Ointment . . ." Thanks to the standards of spelling and punctuation in the eighteenth century this might and probably should be read "Sir George's Green Horse Ointment," but the title goes on to specify its value for aches or shrunken sinews "in Man or Beast, for Strains it's incomparably good, & holds Perfection 40 years," which may account for the quantity manufactured at one time. Besides four pounds of roses and lesser amounts of other herbs, this ointment required twelve pounds of "hogsgrease," thirty-eight pounds of May butter clarified in the sun, and then a gallon of "Sallet oyle" and four pounds of turpentine, plus a few other oddments. The mixture was then tightly stoppered and buried for three weeks three feet deep in a dunghill, after which it was decanted and put on the fire to "boyle a walm or two" (a walm being a bubble). It was then bottled again and ready for its forty years of service.

In order to prove, however, that the eighteenth century could occasionally achieve simplicity an "Eye Water" from the same stillroom book should be quoted. "Red rose water and white rose water of each a penny worth. Two penny worth of powder of Putty a quarter as much white Sugar candy shake it al together in a bottle & drop into ye eyes night and morning."

Part of the fun of using this arbitrary list of medicines is due to the fact that with the next 200-year jump the mid-twentieth century rounds out the story so neatly. Modern science has discovered that rose hips are one of the richest sources of vitamin C in the world. During World War II England needed large quantities of this vitamin. Citrus fruits, the main source of supply, would have had to be carried from overseas in the beleaguered convoys. So England raided her own gardens. Tons of rose hips were harvested and processed. Thus a story of futility that stretches over close to two thousand years ends ironically—and pleasantly—on a note of triumph.

More roses have been distilled for the delight of mankind—and of womankind—than any other flower. To back up such a statement we may take the production figures for a single season at Grasse, in southern France, in the center of the district where flowers are grown for the perfume industry. In one of the years before synthetics cut so deeply into the need for flowers, Grasse harvested nine hundred fifty tons of roses against one hundred forty-seven tons of violets.

But no statistics can tell this story. Nor can it even be sketched adequately in a few pages. The history of perfumes begins with the fact that certain barks and roots emit a fragrance when burned, and these were dedicated to the services of the gods in a very dim past. Certain crude and shaggy individualists must have begun to wonder why they, too, might not enjoy the scents then considered sacred to divinities—or so we may picture the situation. But at any rate man—or, more probably, woman—began early to use sweet-scented substances for his or her personal pleasure. Miniature jars and boxes obviously intended for cosmetic use have been found in Egyptian tombs of great antiquity. Pliny claims that it was the ancient Persians who invented the scented oils called unguents, though not so much for the purpose of positive enjoyment as for the negative use of counteracting "the bad odours that are produced by dirt." He was scornful of those undiscriminating men who drenched themselves in the oil instead of sprinkling themselves with it. One wonders if any of his friends used the famous Roman beauty ointment made from roses and lion's fat!

Perfumes in Europe, as everyone knows, grew into a great industry, especially in France. From the Renaissance on, the combined art and science of making perfumes extended itself from individual mixtures in small, and often famous, shops all the way into modern methods of mass production based now largely on synthetics. To try to follow the rose perfumes through the maze of history, artistry and industrial production would be almost a lifework. In order to bring the picture down to reasonable dimensions the rose, as it has been used in perfumes and cosmetic preparations, is going to be confined here to the stillrooms of England. And lovely places those were in cottage or castle or manor during June and July when most of the work concentrated on roses.

The English never went in for quite the same elaborations that the French enjoyed in perfumes. For more than two hundred years simple rose water was their favorite scent and the published record of the use of roses in homemade cosmetics gives a lively picture not only of how perfumes were made but of where and how they were used. Take, for example, "King Edward VI's Perfume."

King Edward's perfume carries us back to the frail lad whose short reign brightened the years between the death of his father, Henry VIII, and the accession of his older half sister, Bloody Mary. It also illustrates the state of housekeeping at the time. For King Edward's perfume was a sixteenth-century air conditioner made as follows: "Take twelve spoonfuls of right red rose-water, the weight of sixpence in fine powder of sugar, and boyle it on hot Embers and coals softly and the house will smell as though it were full of Roses, but you must burn the Sweet Cypress wood before to take away the gross ayres." If "gross ayres" afflicted palaces, one may well shudder at the thought of the condition of lesser dwellings.

It was not only in young Edward's time that roses were needed as an air conditioner. They obviously continued in that capacity for a very long time. An "Odoriferous perfume for Chambers" appears in *A Queen's Delight*, 1662, and a hundred years later some unknown lady of the manor wrote in her still-room book a receipt for "A Perfume to Burn." In this case rose petals were combined with "benjamin" (gum benzoin) and musk or ambergris to make thin cakes which were dried in the sun. These, burned on a hot shovel, were waved about a room to counteract the gross airs that continued to prevail until people learned that it was not fatal to open their windows occasionally.

"Sweet bags" sometimes helped too. A sweet bag hung on the arm or back of a chair wafted a pleasing fragrance into the nearby atmosphere just as its descendant, potpourri, does today. For sweet bags—usually made of "Taffety"—were filled with much the same mixture of dried flowers, salt and spices that we know today. In potpourri, as well as in sweet bags, the basic ingredient was dried rose petals. Dried rose petals brings us to Hugh Plat and one of the very earliest of the stillroom books to be published. His *Delightes for Ladies*, 1609, is filled with roses. It contains many variations on the theme of how to make rose water and gives directions at great length for the two chief ways of drying rose petals. The common method was to dry them with air "turning them up and downe till they be dry (as they do hay)" but there is a more complicated way of doing the same thing with sieves set in an oven.

In contrast to drying rose petals by air there is the sand method whereby, according to Plat, they or any other single flower may be dried without wrinkles. It sounds simple enough to put a layer of sand in a box, then a layer of petals, more sand, more petals, but it all has to be arranged with the utmost care. Two hot sunny days should see the petals thoroughly dried. Then one lifts them out, one by one, "carefully with your hand without breaking." That last operation sounds, one feels sure, easier said than done. Once you have achieved those unwrinkled rose petals, Plat says, they are pleasant to lay around the house on window sills and in basins all winter long.

The sandbox method of drying roses reminds one of Eleanour Sinclair Rohde's charming little book called *Rose Recipes*. In this she has not only quoted many of the old directions for using roses but tells how she herself has adapted the old methods to her own use. For in addition to being one of the outstanding modern authorities on herbs and herbals Miss Rohde obviously enjoyed putting her knowledge to practical use.

Rose

To return now to Hugh Plat, whose dried rose petals, rose water, rose syrups, jellies, and conserves all serve to let us identify him here with the rose. It is to be doubted that he gives any more rose receipts proportionately than do any other of the compilers of the old stillroom books. But he fits in so well with the subject and he would have been so charmed to be remembered in connection with the rose that it cannot be inappropriate to introduce him here. He was a notable gardener who did pioneer work with soils; he was one of the greatest inventors of the Elizabethan age; and he was a most popular writer on all such domestic matters as household hints and the preservation of food.

Plat's inventive genius still touches our own lives. It is not likely that any modern gambler has tried the ring he invented, a ring with a reflecting sphere in which one player could "discover" the cards in the hand of his opponent. But the spit that turns at every roadside "Bar-B-Q" owes its beginning to one Plat made, and he should be warmly remembered as the man responsible for the alphabet blocks of our nurseries.

Delightes for Ladies is just that, even though after three hundred fifty years the delights are not quite what the author intended. Today it is a delight to read. In its own time it deserved its title because of the large number of perfume and cosmetic receipts it contains. Plat gives eight different receipts for distilling the popular and all-important rose water.

One gathers that the main differences in these directions lie in the point at which you start. You begin with the juice from crushed rose petals if you wish to get "the true Spirit of Roses." "To make a water smelling of the Eglantine" you start with rose petals in "faire-water" and distill that. "To draw both good Rose-water and oyle of Roses together" you "digest" your rose petals for three months in aqua vitae and then distill. And so it goes, not only with Hugh Plat, or Sir Hugh as he became

43

under James I, but with all the early writers on making perfumes in the home.

Rose water was essential. It was not only a perfume in itself but it went into many other cosmetic preparations. Perfumes whose fragrance came from other flowers often had rose water added, whether just for luck, on principle, or as a general base it would be hard to say. Once it was used in a "Water that makes a Face look Young" and one feels that roses were indeed in their rightful place, since they had helped to make that face "so clear and beautiful that all will wonder and admire to kiss it." What more could anyone ask of a cosmetic?

Some of the other perfumes into which rose water went were used to scent gloves and to sprinkle on freshly laundered clothes when they were put away. Rose water perfumed "wash balls" and played its part in what is quite possibly the earliest receipt for a dentifrice published in England. Other stillroom books include all sorts of perfumes and cosmetics but tooth pastes and powders get scant attention. *Delightes* seems to be alone in offering receipts for such preparations. There are two, the second being for a "Sweet and delicate dentifrices or rubbers for the teeth." The "rubbers" were made of gum tragacanth mixed with powdered alabaster finely ground, to be sure, and sifted! Roses added, Plat says, would give the substance a pleasantly tinted veined effect. Rose water, civet or musk, as you please, would scent the preparation. It was then rolled into little sticks about four or five inches long. ". . . if your teeth be very scally, let some expert Barber first take off the scales with his instruments, and then you may keep them cleane by rubbing them with one of the afore said rubbers."

"A delicate washing ball" was the forerunner of our scented soaps. "Castile sope" dissolved in rose water had powdered sweet herbs added to it—rose, lavender, orris root and suchlike—and these were incorporated by "laboring them all in a mortar."

Rose

Besides the perfumes of the stillrooms there were, of course, those made and sold by professionals. Wash balls bring to mind Mr. Charles Lillie, who rather specialized in them. Mr. Lillie was "That Celebrated Perfumer at the corner of Beaufort Buildings in the Strand" who was often mentioned by Steele and Addison in *The Tatler* and *The Spectator*, much as a similar figure might be mentioned today in *The New Yorker*.

By the end of the eighteenth century the popularity of perfumes had reached a pitch that brought them to the attention of Parliament. It is hard to believe that there were such timid souls in England, yet in 1770 an act of Parliament decreed "That all women of whatever age, rank, profession or degree, whether virgin, maid or widow, that shall from and after such Act impose upon, seduce and betray into matrimony any of His Majesty's subjects by means of scent, paints, cosmetic washes, artificial teeth, false hair, Spanish wool, iron stays, hoops, high-heeled shoes or bolstered hips, shall incur the penalty of the law now in force against witchcraft and like misdemeanours and that the marriage upon conviction shall stand null and void."

Yet most of the women against whom this statute was directed worked hard for their beauty preparations. They were not lazy trollops. They were willing to stand over hot stoves and stills on a summer's day tending the concoctions that needed attention. They did the tedious job of cutting off the "nails" from the petals of bushel after bushel of roses. They handled delicate jobs like removing the smooth petals from sand. But, to be sure, this was work that offered compensations in the doing. Inside and outside the stillroom must have been such tumbled masses of sweetness as moderns rarely see and fragrant with scents that only the old damasks and centrifolias could give. As the girls labored through the flowery abundance to make their beauty preparations it is doubtful if many of them had any more sinister ambitions than for the fulfillment of a dream—the dream of a face that all would want to kiss!

A pudding made of rose petals and calf's brains opens the story of the rose in the kitchen. There is such a flavor of sophistication about this dish that it is difficult to believe that its receipt comes from the most ancient of European cookbooks.

A Roman named Apicius was credited with compiling this book although there is no certainty about it. He was unquestionably a famous gastronome of his time but there is no way of being sure that the title given the English translation is a fair one: *Apicius: Cooking and Dining in Imperial Rome.* Marcus Apicius was born in 80 B.C. and died in A.D. 40. According to legend, his death by poison took place at a banquet which he had carefully planned for the occasion. He had already spent a hundred million sesterces on his appetite, which would amount to $8,090,000 today. Now he had no more than $809,000 left. Life under such circumstances was not worth living, so he arranged an appropriate exit. Joseph Dommers Vehling, translator of this earliest of cookbooks, makes the rather contradictory statement that he does not believe this story about Apicius' death, but has to accept *facts* as they were reported.

It seems probable that, like so many of the other civilized amenities of Roman life, good cooking came from Greece. From internal evidence Mr. Vehling concluded that this was true and that this book was a sort of gastronomic bible in Imperial Rome. Apicius might have compiled it but it seems more likely that it was simply dedicated to him by an unknown hack who knew that the great epicure's name would carry more weight than his own.

To make *Patina de Rosis*: "Take roses fresh from the flower bed, strip off the leaves, remove the white [from the petals and] put them in the mortar; pour over some broth [and] rub fine.

Rose

Add a glass of broth and strain the juice through the collander. [This done] take four [cooked calf's] brains, skin them and remove the nerves; crush 8 scrupples of pepper moistened with the juice and rub [with the brains]; thereupon break 8 eggs, add 1 glass of wine, 1 glass of raisin wine and a little oil. Meanwhile grease a pan, place it on the hot ashes [or in the hot bath] in which pour the above described material; when the mixture is cooked in the *bain marie* sprinkle it with pulverized pepper and serve."

It does not sound too bad. One is almost tempted to try it!

The gap between this Roman receipt and the next one is a mere fourteen hundred years. Needless to say, other receipts were committed to parchment or paper in the interim but the fall of Rome swept such niceties as good cooking into limbo for several hundred years. It was not until the feudal order was established that men once more had time to think of food as something more than a bare necessity. Fumbling and awkward, they began to try to make their meals savory and attractive. We would not think that they succeeded but we can respect the hard labor that went into their efforts.

Take, for example, the banquet given by Henry V to celebrate the joint coronation of himself and "the Faire Ladie Katharine." The ceremony took place on February 24, 1421, and the banquet followed. The Countess of Kent, we learn, and the Countess Marshal sat to the right and left of the newly crowned queen "under the table." Actually, the phrase is more picturesque than the fact. These ladies simply sat at tables set on a lower level than that of the queen. Great nobles acted as carvers, cupbearers, "bottlers," "naperers," and as various other menials. We are told precisely which ones stood and which ones knelt throughout the meal. Life was easier for the Earl Marshal. He rode around and around the hall on a great charger throughout the banquet to keep order.

Flower Chronicles

At the end of each course a "sotyltye" was set upon the table—whether to be eaten or just admired is unclear. But it is with the "subtilty" that we return to the rose in cooking.

A "sotyltye" was a monumental piece of culinary sculpture constructed out of paste, sugar and gelatine. The first one to appear at Henry's feast was designed as "a pelly cane sytting on hyr next, with hyr byrdes, and an image of Saynte Katharyne holdying a boke, and disputing with the doctors, holdynge a rason in her ryghte hande. . . ." The "rason" seems to have been a posterlike affair that carried a legend to the effect that the pelican had an answer (to what is not stated) and that the king wished all his people to make merry. Although the saint was obviously the queen's patron, the significance of pelican, doctors and book are too subtle for the modern mind!

Judging from the cookbooks of the period it seems likely that the making of "sotyltyes" was a carefully guarded professional secret. Even so, scattered through those early English cookbooks are receipts that give us an inkling as to how the majestic structures were created. One receipt describes the making of a paste flavored and colored—"y-paynted"—with either roses or violets. The flowers were boiled and then incorporated with the flour, sugar and "almonde mylke, or gode Cowe Mylk." The last touch was to add flower petals—whether fresh or dried is not stated—to give the desired color.

Another fifteenth-century receipt describes how to make a "gelye" colored with columbines and, as will be made clear in the chapter on the crocus, saffron was ubiquitous in kitchens of this period. Thus the artists of the "sotyltye" had red and purple and blue and yellow to work with, all owing their colors to flowers.

We see, then, that roses played a role in medieval kitchens but it was a very minor role. It was not until the seventeenth century that they assumed any importance in cooking, but when

The grete herball

lohiche geueth parfyt knolblege and vnder
ftandyng of all maner of herbes ⁊ there gracyous bertues lbhiche god hath
ozdeyned foz our pzofperous lbelfare and heilth/foz they hele ⁊ cure all maner
of dyfeafes and fekeneffes that fall oz myffoztune to all maner of creatoures
of god created/pzactyfed by many expert and lbyfe mayfters/as Anicenna ⁊
other.⁊c. Alfo it geueth full parfyte vnderftandynge of the booke lately pzen
tyd by me(Peter treueris)named the noble experiens of the vertuous hand
warke of furgery.

Title page of *The Grete Herball*. (*The Pierpont Morgan Library*)

49

they did they were to continue as a staple flavoring for at least two hundred years.

Vanilla seems not to have come into common use until the early nineteenth century and even after it had arrived on the scene the familiar and popular rose flavor continued to be used. "W.M.," who was cook to Queen Henrietta Marie, published *The Queen's Closet Opened* in 1655 and in it tells how "To Make a Cake with Rose Water the Way of the Royal Princess, the Lady Elizabeth, the Daughter of Charles the First." The title of this suggests that rose water as a flavor was something of a novelty at that time. But from about then on it ceased swiftly to be a novelty and was soon a regulation flavor for practically all sweet dishes.

In addition to its use as a flavor for desserts the rose was important in candymaking right down to within the memory of the present older generation. Today it is rare indeed to see candied violets or candied rose petals, but no box of candy from a good confectioner of the early nineteen hundreds would have been sent out without the final touch of candied flowers tucked in the top layer between the nuts and chocolates. These pretty and tasty sweetmeats are tedious to make and do not lend themselves to mass production, so they are disappearing from the modern scene. They date back to such confections as one Miss Rohde quotes in her *Rose Recipes*. It is from *The Whole Body of Cookery Dissected*, 1675, and tells you how "To Candy Rose Leaves Natural as if They Grew on Trees."

Other early forms of candy were "sugar plates," made with sugar colored and flavored with roses or other flowers, and many forms of sugar paste. Hugh Plat gives a number of receipts for the latter and, for all that his earliest book did not appear until 1594, his directions may be much the same as those that were used to make the "sotyltyes" of a century and a half before his time. "A most delicate and stiff sugar paste, whereof to cast

Rose

Rabbets, Pigeons or any other little bird or beast, eyther from the life or from carved moulds" was made with "issinglasse," but usually gum tragacanth served as stiffening.

Syrups, conserves and jellies made of roses, originally designed as medicines, gradually made their way to the table as pleasant sweets. There must be hundreds, perhaps thousands, of receipts for making them. One that Sir Kenelm Digby recorded was given him by "Doctor Bacon." Now, the life of Digby, the philosopher and epicure of Stuart times, overlapped the life of Bacon, the Elizabethan philosopher, so "Doctor Bacon" could have been the great Francis. Whoever he was, he used, Digby says, to put his rose conserve into a "pleasant Julep." Modern authorities on the julep, i.e., Virginians and Kentuckians, will be entertained to learn that the rest of Doctor Bacon's drink called for no more than lemon juice into which you clip "a little rinde of the Limon" and spring water.

There are a rather surprising number of modern, or comparatively modern, receipts that use roses. A jam to be made from the hips of the wild dog rose is described by Princess A. Gazarene, a czarist refugee who compiled and published a Russian cookbook in 1924. Miss Rohde gives receipts for a rose petal conserve, a rose petal jelly, a sauce eglantine, and a rose hip marmalade. The last two receipts were approved by Queen Victoria, who often had the sauce and the marmalade served at Balmoral. Mrs. Maud Grieve whose *Modern Herbal* was published in 1931 rounds out contemporary rose receipts with

Rose Petal Sandwiches

Put a layer of Red Rose Petals in the bottom of a jar or covered dish, put in four ounces of fresh butter wrapped in waxed paper. Cover with a thick layer of rose-petals. Cover closely and leave in a cool place overnight. The more fragrant the roses, the finer the flavour imparted. Cut bread in thin strips or circles, spread each with the perfumed butter and place several petals from fresh Red Roses between the slices, allowing the edges to show.

Between the calf's brain pudding and those sandwiches lie two thousand years, during most of which the rose has had its share of work to do in the kitchen.

"The Plant of Roses, though it is a shrub full of prickles, had bin more fit and convenient to have placed it with the most glorious floures of the world, than to insert the same here among base and thorny shrubs: for the Rose doth deserve the chief and prime place among all floures whatsoever; beeing not onely esteemed for his beauty, vertues, and his fragrant and odoriferous smell; but also because it is the honor and ornament of our English Scepter. . . ." Thus Gerard sums up the respect as well as the affection that Englishmen feel for the rose as the accepted symbol of their country.

If heraldry did not begin with the rose in England, the rose was right there from its earliest formal beginning. For, while heraldry reached England in the latter part of the twelfth century, it was not systematized with a language of its own until a few decades later, during the reign of Henry III (1216–1272). It was Henry's second son, Edmund Crouchback, first Earl of Lancaster, who brought home from France the red rose that became the badge of the House of Lancaster. His brother, Edward I, perhaps inspired by Edmund's example, chose a golden rose for his device.

Edmund Crouchback was the son of a man who was "a patron of artists and men of letters, and himself skilled in the gay science of the troubadours." When he went to Provins, that land of the troubadours, Edmund was perhaps the readier to choose the Provins rose as his badge because he had been reared during a great upsurge of artistic and intellectual activity. Roses always seem to fit in with a high degree of civilization and the scholastic movement of the thirteenth century touched the highest point Europe had reached since the fall of Rome. Albertus Magnus, who was the teacher of St. Thomas Aquinas and Bartholomaeus Anglicus, belonged to this period. So did the early English historian Matthew Paris who was artist enough to illustrate his own works and who has left us a most engaging picture of Edmund in his cradle.

As a man in his thirties, Edmund was sent to Provins by the king of France who had become his feudal overlord when Edmund married his second wife, the heiress of Champagne. The mayor of Provins had been assassinated in some local uprising and the king wanted revenge. How Edmund handled his political errand is no concern of ours, but he must have liked that part of the world as he lingered there far longer than his mission demanded. When he returned to England he took with him as his device the Provins rose. Authorities differ as to exactly what the Provins rose was. A parti-colored one is sometimes so called. Some claim that it was the damask rose, others the centrifolia. But by whatever name, the red rose of Lancaster was to play its part in English history.

According to Shakespeare's *Henry VI* the roses that gave their name to a civil war were chosen in the Temple Garden. He who was "a true-born gentleman" plucked a white rose with Richard Plantagenet and he who was "no coward and no flatterer" plucked a red rose with Somerset. It is a colorful scene charged with drama but not necessarily founded on fact. In some such way, however, the white rose of York could have been chosen in contrast to the already accepted red rose of Lancaster.

When the bitter struggle between York and Lancaster, white rose and red, finally ended, the two families—originally descended from a common ancestor—were once more united. Elizabeth of York, daughter of Edward IV and sister of the little Edward V murdered in the Tower with his younger brother, married Henry Tudor, descendant of the Dukes of Lancaster. He reigned as Henry VII and for the first time the royal arms carried the Tudor rose, which is a double rose, the outer circle of petals usually red, the inner white.

Besides the Tudor rose a common heraldic one is a single five-petaled flower with stamens in the center and five pointed sepals showing between the petals. If the center and the sepals are displayed in a different color from that of the petals they are referred to as "seeded" and "barbed," respectively. A *rose en soleil* is usually a single white rose, though it could be a double one, displayed against a golden-rayed sun. A slipped rose has a bit of the stalk and leaves attached. The roses of heraldry are colorful and varied and romantic.

As no other flower has ever done, roses wear the costume of their time. Recently a friend who is working with old roses brought me a Provins rose. It was a small flower no more than two inches across. It was double but not in a tumbled fashion— its petals lay neatly shingled one over another. On each white petal were stripes—some mere pin stripes, some almost an eighth of an inch wide. If anything ever was, this was a parti-colored flower.

However dangerous such loose generalizations may be, it is a safe guess that to most people the word "parti-colored" suggests the Middle Ages, when clothes were so often described as parti-colored. A man's shoes, hose and breeches might be scarlet on one leg, dull green on the other; his jerkin ultramarine blue with a triangle of lemon yellow over one shoulder and down a sleeve. Equally for most of us the word "Provins" also suggests the Middle Ages with an overlay of troubadours. The name and coloring of that little rose from a New Hampshire garden carried one straight back into medieval times—to old books of hours and the miniatures that were the contemporary illustrations of the age.

Needless to say, this pleasant game of matching the dress of the rose to a period cannot go on indefinitely but there are one or two more worth noting.

Whichever one of the great roses of Malmaison was the Empress Josephine's favorite, we may be sure that it fitted to perfection her thin white muslin dresses, high waisted and long skirted in the style of the day.

The fussy little moss rose was ideally suited to the ruffles and frills of the Victorians, who loved it.

In the early days of this century there was the unlamented American Beauty. Coarse of stem and leaves, of giant size and a peculiarly ugly color, it had its vogue during a period when clothes, furniture and decorations reached a nadir of bad taste.

Today, at mid-century, we have our characteristic rose, the floribunda, crisp, slim, in beautiful colors, the streamlined rose of the twentieth century.

"The Winged Stags." Drawing by Wilson T. Airey, Jr., of a detail from a fifteenth-century tapestry in the Musée Départmental des Antiquités, Rouen, France.

Iris

Namesake of a goddess; symbol of a Bronze Age religion; heraldic device of the kings of France; "soveraigne" remedy for a vast number of ailments from weak eyes to insanity; flavor for various beverages hard and soft; basis for countless perfumes and powders; ornament of our gardens. The *Who's Who* item of the iris is a long and distinguished one.

Iris, the Greeks believed, was the messenger of the gods and the personification of the rainbow. Among her duties was that of leading the souls of dead women to the Elysian Fields. And in token of that faith the Greeks planted purple iris on the graves of women.

It would be easy to drop into whimsey and express the pious hope that Iris has now brought together Grace Sturtevant, Louise Beebe Wilder, Gertrude Jekyll, Madame Chereau, Freda Mohr and the host of other women who have shared their loves. But what about the gentlemen who have as much right to iris on their graves as any woman—and more than most? They range, to take only a few at random, from Gerard and Parkinson, who boasted of their "flower-de-luces," on and along through Sir Michael Foster, who began the modern work on the iris; J. G. Baker, whose description of the family is standard; W. R. Dykes, who wrote the definitive book on the genus; Robert Fortune, Reginald Farrer and other collectors who brought back choice iris from far places; through and beyond such iris breeders as William Mohr, who went out with his wife at that grade crossing to whatever darkness or bright fields awaited them, leaving us the heritage of blue and purple, white and gold that bear their names.

The Greek symbolism for the iris comes down to us by word of mouth in the form of a myth that was old in Homer's day. In Crete we find the iris appearing visually in that misty period, the Bronze Age, where history and prehistory meet.

Somewhere between three and four thousand years ago an artist was commissioned—more probably commanded—to model in stucco on one of the walls of the great Minoan palace at Knossos a representation of the priest-king. When he had finished the vigorous figure of a youth in low relief he painted around it a background which may have been intended to suggest the Minoan version of the Elysian Fields. For the young priest-king strides forward, iris to the right and to the left of him. Since the iris appears elsewhere as a sacred flower, Sir Arthur Evans believed that these, too, had a religious significance, "and may indeed," he adds, "have been suggested by *I. reticulata* which today blooms abundantly over the site of Knossos, the fairest harbinger of the Cretan spring."

There are other iris in Knossos painted during that period. In the House of the Frescoes, already mentioned because of the rose pictured there, we find our iris again. It is conventionalized a little, but very little, for the swordlike leaves and crested flowers look so familiar, so natural, that we are driven to wonder about their owners—what sort of man and woman and children enjoyed them as part of home three and a half millennia ago?

A comparatively short time after iris bloomed on Minoan walls it appeared sculptured in stone at Karnak in Egypt. Thutmosis III (1504–1450 B.C.) celebrated the conquest of a large slice of Asia Minor by having a garden built near one of his palaces to display some of the plants he had brought back from his campaign. A number of these seemed exotic enough to be perpetuated in stone, so he had them carved on a great wall of the temple of Amon. Unmistakable among them are some iris. Even to the lay eye they look like iris, and W. R. Dykes has identified them as *I. oncocyclus*. But we also have assurance from Thutmosis himself of their authenticity. He had an inscription carved near his flowers which reads in part: "Year 25 of the King of Upper and Lower Egypt, living forever. Plants which his Majesty found in the country of Syria . . . His Majesty saith, 'As I live, all these plants exist in very truth; there is not a line of falsehood among them. My Majesty hath wrought this to cause them to be before my father Amon, in this great hall for ever and ever.' "

For ever and ever is a long time but thirty-five hundred years is a good start.

The later symbolism of the iris carries us by a long leap out of antiquity into European history. The fleur-de-lis as a conventionalized form long predated its association with the kings of France, but its significance lacked the weight of meaning that accumulated with time around the French national emblem.

There are various legends as to how the iris came to represent the French monarchy but most of them center around one or the other of two historical incidents separated in time by six hundred years.

The first of these concerns Clovis, who, in A.D. 496, is said to have abandoned the three toads on his banner in favor of the fleur-de-lis—no bad swap either, as any gardener will admit. His Christian queen, Clotilda, had long sought, so runs the tale, to convert her heathen husband. But Clovis ignored her pleadings and prayers until faced by a formidable army of Alamanni, the Germanic tribe invading his kingdom. In that critical hour he told his wife that if he won the coming battle he would admit the efficacy of her God and be baptized. He did win, of course, and the toads whose symbolism it might be interesting to know disappeared into limbo.

The second incident, according to tradition, occurred in 1147. Louis VII of France, shortly before setting out on his ill-fated crusade, is supposed to have adopted the purple iris as his device in obedience to a dream. Thus, according to this version, the fleur-de-lis came to the banner of France.

For close to six hundred years then, if we take the date from the time of Louis, nearer twelve hundred if we take it from Clovis, the iris was the living symbol of a great nation.

> Now by the lips of those you love, fair gentlemen of France,
> Charge for the golden lilies! Upon them with the lance.

This was more than a mere romantic couplet. Over and over again it was in grim and bloody earnest. Men charged and fought and died for the land the fleur-de-lis represented. Today, on a piece of "junk" jewelry, on an upholstered chair, wallpaper, dress material, we see a conventionalized ornament. It is hard to realize that for many generations of Frenchmen that symbol held the same emotion with which we first saw the photograph of the six marines planting the Stars and Stripes on Iwo Jima.

So potent was the fleur-de-lis as the device of French kings that the Revolutionaries of 1789 set out to obliterate it as the symbol of the hated monarchy. It was chipped off buildings and torn from draperies. Men were guillotined for wearing a fleur-de-lis, however incidentally, on their clothes or jewelry. And the Revolution succeeded, for the fleur-de-lis is a symbol now in memory only and passed, as such, into the realm of conventionalized ornament.

Throughout the above section on the fleur-de-lis readers will have noticed that it is accepted as a conventionalized iris. Yet in

Iris

the couplet quoted French knights were exhorted to "charge for the golden lilies." "Much learned ink has been spilled," said H. N. Ellacombe, "in the endeavor to find out what flower, if any, was intended to be represented."

Undoubtedly, the difficulty of finding the origin of the fleur-de-lis is due to the antiquity of the conventionalized form. It was ancient when Louis VII adopted it—ancient even when Clovis used it. The form appears at least as far back as Etruscan art though it cannot be traced into ancient Egypt.

So many authorities have mentioned the fleur-de-lis on the head of the Sphinx that it is high time for the matter to be cleared up. It all started with Henry Phillips, who published his *Flora Historica* in 1824. "The ancients used the iris or flag-flower," he wrote, "as the symbol of eloquence and it was on that account, we presume, that it was placed by the Egyptians on the brow of the Sphinx."

The cobra—the ureus—is what actually appears on the head of the Sphinx in a slightly conventionalized form. At the time Phillips was writing, the Napoleonic archaeological discoveries in Egypt were new and exciting. Books published then were naturally innocent of photographs, but many contained drawings. If you were to draw a sphinx at a slight angle, the cobra's head with the raised hood showing a little on either side might quite easily be mistaken for a fleur-de-lis.

That, at any rate, is the best explanation that a modern Egyptologist can suggest when faced with the problem. For he knows beyond all question that there is no fleur-de-lis on the head of the Sphinx and never has been.

It is doubtful that the origin of the fleur-de-lis can ever be traced. At different times and in different places it was casually assumed to have sprung from an iris, lily, toad, sword hilt or spearhead. Then somewhere along the way it became most often associated with the iris—not all at once, but gradually over the years.

Abandoning details about the origin of the fleur-de-lis, many writers hurl Chaucer, Shakespeare, Spenser and Ben Jonson at each other—on the one hand, Shakespeare's "lilies of all kinds, the flower-de-luce being one," with Ben Jonson in rebuttal, "Bring rich carnations, flower-de-luces, lilies." But actually the matter had been settled by the time Shakespeare was four years old, if not authoritatively, at least by popular consent. "From the time of Turner, in 1568, through Gerard and Parkinson to Miller, all botanical writers identify the iris as the plant named, and with this judgment most of our modern writers agree," wrote H. N. Ellacombe in *Plant Lore and Garden Craft of Shakespeare.*

I think I may have pushed the identification of the iris with the fleur-de-lis back in time a little. All those who saw the magnificent exhibition of French tapestries sent to the United States in 1948 will remember the one called the "Winged Stags." On this tapestry the stags have the crown and arms of France hung around their necks, both lavishly adorned with the fleur-de-lis. Conspicuous in the pattern, and so placed as to suggest a deliberate juxtaposition, are beautifully executed naturalistic tall bearded iris. One cannot escape the deduction that the flowers are there to emphasize their relationship to the French royal emblem. The tapestry is dated 1450–1469, almost precisely a century before Turner's herbal appeared. Thus the fleur-de-lis can be identified with the iris for close to five hundred years, which should be long enough to make the identification stick.

A careful search through pictures, manuscripts and textiles may well carry the date further back. But this researcher is frankly partisan and hopes that any future discoveries continue to favor the iris.

Iris

We can now leave the iris as a symbol and turn to early medicine to pick iris with the men who used them hopefully to heal their fellows.

"If one suffer mickle hreak [a great collection of phlegm in the throat], and he may not easily bring it away from him for thickness . . . let him take the dust of a root of this wort [*I. germanica*], pounded small, by weight ten pennies, give to drink to the sufferer, fasting, in lithe beer, four draughts for three days, till that he be healed."

Hreak! Such a beautiful onomatopoeic word. What a pity it did not come down to us—along with less desirable ones—from the Anglo-Saxon. It, together with that naïve prescription, delights us. But somehow, too, one's imagination slips away to a woman long ago pounding orris root, her ears strained for the terrible choking of a child that has diphtheria. Nature, not orris root in lithe beer, must have healed those who did survive the more virulent forms of *hreak*.

Anyone who reads old herbals must be impressed by that fact. Until modern chemistry came along to analyze the tissues of our bodies and the substances supplied to heal or nourish those tissues, there were only two ways to meet medical problems: tradition, and trial and error.

Tradition reigned supreme until after the intellectual revolutions created by the Reformation and the Renaissance. It was still powerful long after that. And tradition in the case of the iris centered around the work of Dioscorides.

De Materia Medica begins with an article on *I. germanica* and is followed by one on *I. pseudacorus*. When Dioscorides led off his great work with iris, that meant that iris went into official medicine to stay for close to nineteen hundred years. Through all the squalor and violence that followed the fall of Rome, through the Middle Ages when men had neither the time nor

Irus is an herbe lo named. It is
hote and dzye in the thyzde degre
It is allo named aaron / z calues
fote. Some call it pzelles hode / foz it hath
as it were a cape z a tongue in it lyke ler-

Woodcut illustrating iris in *The Grete Herball*.
(*The Pierpont Morgan Library*)

the taste for gardening, iris were cherished in the only gardens
there then were—the physick gardens.

After telling how to dry and treat the root of iris, Dioscorides
goes on to say that *I. germanica*, drunk with honey, vinegar or
wine was a specific for coughs and colds, for "torments of the

belly . . . & for such as let fall their food, for women's fomentations which do mollify & open the places," for sciatica, fistulas, "& all hollow sores which it fills up with flesh." Laid on as a poultice orris root was good for various kinds of tumors and ulcers, broken bones and headache. Mixed with honey and hellebore, it removed freckles and sunburn and finally, summing up the value of the roots, "in a general way they are of very much use."

That settled the matter for centuries to come.

Although Dioscorides made some acute original observations on a number of plants (notably myrrh, opium and the squill), the bulk of his book derived from earlier Greek herbalists whose work is now lost. Iris came down, along with other healing herbs, from primitive times when magic and medicine were one.

The rhizotomi (root diggers) were the druggists of primitive Greece and possibly even its doctors. From them came ideas which had aroused the scorn of Theophrastus, whose work Dioscorides must have known. With the beautiful clarity of the Greek mind disciplined to careful and honest inquiry Theophrastus thought that on the whole it might not be unreasonable to bid a man to pray when digging iris roots. But he went on to claim that it was absurd to insist that it be done with a two-edged sword "first making a circle around it three times and that the piece first cut must be held up in the air while the rest is being cut." This difficult gymnastic feat undoubtedly added to the magic potency of the iris so garnered.

Even down into Dioscorides' own day magical ideas continued to haunt the iris. Pliny, a contemporary, could add to his own medical recommendations for iris the injunction that it must be gathered only by those in a state of chastity.

Deplorably few books survived the fall of Rome. Thousands were, of course, destroyed in the long-drawn-out chaos. Happily for the future, a large number of manuscripts were swept up by scholars who carried them off to Constantinople for safety. But it was the far future that would benefit by that exodus.

Medical books, however, have a utility that makes men cherish them even during the darkest days. A number of copies of *De Materia Medica* did somehow survive and these were treasured in monasteries, which were the only places where learning was respected during the Dark Ages. Scholarly monks made translations and copies of their own manuscripts to enrich the libraries of other monasteries. From such a copy came the medication to cure *break* quoted above. It shows, too, the "improvements" and changes made in Dioscorides' text by well-intentioned scribes as manuscripts passed from hand to hand. This prescription is an English translation of an Anglo-Saxon translation of a Latin translation of the Greek herbal of Dioscorides.

I. germanica continued in use in European medicine until modern times. It, along with our own beautiful *I. versicolor,* was listed in the U.S. Official Pharmacopoeia as recently as 1938. But it had lost its medical importance and was relegated to nothing more than a flavoring substance for toothpastes and tooth powders. Our native iris, however, was used medically— for dropsy, syphilis, and some forms of scrofula.

Even though we now know that the virtues Dioscorides attributed to iris were nonexistent, a little orris root more or less never hurt anyone and the belief that it would cure was at least psychologically helpful. As herbal medicine goes, the record of the iris is a long and honorable one.

Iris never seems to have got into the kitchen, but it did make its way into beer barrels and wine casks. In Germany orris root used to be suspended in beer barrels to keep the beer from getting stale. In France it was hung in wine casks to enrich the bouquet of the wine. In England orris root was used to give "the peculiar flavor" to artificial brandies made there. (One somehow feels that the adjective used to describe that flavor was aptly chosen.) In Russia, in czarist days, orris root flavored a soft drink made of honey and ginger that was sold on the streets.

The iris came onto the stage of human activities with all the dignity of a religious symbol, only to leave it after taking part in what was probably the most frivolous performance ever put on by mankind.

The earliest appearance of the iris, however, was in a serious role because the first perfumes were offerings to the gods. Since dried iris root flung on a fire gives forth a pleasant odor, it is more than likely that the iris figured in some of the sacred burnt offerings of primitive times. Be that as it may, a number of men and women very early failed to see why the gods should monopolize all sweet scents. In Egypt, Persia and Greece perfumes of one sort or another were known and valued from very early periods. Theophrastus mentions iris among the plants used for perfume in Athens and down in Corinth an iris water called *Irinen,* which had the fragrance of violets, was distilled from the rhizomes.

This peculiar property of orris root should be emphasized. Its odor is not that of iris but of violets. Until the synthetic *ionone* was discovered a little more than fifty years ago all violet powders and perfumes were based on orris root. In the more expensive perfumes, a little violet leaf extract was added.

A second property of orris root is no less important. It has the quality of being able to strengthen the odors of other perfumed substances. Thus, as a fixative, it has for centuries held a place in the making of powders and perfumes.

When civilization had staggered to its feet after the fall of Rome, during the ensuing Dark Ages, all through the feudal period, in the Renaissance, and up to comparatively modern times, orris root has played a major role in helping to make social intercourse bearable. Clothes, even gloves, were soaked in perfume. Orris root itself, as a perfume for linen, is mentioned as early as 1480 in the wardrobe accounts of Edward IV.

It is possible, too, that the "swete cloth" famous in Queen Elizabeth's day was achieved by the same method French peasant women have long used to make their household linen fragrant. Several pieces of dried orris root strung on a string would be plunged into the boiling water with the clothes. Then taken out and dried, the roots could be used again and again. It remains to be seen whether or not this would work in a modern washing machine.

"Swete cloth," if so achieved, could only have been linen. However pleasant that might have been next one's skin it could hardly have been efficacious in itself. Look at the portraits of the time. There was wool, of course, but if one was a person of any importance at all one wore silk, satin or velvet. Dry cleaning was a long, long way in the future. "Swete cloth" underneath and a great deal of perfume on top was about the best the fastidious could do, since bathing was considered dangerous.

So for centuries orris root played an important social role. It remained for the eighteenth century to see that role brought to the extreme of absurdity when, at the beginning of the century, men and women started to powder their hair.

For the first fifty years the new hair arrangements were fanciful and elaborate enough, but they grew more and more so until by the seventies and eighties they had reached heights—and literally!—that are hardly believable. It was not at all unusual for a lady of fashion to have a coiffure that towered two feet above her forehead—and three was far from unknown.

Orris root was not, in this case, the basic powder used. It

Iris biflora Lusitanica. Woodcut from Rembert
Dodoens' *Pemptades,* printed in Antwerp in
1616. (*Horticultural Society of New York*)

was simply added as a perfume to flour or starch—and later to a powdered white earth. Until the latter was discovered, one of the grievances of the hungry peasants of France before the Revolution was that so much of the flour they needed for food went to dress the hair of the nobility.

Hair powder was not so simple a commodity as the words "flour" and "starch" suggest. Mr. Charles Lillie, "that Celebrated Perfumer" of the early eighteenth century, warned his customers against buying starches which have been "so adulterated as to be damp and mouldy" or "very bad indeed," in what way he does not specify. Whether they were "light and flying" or "damp and mouldy" they were always perfumed by the addition of orris root either for its own scent of violets or as a base for some other fragrance.

Even aside from the olfactory offense of moldy powder the need for perfuming these coiffures is crystal clear when one reads a contemporary description of a hairdresser asking a lady "how long it was since her hair had been opened and repaired. She replied, not above nine weeks; to which he replied that that was as long as a head could well go in summer and that it was therefore proper to deliver it now." The gentleman who gravely reported this conversation to the Cambridge Antiquarian Society in 1909 added that "the description of the said opening of the hair and the disturbance that it occasioned to its numerous inhabitants is best left to the imagination."

There, too, let us leave it. But possibly the reader will find as much interest as did the Cambridge antiquarians in learning how the structure was built. "The substratum was composed of wool, tow, pads and wire, over which was drawn the natural or false hair." Once this had been done the powdering must have followed. Then, artistically arranged on the basic structure, came such trimmings as ribbons, plumes, ropes of pearls or beads, artificial flowers. As a finishing touch objects

la Candeur

Eighteenth-century coiffure stiffened with powdered orris root. From *Galerie des Modes et
Costumes Francais,* 1778.

of blown glass were often added—insects, birds, ships, animals—
a sow is mentioned in one list. One wonders—were the little
pigs attached?

The French Revolution, when so many lovely ladies lost not
only their headdresses but their heads, brought an abrupt end
to the grotesque fashion, not only in France but all over Europe.
So, as a very minor result of the great political upheaval, some
hundred seventy-five years ago, the iris sank back once more to
its normal uses in pharmacy and the cosmetic industries. Modern chemistry has now eliminated iris as a medical drug, and
with the coming of synthetics the need for it in perfumes and
cosmetics has dwindled to negligible quantities.

Today the iris is an ornament in our gardens. But over thousands of years it has served mankind. If it began its service with
solemnity as a religious symbol it traveled to an ultimate
frivolity. Now perhaps, to those of us who care for it, it may
go full circle and take on a symbolic meaning again—different,
but our own.

When Edna St. Vincent Millay wrote *The Blue Flag in a
Bog*—far from one of her best poems but one which gardeners
tend to remember with affection—she visualized a sort of Sun-
day-school version of the end of the world. With grim and
horrible possibilities of man-made cataclysm facing us, her iris
as a symbol once more has validity:

* * *

There encompassed round by fire
Stood a blue flag in a bog.

* * *

It was all the little boats
That had ever sailed the sea,

Iris

It was all the little books
    That had gone to school with me.

On its roots like iron claws
    Rearing up so blue and tall,
It was all the gallant Earth
    With its back against a wall.

Lilies and roses in bronze. Detail from Ghiberti's north door of the Baptistery in Florence completed in 1424. (*Horticultural Society of New York*)

Lily

The Leyle is an herbe wyth a whyte floure. And though the levys of the floure be whyte: yet wythin shyneth the lykenesse of golde."

There are pink lilies and red lilies, orange lilies and lilies of every shade of yellow from buttercup through lemon to ivory; there are lavender lilies and purple lilies. But for most of us the word "lily" alone calls up the picture that the English monk Bartholomaeus Anglicus drew for us seven hundred years ago.

It is not likely that the primitive form had the size and magnificence that thousands of years of cultivation have given the Madonna lily, *L. candidum*. But even when it was a common wild flower the "levys" must have had that characteristic whiteness and, beyond a doubt, within shone the "lykenesse of golde." It was a flower to lift the heart and stir the imagination of even barbarous men.

In the story of the lily we can go back to an almost unbelievable antiquity—back for only a moment when we think we can catch a glimpse of the white and gold flower among half-civilized men struggling to build some sort of stable existence only to lose it to invading barbarians.

At least five thousand years ago a culture as early or earlier than that of Egypt was established in the Tigris-Euphrates Valley by a people we call Sumerians. At its peak their power overflowed into what is now Iran, including a city that lay roughly about a hundred miles from the Tigris. Beyond Sumerian jurisdiction roamed nomad tribes that were, in the latter part of the third millennium B.C., united by one Sargon who conquered the Sumerians and set up an empire of his own, the Semitic empire of Akkad. Contemporary tablets of his reign have been deciphered and on one of them we get a reference to the Iranian city Susa—the Lilies. A ruthless conquest is described in words that seem the essence of tact and understatement: "At Agade . . . Sargon, a gardener and cup-bearer of Ur-Ilbaba, having been made king." These inscriptions date from about 2872 B.C.

Since the conquerer was also a gardener, one is tempted to suggest that it was he who named the city so newly won after the conspicuous local flower. But scholars would consider this a frivolous speculation.

Meantime, the scholars themselves carry on a brisk argument about the name "Susa," not because of the horticultural implications but because the relationship of the word to other Middle Eastern languages may throw light on various ethnic and linguistic problems. According to some scholars, "Susa" came to mean "the Lilies" long after Sargon's time. According to others, the word was originally applied to both the city and the flower. If this latter group is correct, then the "Susa" of the Sargon tablets is the earliest reference to the lily yet found—a reference that is nearly five thousand years old.

One is indebted for this excursion into the dim reaches of prehistory to the valuable and interesting book, *Garden Lilies,* by Alan and Esther MacNeil. They have done a masterly job of research on the flower in which they specialize and it would be an impertinence to continue to quote them, as their book is recent and still in print. They carry the lily briefly but with authority from what was probably its original habitat in Iran through Asia Minor into Egypt, Greece, Rome and down into more modern times. So let us turn off into one of the Mediterranean byways where, like the iris and the crocus, the lily played a part in the Minoan religion of ancient Crete.

Lily

"The lily," Sir Arthur Evans stated without qualification, "is pre-eminently the Minoan sacred flower." And again, it is "a special attribute of the Great Minoan Goddess." This goddess, Britomartis (sweet maiden), or Dictynna, to give her both her names, had her origin in Neolithic times. She maintained unchallenged supremacy in Crete until, after the mysterious cataclysm that befell Minoan civilization in the middle of the sixteenth century B.C., her cult was gradually assimilated into the religion of the Greeks, and she became the precursor of the Greek Artemis.

Now, the interesting thing about Minoan religion was that it was monotheistic. In Greece, as elsewhere in the ancient world, a multiplicity of gods and goddesses developed a disunited pantheon of clannish deities who carried on feuds among themselves as enthusiastically as did their worshipers below. "Surveying the whole field," says Sir Arthur, after discussing some of the cults of antiquity, "it may be confidently said that so far as the evidence goes, of all these kindred religious systems, that of ancient Crete and the Minoan world stands out as the purest and best. . . ."

Naturally we do not know at just what date the lily became the symbol of the Minoan goddess, nor do we know with what other goddesses of the far past it may have been associated until we get into the familiar field of Greek mythology. There it was clearly attributed to the chief Greek goddess, Hera. From Greece it was passed on as a symbol to Hera's Roman prototype, Juno. In the Christian era, however, it has become associated with the Virgin Mary, from whom it gets its modern name, Madonna lily. So for literally thousands of years the lily has figured in human history as a religious symbol, typifying with its white and gold all that man could imagine of goodness and purity.

On a less exalted plane the lily has played a part in the specialized symbolism of heraldry and, for a few brief moments here and there, as a political symbol.

In the chapter on the iris it has been explained why I am convinced that it was the iris that served as a model for the fleur-de-lis, which must be taken into consideration in any discussion of flowers in heraldry. But for the benefit of those who believe, or hope to believe, that the fleur-de-lis originated in a lily, there are books on heraldry by an eminent modern authority, Arthur Charles Fox-Davies, who favors the lily.

There are, however, in heraldry plenty of lilies that are drawn so naturalistically that there is no doubt whatever about them. It is obvious why they occur on the arms of Lilly of Stoke Prior, or Lilley of Harrow, but the reason for their appearance on the arms of various families named Chadwick is obscure. Possibly a sentimental or romantic family legend accounts for the Chadwick lilies. It would be interesting to know it, but most books on heraldry hold themselves sternly aloof from matters of mere human or horticultural interest.

The frequency of lilies on the arms of educational institutions recalls the time when all schools and colleges were under the jurisdiction of the Church and the Virgin's lily seemed a natural symbol for institutions devoted to youth. The University of Aberdeen, King's College of Cambridge, and the schools of Winchester and Eton all display lilies on their arms.

Eton and King's were both founded by Henry VI, that pathetic son of the hero of Agincourt. Succeeding to the throne at the age of nine months, he grew up lacking the warlike and statesmanlike virtues of his father. In an England harried by the Wars of the Roses those virtues were sorely needed. Temperamentally he was probably more scholar than statesman, more student than warrior. In the course of a harassed life that ended on a block in the Tower of London, the establishment of two such schools as Eton and King's must have been among his few pleasures. He seems to have enjoyed working out detailed plans for them. Both were given almost identical coats of arms except that whereas white roses appear on King's, Eton has white lilies.

On May 23, 1471, Henry repeated his Latin prayer and bowed his head to the ax. Now each year on that day Eton and King's celebrate the Ceremony of the Roses and Lilies. There is a service which includes Henry's own prayer and ends when the provosts of the two schools lay the white roses of King's and the white lilies of Eton on the spot where the king was beheaded.

It would be interesting to know why Henry, last of the Lancastrian kings whose badge was a red rose, chose white roses for his college at Cambridge.

In comparatively modern times an orange lily became briefly a political symbol. Sometime before the French Revolution there was so much antiroyalist agitation in Holland that the members of the House of Orange had to flee the country. Along with the royal family Turk's-cap lilies came in for trouble. Radicals went so far as to prohibit the sale of oranges and carrots in the markets while the gardens were despoiled of their marigolds and the bulbs of all orange lilies.

In Ireland, too, there have been flying shillelaghs and broken heads because some Protestant Irishman invited trouble by sporting an orange lily in his "bonnet."

Naturally, myths and legends gather around so potent a symbol as the lily.

The most famous of these is the Greek myth which accounts for the origin of both the Milky Way and the lily. Since Hercules was his son by one of his numerous extramarital adventures, Zeus wanted to make the infant a god. When Hera understandably objected Zeus ordered Somnus, the god of sleep, to give Hera a sleeping draught. While she slept, Zeus put the child to her breast and the greedy baby sucked so lustily that the milk flowed faster than he could swallow it. Some drops splashed over the heavens to become the Milky Way. Others fell to earth and from these sprang the white lily—the emblem of purity.

The sight of its whiteness—thus a related myth continues— set up such a lively jealously in Aphrodite, who had herself issued from the whiteness of sea foam, that out of pure spite she had a huge pistil set in the center of the flower. The Freudians may take over from there, weaving together as they see fit such scattered items as that the lily was sometimes associated with the Satyrs; that St. Louis de Gonzague, protector of youth, is usually pictured with a lily in his hand, while a lily is attributed also to St. Anthony, protector of marriages; and finally, according to Albertus Magnus, the great thirteenth-century Schoolman and Dominican monk, you can tell with a lily whether or not a young girl is a virgin.

Now, it seems very unlikely that the great cleric busied himself with such matters, however interesting they may be to the lay mind. It seems far more probable that this particular item came from a curious old book, libelously attributed to him, *The boke of secretes of Albertus Magnus*. This spurious collection of herbal lore, magic and superstition was immensely popular during the Middle Ages and was generally accepted as gospel.

Anglo-Saxon folklore has a pleasant contribution to make in regard to the lily. With a lily and a rose you can foretell the sex of an unborn child. You approach the expectant mother carrying a lily in one hand and a rose in the other. If she chooses the rose her child will be a girl—if the lily, she will bear a son.

Lily

Even the white and gold of the lily fails to lighten the terrible period of history known as the Dark Ages. After the fall of Rome the accumulated knowledge of mankind was, for all practical purposes, lost. Medicine, like all other branches of learning, had to fall back upon such manuscripts as the local monasteries afforded. The monasteries cherished the few books they possessed and the monks made copies of them but without venturing into any critical or creative activities.

Outside the monasteries the world fought endless wars, from local raiding forays to large-scale hostilities. Men toiled under almost intolerable handicaps to get enough food and clothing and shelter to sustain life. Only after the feudal system had begun to bring some order out of the chaos was it possible for humanity in Europe to start again, almost from scratch, the slow business of learning to reason and to create.

Under such circumstances only a few literate men had access to such bits and pieces of classical medical knowledge as were to be found in monastic libraries—a battered manuscript of the herbal of Dioscorides here, a miserably transcribed copy of Galen or Celsus there. Most leeches knew nothing even of these authorities, but practiced the folk medicine which had for centuries come down from leech to leech by word of mouth. Reading and writing were no necessary part of a doctor's education in the Dark Ages.

Naturally, the very few medical manuscripts we have dating from this time were the work of men of exceptional mental vigor—men who had taken the trouble to read, or have read to them, such classical medicine as was locally available. What they remembered they proudly incorporated into their own work, and it is easy for even the layman to pick out such pieces. Directness and simplicity mark the medical writing of the great Roman tradition, while primitive folk medicine depended

Liliũ albũ   wyſz lilien   ⸿ Cap·lxxxix·

Ilium latine·arabice anſea uel aſtoſcam·grece Licina uel
ſyrion· ⸿ Der meiſter Serapio in dem bůch aggregatons
in dem capitel Anſea id eſt liſlum beſchribet vns vnd ſpriche
daʒ liſlum ſy heyß vnd druckener natuer in dem temperament· vnd
der iſt ʒweyerhande·Eyn wilde·die ander ʒame·⸿ Der meiſter Gas
bienus ſpricht daʒ die wilden liſten mancherhande blomen haben·

Lily from Peter Schoffer's *Hortus Sanitatis*, printed at Mainz in 1485.
(*The Pierpont Morgan Library*)

82

on the magic of charms and spells as much, if not more, than on any herbal remedy.

The Leech-book of Bald, for instance, gives a prescription for a burn medication which may well have come from one of the versions of Dioscorides.

"For a burn . . . take lily and yarrow, boil them in butter, smear therewith."

To make a "holy salve," on the other hand, you needed fifty-eight herbs, including the lily and the dust of a black snail. Butter must be made from the milk of a cow all of one color, red or white—no spots. Water was then hallowed in the baptismal font, but when or how it was incorporated is unclear. The butter went into a jug on which the names Matthew, Mark, Luke and John were written and was then stirred with a spoon "formed into a bristle brush"—whatever that may mean. Over this two psalms were sung three times. After that the *Gloria,* the *Credo, Deus meus et pater* and *In principio* were intoned. These sacred exercises were followed by the singing of the "worm chant," a mélange of Latin, Anglo-Saxon and gibberish which must have been so old even in Bald's time that its meaning had long been lost though its potency was still revered. We then return to the herbs which were "laid by the jug," spat upon, blown upon and hallowed (perhaps with the forgotten water). Finally the priest said Mass over the brew.

Here, it is clear, very ancient magic has been made respectable by the Church itself. Few ecclesiastics of the time were much more enlightened than their flocks, so it seemed to them best to let the local doctors go on with their practice of folk medicine, provided Christian prayers were substituted for heathen charms. The worm chant was an unusual exception but no one could understand it and there was always the chance it might bring good luck.

Even two hundred years after Bald the situation had changed very little. Information and ideas were disseminated with glacial slowness until after the invention of printing. In 1161 Odo of Meune, a town on the Loire, wrote a rhymed treatise on the properties of herbs that became famous under the name *Macer's Herbal.* Since an herbal was a necessary part of the equipment of every great lady, a copy of this highly esteemed authority was given to Phillippa of Hainault when she married Edward III of England. Even a queen, in those days, must know how to dose her household.

The manuscript that the young bride brought to her new home was an English translation of Odo's Latin original. For the white lily he gave conventional prescriptions that probably derive from Dioscorides. One tells how to make a plaster that will "rypyth ye sor sothly." But the native lily of the field that is described as being yellow as saffron served for some rather sinister magic. It must be gathered when the sun is in Leo, between the 15th of July and the 13th of August. If, then, it is mixed with some laurel leaves and buried under a manure pile it will breed worms that are big and fierce. Of these worms a powder can be made which, dusted on the clothes of an enemy, will prevent that unfortunate person from sleeping by night or by day. Or fed to the victim in milk, it will cause him or her to come down with fever. Fed to cattle, their milk will be dried up.

The later history of the lily in medicine is rather monotonous. With the exception of snakebite, for which he directed that lily seed be administered in a drink, Dioscorides had used lilies only externally. Medical practice up into the nineteenth century followed his lead, for, with negligible exceptions, lilies appear only in prescriptions recommending them as ingredients for plasters, salves and ointments.

Lily

The ointments carry us neatly from professional medicine into the stillrooms of castle and manor house where lilies were of vast importance. For Dioscorides had made a statement that was to echo through aging female hearts for eighteen hundred years: lilies, he said, "being beaten small with honey . . . cleareth ye faces & maketh them without wrinkles."

Woman, being the complicated creature she is, would probably have preferred to use "Susinon," an oil of lilies also recommended by Dioscorides as a cosmetic. But many a lady in Northern Europe must have been forced to fall back on the simpler lily-and-honey formula for lack of three thousand lilies. The making of the oil was a fabulous undertaking requiring days of mincing, boiling, straining, scumming and pressing the mixture. The final achievement yielded three batches of oil of a strong, medium and weak fragrance.

The statement that Dioscorides' recommendation about wrinkles was to echo through eighteen hundred years is quite mathematically exact. Not long ago a New Hampshire neighbor lent me a cookbook called *Old Dr. Carlin's Receipts* that had belonged to her grandmother. Like many another book of the period, this gives not only receipts for food and medicines but takes all kinds of useful information as its province. From it one can learn how to etch on ivory; how to caponize a fowl; how to hang wallpaper; how to decorate a carriage with decalcomania.

The exact date of Old Dr. Carlin's book had disappeared along with the title page, but leafing through it I found a newspaper clipping on how to make a cracker pudding. On the other side of the clipping, I read: "Sweeter words were probably never heard by Mrs. Seward and her son and daughter . . . When did I hear of Pres. Lincoln's assassination? When Surg. Gen. Barnes came . . . The surgeon general came to take my place at the bedside. As he did so . . . ." The cracker pudding ended on the other side and we shall never know what the surgeon general said to the writer—whoever that may have been.

A clipping, of course, cannot date a book, but along with the paper and format it is an indication that *Old Dr. Carlin's Receipts* probably appeared in the late 1850's or early 1860's.

Among the oddments described by the old doctor is a "Pomade to Remove Wrinkles." Two ounces of onion juice, two ounces of white lily (part not specified), two ounces of honey and one of white wax are put in a warm place to melt together. Then after stirring with a wooden spoon the mixture is allowed to cool. "Apply at night and do not rub off until morning."

The New Hampshire housewife who cherished the receipt for cracker pudding may well, as the years began to overwhelm her, have made up a batch of Old Dr. Carlin's ointment unaware of the fact that the use of the white lily to combat wrinkles dated back to another doctor who had practiced in the days of Nero.

Between Dioscorides and Old Dr. Carlin the same idea came in for some very fancy elaborations. As early as the fourteenth century there was a receipt for making "a face whit." Beans that have been steeped in eggs and wine for twenty-four hours are hulled, dried and powdered. This and hot water are added to the root of a lily pounded to a pulp and one is assured that this mixture will "do a-way the spottys."

Sir Kenelm Digby, in his mid-seventeenth-century stillroom book, had nearly as many claims for his "Precious Cosmetick, or Beautifying Water" as any modern "beautician" would advance for a facial treatment. He says that lilies, distilled along with some seventeen other ingredients, make a water that "Smoothes, whitens, beautifies & preserves the Complexions of Ladies. They may wash their faces with it at any time, but especially Morning and Evening."

Lily

It remained for the eighteenth century to carry the lily's cosmetic use furthest away from the original wrinkles. Along with various other plants, ashes and lye, these were boiled to make a water in which the hair must be frequently washed if the anxious operator hoped to have it "change in a little time to a beautiful flaxen color."

Lilies in the stillrooms were not confined, of course, to cosmetic receipts but their homemade medical aspects in most cases differed hardly at all from the professional herbalists' remedies. Elizabeth, Countess of Kent, however, used white lilies among other herbs in one of those pathetic prescriptions that run so futilely, so tragically, through all the old medical books: "For the biting of a mad dog."

There is a dearth of material about the use of lilies in the kitchen, and from the remote past we shall never get anything but theories. The MacNeils have one which is especially logical and interesting. Their suggestion is that the spread of *L. candidum* throughout the Near East was effected accidentally by nomads who carried the bulbs as food on their wanderings. Wherever a bulb, or even a scale of a bulb, was dropped a colony of the plants might spring up.

In China and Japan the bulbs of the tiger lily are commonly used as food and in Japan those of *L. auratum*—however sacrilegious this may seem to American gardeners—are often eaten. Mrs. Helen M. Fox, in her book *Garden Cinderellas*, gives a number of receipts for lilies as they are cooked in the Orient.

But when it comes to England and Europe there are only tantalizing hints that lilies were used in the kitchen. At the beginning of that fifteenth century cookbook quoted so often by Alicia M. Rockley, Baroness Cecil, in her *History of Gardening in England*, Turk's-cap lilies are listed among the herbs for pottage and among those for "Savour and beaute." A "Pottys of lylys" was served in the third course of the banquet given after the coronation of Henry IV in 1399. But a careful search in a good number of early cookbooks fails to reveal a single receipt that called for lilies. Obviously some must exist, but the field is so vast that it must be left to some other curious searcher who may one day turn up with a whole series of lily receipts. It would be interesting to see them.

When and how the Madonna lily reached Northern Europe is an intriguing speculation. The MacNeils' theory as to how it was disseminated through the Mediterranean area makes good sense but it throws no light on the question of when and how a flower native to the Persian Gulf area learned to flourish in the cool, damp gardens of England and Northern Europe.

One writer has made the inevitable guess—it was brought home by the Crusaders. It would be interesting if someday someone were to find documentary evidence that a specific plant found its way north in the shape of seed or bulb in the loot that some Crusader brought home. Although such factual data are still unfound, this has proved no deterrent to the theorizers. Whenever there is a gap in the history of some Mediterranean plant which eventually succeeded in the north of Europe, the Crusaders get the credit for its introduction. No one, one suspects, would be more surprised than they who looked rather for jewels and precious metals, ornate weapons and fine textiles.

In the case of the Madonna lily, however, we cannot get off with an easy guess about the Crusaders. Wahafrid Strabo (809–848) counted it as equal to the rose in his German garden in the Benedictine Abbey at Reichenau. The First Crusade did not get under way until 1096.

The explanation of how the lily reached Germany so early may lie in a theory suggested by Baroness Cecil. She had no

Lily

Lily from Dodoens' *Pemptades* (*Horticultural Society of New York*)

doubt that *L. candidum* came to Britain with the Romans. The homesick men who garrisoned that far outpost of empire built villas and baths and temples as much as possible like those they had known in Italy. Near their villas, reasoned Baroness Cecil, must have stood the gardens where they grew plants imported from home.

Flower Chronicles

In A.D. 410 came the order to evacuate the Roman forts in Britain and the legions hurried south to defend the homeland from invading barbarians. Only those flowers which were thoroughly acclimated could possibly have survived the ensuing centuries of neglect, for the Northmen swept into England in wave after wave once the Romans were gone. Angles, Saxons, Jutes and Danes came and conquered. In the scanty intervals between invasions, internal upheavals kept the unhappy island in a state of constant turmoil until the Normans came and a sort of order was restored.

Baroness Cecil supports her theory by pointing out that the Anglo-Saxons knew Roman names for many plants and so those foreign ones to which they gave Anglo-Saxon names must have been, as she called them, "the hardy survivors" of the Roman occupation. The same argument might well apply to Germany and explain how Strabo came by his lily.

If Baroness Cecil is right, then it is possible that the ancient Britons, who painted themselves blue and practiced human sacrifice, may have admired the same white and gold that Sargon's men had known in ancient Iran.

In curious and exciting ways wild lilies have come to be tamed to our gardens. Some of the more popular ones have reached us from Asia, many within the past fifty years. Few stories of travel and adventure can equal those of the plant collectors working along the Chinese-Tibetan border, where many of the lilies we know grow wild at extremely high altitudes. It is incredible country—beautiful, wild and isolated from anything we call civilization. The men who traveled there and in similar remote parts of Asia are not only interesting to gardeners everywhere but should be remembered and honored for the risks they have run, the hardships they have endured, and the perseverance they have displayed in the face of what must often have seemed insuperable obstacles.

Lily

A fine staff of regal lilies reminds us that in 1904 one of these men nearly lost his life getting these lilies from the Chinese-Tibetan borders to American gardens. Eighteen hundred miles up the Yangtze to the Min River, then two hundred fifty miles north where "in narrow, semi-arid valleys, down which torrents thunder, and encompassed by mountains . . . whose peaks are clothed with snow eternal, the Regal Lily has her home." On the return journey E. H. Wilson was knocked off his feet by a rockslide which gashed his thigh and broke his leg in two places. When he reached the nearest medical missionary, after having been carried for three agonizing days in a sedan chair by his Chinese attendants, the leg was infected. By some miracle he survived without amputation, but he walked with a limp for the rest of his life.

In books easily available today, the books of E. H. Wilson quoted above, in those of Reginald Farrer, who died of fever while on the job, of Frank Kingdon Ward and E. H. M. Cox, those who are interested can read the stories of those adventurer-botanists.

They were professionals, these men, and they were paid to do the work. But, like true professionals the world over, they were earning their livings at the jobs they loved. They often risked their lives to gather flower or seed—sometimes on a precipice, sometimes by crossing a flimsy bridge over a wild gorge, sometimes at the hands of angry natives. The latter, especially those on the Tibetan side of the border, were convinced that no one in his right mind would dare the heights except for gold. All this talk about flowers was just a red herring. There is gold in the Tibetan alps and the lamas who rule the country have made it clear that evil spirits will punish with thunder and lightning, sleet and hail, those impertinent men who invade the high fastnesses. Reginald Farrer tells how afraid he was after a storm to return to a native village he had left below. If hail had destroyed the scanty harvest, who could be to blame but the foreigner who had obviously called down the wrath of the mountain demons?

But between the ancient and modern introductions of lilies is a little-known chapter in the story of men and flowers that closely concerns us as Americans.

The three great lilies of our eastern seaboard, *L. canadense,* *L. superbum,* and *L. philadelphicum,* were early valued in European gardens.

It is not quite certain when *L. canadense* reached Europe. If it is true that it was brought from the New World by the French explorer Jacques Cartier, it is understandable why no special record of its arrival remains. It would have been merely a trivial item among the curiosities brought back from an exciting new continent.

L. superbum came next—after some two hundred years. According to a Belgian botanist who has done a great deal of research on lilies, it was sent to Peter Collinson in London in 1727 by Benjamin Franklin. Now, in 1727 Franklin was, it is true, an up-and-coming young man around Philadelphia, but he had not yet reached that point in his career when he was in correspondence with notables abroad. It was his friend and fellow townsman, John Bartram, the first and one of the greatest American botanists, who sent the *L. superbum* and, later, *L. philadelphicum* to Collinson.

"I have the pleasure to tell thee," Peter Collinson wrote Bartram from London in September, 1736, "that the noble Marsh Martagon flowered with me, which thou sent me this spring. It is a delicate flower." Somewhat later *L. philadelphicum* figures in the correspondence and Collinson inquires of Bartram whether the plant in its native habitat always produces only a single flower to a stem, as his specimen does.

In the informal letters between Bartram and Collinson one

steps completely into the feeling and spirit of two hundred years ago. Both were members of the Society of Friends and both were passionately interested in natural history, but there the resemblance ends. Collinson was a rich and busy merchant in a great metropolis, a member of the Royal Society, a friend of Linnaeus, of the—at that time—even more famous Dr. Johann Gronovius of Holland, and of a number of British peers who shared his interests—especially in new botanical specimens for their gardens. Bartram, who lived not far outside Philadelphia, was no frontiersman, but he was still the son of a new world, a sparsely settled country, innocent of sophistication, where most men were still hard at work on the land.

It is the very difference in background that makes for the amusing paradox in the letters. For Collinson, the man of the world, is the inquirer and Bartram, the farmer-turned-naturalist, is the mentor who explains and elucidates.

In spite of the gains, we have lost much in our own time by specialization. One rarely hears of "natural history" today. One man is interested in birds, another in flowers, still another in fungi. The amount of data now available about such things is so great that a man can spend a lifetime studying one species in a genus. In the early eighteenth century most of that data was still to be collected, and men of lively minds were free to scatter their interests far and wide. And they did. To read Collinson's letters is to be reminded of an exceptionally intelligent small boy wild with excitement about all the wonderful things the world contains.

Yet now and again Collinson's urban sophistication slips through, as when he wrote Bartram about a plant-hunting trip the latter was to take into Virginia. Bartram was to call on various prominent Virginians with whom Collinson was in correspondence and to whom he had written about Bartram. To Bartram himself he wrote:

"One thing I must desire of thee, and do insist that thee oblidge me therein; that thou make up that druet clothes, to go to Virginia in, and not appear to disgrace thyself or me; for though I should not esteem thee the less, to come to me in what dress thou will,—yet these Virginians are a very gentle, well-dressed people—and look perhaps more to a man's outside than his inside. For these and other reasons, pray go very clean, neat and handsomely dressed to Virginia."

It may be added that whatever clothes Bartram wore he had no difficulty whatever in making friends with such men as Colonel Byrd and Colonel Custis of Williamsburg. In fact the latter complained peevishly to Collinson that Bartram's visit to him was entirely too short.

The greater part of Collinson's letters, however, reflect that intelligent, quivering small boy who was the essential spirit of the age. He was repelled by the stories of rattlesnakes but fascinated and eager for more details. He wanted Bartram to send him seeds, bulbs and roots of every conceivable wild flower shrub and forest tree. But his restless interest was not confined to botany. He wanted birds' nests and eggs, hornets' and mud-daubers' nests, shells, insects, butterflies, terrapin and tortoises, fossils, ferns, fungi, animal skins and horns.

The birds' nests, fossils, shells, insects, and all the other items Bartram sent Collinson may seem a far cry from our two native lilies. But at that time hundreds of fine plants were reaching England and Europe all because of the eagerness of men like Collinson. "Curious" men they called themselves with pride—meaning not that they were eccentric but that they were men of wide-ranging interests. All gardens are the richer for the plants the curious men had shipped from far places and which they brought under cultivation. American lilies were part of the wealth so garnered.

Lily

We have now come through nearly five thousand years and entirely around the world with lilies. Even though those of Palestine are believed to be the brilliantly colored anemones, lilies live for all of us, forever, not only in our gardens but in the beautiful ageless words: "Consider the lilies of the field, how they grow; they toil not, neither do they spin: and yet I say unto you, That even Solomon in all his glory was not arrayed like one of these."

Pionia benonien korner oder wne
dicten korner ⸿ Capitulum·ccxcviij·

Ionia latine·arabice pynuser· ⸿ Die meister sprechen ge
meynglich das der stam dar uff disser same wachs habe groß
blumen die synt roit und synt gemenglich genāt benedicten
rosen· Disser stam ist uns wole bekant der wurtzeln dogent ist uns
beschriben in dē capitel pionia· ⸿ Platearius spricht das diß korner

Peony from *Hortus Sanitatis* of Mainz. (*The Pierpont Morgan Library*)

Peony

n a rugged mountainside in prehistoric Greece a shepherd sat one night keeping watch over his flock of scrawny beasts. Staring vacantly about him, his eye was caught by a trick of moonlight—its sheen on the satiny petals of a nearby clump of peonies. Cause and effect as we know them were concepts for the distant future. The dim, slow brain that received that sensory impression marveled. Here was a familiar flower that shone by night, that glowed in the dark! At the first opportunity the shepherd told his comrades about the wonder.

In some such fashion, down through ages that predate written records, from father to son, from tribe to tribe, went the word that the peony shone in the dark, that it must be of divine origin and possessed of most potent magic.

Quite possibly the first magic the peony performed was to drive away devils and the fear of devils from which the mountain shepherds suffered. Again a faulty chain of cause and effect operated. Peonies "shone" at night only when the moon was near the full, and the assaults of devils and fear of devils notoriously occur in darkness. But since the magic power to banish evil was associated with the peony, the very proximity of the flower on the darkest night must have brought comfort to many a fearful man.

The next step may well have been to reason that if this flower was so potent against devils and evil spirits when it was growing in the ground, a piece of the plant worn on the person might be equally potent as protection from devils and evil spirits wherever he might be.

Flower Chronicles

The magic of primitive man, anthropology has now shown us, was not mere mumbo-jumbo but a legitimate science. However childish the reasoning may seem to us today, our remote ancestors had soberly worked out methods for influencing transcendental powers with which they could not otherwise cope. Not for a moment can we assume that modern man has solved the problems of understanding or influencing the transcendental; it is still high and far for us to seek, but its boundaries are different. Devils and evil spirits who can be placated with animal or herbal offerings are no longer believed to be the primary cause of disease and insanity, earthquake and famine. We have found physical laws that bring much illness, many mental aberrations, and even some aspects of the weather under man's control.

Reasoning as he did, primitive man naturally claimed great and supernatural powers for a flower that shone in the dark. Myths and legends cling to such a magic flower. A plant of such immense potency was no common thing to be pulled up casually by anyone who wanted or needed it. It had to be dug by night, for should a man attempt to do so by day he risked the loss of his eyes from the woodpecker who guarded the magic herb. Theophrastus, ever true to the great intellectual tradition of his time, always tried to base his theories on facts. He characterized this fear of the woodpecker as "far-fetched and irrelevant."

One wonders if Theophrastus' comment would have been so temperate had he known the elaborations that time was to add to the digging of peony roots. Gerard cites two authors from Roman times who illustrate these elaborations. Josephus (c. A.D. 37–90) thought that those who wanted to gather the plant should do so only after they had poured a woman's urine or menses upon it. Aelianus (c. A.D. 220) claimed that even under cover of darkness it was dangerous for a man to dig peony root. As with the mandrake, a hungry dog must be tied to the plant with roasted meat set nearby so that the dog would drag the peony from the ground in his efforts to reach the food.

These legends lend color to Pliny's remark that "the paeonia is the most ancient of them [herbs] all," and he goes on to say that it still bears the name of him who first discovered it.

As usual, accuracy was not Pliny's forte. For, according to Greek mythology, Paeon did not discover the potent herb but was given it by Leto, the mother of Apollo. It was with the peony that Paeon was supposed to have healed Pluto of the wound he received during the Trojan War. Presumably peony was also among the herbs with which he cured Mars of a wound. These successes so aroused the jealousy of Aesculapius, whose pupil he had been, that Aesculapius plotted the death of Paeon. (Probably, as Mrs. Edward Harding remarked in her invaluable book on the peony, this was the first recorded instance of professional jealousy.) Pluto was so grateful to Paeon for healing his wound that, when he heard of the plot, he saved his doctor from death by changing him into the flower that bears his name.

Magical attributes, myths and legends are all we might expect to find about the peony in the remote past, so it is at once surprising and delightful to run across peonies in ancient history. It is a tenuous reference, but most gardeners will be charmed to discover that there was once a country—a separate national entity with a king, a government and an army—that was called Paeonia. Whether the land was named for the native flower or the flower took its name from the land we do not know and probably never shall.

There is a tradition that in pre-Homeric times a people from the neighborhood of Troy migrated in great numbers to Europe. They settled in what is now northern Greece and at the height of their power controlled a crescent-shaped area reaching from the Aegean up through a bit of modern Bulgaria, then along the northern part of Greece to that western corner where, in the neighborhood of four lakes, Greece, Albania and Yugoslavia now meet.

Homer speaks of Paeonians from the Axium (Vardar) who fought on the side of their Trojan kinsmen.

Later, during the Persian Wars, much of Paeonia was conquered. Herodotus tells how Darius (c. 521 B.C.) disposed of two whole tribes of Paeonians by mass migration. Resting in Lydia (now Turkey) after one of his campaigns, he was intrigued by a woman he saw. Not only was she beautiful but her industry delighted him. She was walking along leading a horse to water, a pitcher on her head and spinning flax with her free hand. On learning that she was a Paeonian he immediately sent word to his military commander in Thrace to deport two tribes of these hard-working people straightway to Asia.

The part of Paeonia that escaped the Persian inroads lay to the west. There in mountainous country, dotted with lakes, where peonies flourished, a group of fiercely independent tribes made their home. Their dwellings, according to Herodotus, were built on platforms in the lakes and parents "tied their baby children by the foot with a string to keep them from rolling into the water." A trap door in the floor of every house offered access to an inexhaustible supply of fish below.

These Paeonian tribes were conquered by Philip of Macedonia, and thereafter such history as the country had was that of a province, not of an independent state. It is possible that the Persians named a city for the lily, but Paeonia was the only nation ever to bear the name of a flower.

Peony

It may seem a far cry from a prehistoric shepherd's simple wonder at a moonlit peony to the teething necklace of a nineteenth-century baby. But the extraordinary fact is that a traceable thread runs back through the medical history of the peony to the magic that was primitive man's only means of coping with phenomena that he could not understand. Because of the persistence of that magical aspect of the peony, its medical history is far the most interesting of any flower in this book —and the most amazingly consistent.

Many plants have been credited with the same "vertues" over the centuries, but usually the reason they were so credited is unclear or has been wholly lost to us. In the course of time, the original virtue accorded one flower has been confused with that of some other flower, as in the case of the cornflower and the centaury. The more herbals one reads the more confused the picture becomes: a flower that one has pinned down in antiquity as a specific for respiratory troubles may turn up in the sixteenth or seventeenth century as a sure cure for the itch.

The peony, of course, was no exception to the rule that a plant valuable for one ailment might well serve for others. In the course of its long medical career it has been used for childbirth and female complaints (practically every herb seems to have been tried out for these at one time or another), for stomach-ache, kidney troubles, sciatica, fever, gout, dropsy, headache, and various other maladies. But along with the prescriptions to combat these ills has gone, in practically all the old medical books, the assurance that peony root or seed would be effectual in coping with epilepsy and such "related" illnesses as convulsions and "the Incubus we call the Mare." That was William Coles's phrase in *The Art of Simpling* (1657). A more modern physician described it as "that disagreeable disease the night-mare."

More than seventeen hundred years before Dr. William

Flower Chronicles

Meyrick, in his *New Family Herbal* (1790), described night-mare as a disagreeable disease Pliny wrote that peony is "a preservation against the illusions practiced by the fauni in sleep."

Pliny, as already noted, based much of his information on ancient Greek herbals now lost, and those herbals had evolved, as have all herbals, from the folk medicine of an earlier time. Ancient folk medicine was based on the only science primitive man knew—magic. So we find in Pliny's writing, as well as in that of his contemporary Dioscorides, material now undocumented that can be traced back—at least by logical deduction—to a folk medicine of undeterminable antiquity.

Pliny's *fauni* were the Roman version of the more ancient Greek devils and evil spirits. Even Dioscorides, whose herbal is singularly free of magic, devotes his last words on the peony to remarks about its potency against "bewitchings and fears and devils and their assaults . . . and it is said that sometimes growing on an hill where there are devils, it drove them away." There was then only a single short step to take from devils and evil spirits that objectively "assault" a man to the subjective "possession" of a man by devils and evil spirits. Surely nothing less than a devil could be responsible for the writhings and rackings of the human frame in epilepsy or convulsions; nothing less than evil spirits could drive an otherwise courageous man out of his bed at night sweating with terror. The peony offered an obvious remedy. Had it not been held from time immemorial as powerful against devils and evil spirits and the terror by night?

We do not know exactly when that step was taken but it must have been early because Galen, writing in the second century of our era, speaks as if the peony had long been used in cases of epilepsy. "I do not entirely relinquish the hope," he wrote, "that it may have been reasonable to rely on it [the

peony] to cure epilepsy in children, even if used as an amulet."
It would appear that one of the greatest doctors of all time fell
back on magic as lesser men were to do for centuries to come.
But we cannot be dogmatic about it. Galen had done some ex-

A barber-surgeon with his equipment. *The
Grete Herball.* (*The Pierpont Morgan Library*)

perimenting with peonies in an entirely rational fashion and
the word "amulet" did not carry in his time quite the same
magical connotation it has today. But that last phrase "even
if used as an amulet" does suggest a reservation in Galen's
mind. Magic or medicine, he used peonies for epilepsy and we
can feel sure that as a doctor it comforted him to have a specific he could recommend. In that respect he was better off
than are modern physicians.

It is possible to pass from classical medicine to that of the

Middle Ages without being surprised to find that the peony continued its career as a cure for epilepsy—sometimes in straight magical fashion as an amulet, sometimes as a drug administered internally.

It is doubtful that peonies had reached England by the tenth century, for none appear in the Anglo-Saxon leech-books except those that are translations from Dioscorides and Apuleius. In those, of course, peonies were mentioned along with numerous other Mediterranean plants that posed such riddles to northern students in those early innocent days. But by 1161 *Macer's Herbal* could specify that five "grynes of pionys" added to vervaine and gathered with *pater nosters* and *aves* would, after the patient had been cleansed "owt of dedly syne," cure him of the falling sickness.

Saints in medieval times were patrons of various diseases. While a number of them presided over epilepsy, the most interesting patrons were not saints but the Three Wise Men. These "when they were come into the house, they saw the young child with Mary his mother, and fell down, and worshipped him." As Dr. Owsei Temkin points out in his fine book, *The Falling Sickness*, it was probably because they *fell down* that they came to be associated with epilepsy. At any rate they, together with the peony, figure in a prescription written about 1412 by John of Ardene: "Against Epilepsy write these three names with blood taken from the little finger of the patient—Jasper, Melchior and Balthazar—and put gold, frankincense and myrrh into a box. Let the patient say three *pater nosters* and three *ave marias* daily for the souls of the fathers and mothers of these three kings for a month and let the patient drink for a month of the juice of peonies with beer or wine . . . and without doubt this remedy never fails."

During the Renaissance, when the use of reason as against the acceptance of tradition became common, this sort of mumbo-jumbo gradually disappeared. But the peony remained, and with more old source books in circulation there was a return to one of the peony's original uses. William Turner recommended fifteen black peony seeds for "the stranglying of the night mare," and Gerard gives the "disease" a fine Greek name—*Ephialtes*. The latter also quoted Galen as his authority for using an amulet of peony for small children but thought that those who are "growne up in more yeares" should be given peony root internally. Parkinson thought it valuable for all Epilepticall diesease" and that the roots hung "about the neckes of the younger sort" might serve as a preventive. Here still is magic, mixed now with a tendency to use a drug in what we would consider more orthodox fashion.

In home medicine as well as in professional practice the peony played an important role. Those frightening manifestations we call convulsions seem to have been, for instance, an especial problem of that unknown English family whose stillroom book we know as *A Book of Simples*. For it contains no less than five prescriptions for this state, which take peonies and several more besides made up without benefit of peonies.

There is the "Hysterick Electuary the Lady Gerard's Rect." which includes "surrop of pioneys" and purports to have cured "both old and young of convulsions Hysterick vapours fitts and falling sickness." There is "A Very excellent Receipt against Convulsions which cur'd one who had nine Fitts in a day," which also included syrup of peonies as does another "For Convulsion Fits." Dried peony roots powdered make a medicine to cope with "Very strong Fitts or Fitts in Great People." Finally, there is "The Convulsion Water," which takes green peony roots and is of such frantic complexity that one feels sure it was copied down by some desperate woman who had already tried everything else and was at her wit's end.

That she was willing to try anything is witnessed by a revolting prescription which is as innocent of peonies as it is of punctuation and spelling. "Take three drops of cats blood in breast milk or cowes of the milk one spoonful blood warme mingle the blood and milk together putting thereto a grain of musk and give it to the patient an hour before the fit if you know at what time it comes if not then as soon as they find it coming let them drink it. this is aproved."

Perhaps all families did not have such dire need for remedies for convulsions as did this unknown English family but in other stillroom books there appear similar prescriptions that used peonies consistently for both convulsions and epilepsy. So throughout informal as well as professional medical practice peonies held to the reputation that had been given them when medicine and magic were one.

Meantime, during the latter part of the seventeenth century, the magic aspect of peonies took a very fancy turn. The "Anodyne Necklace" came into its own. Some sharp-witted quack seized upon the idea, already very old, that peony worn about the neck had medicinal value and others swiftly exploited the possibilities of this "cure." "Miraculous necklaces"—thus runs an early eighteenth-century handbill—"for children breeding teeth, preventing (by God's assistance) feavers, convulsions, ruptures, chincough [whooping cough], rickets and such attendant distempers." Prehistoric ideas of preventive magic had raised their heads once more even in the face of the growing body of empirical knowledge that was being accumulated by men with scientific minds.

As late as the nineteenth century faith in the age-old theory in the value of the peony for epilepsy still hung on here and there. But there is an indication of the new scientific caution in Dr. Robert John Thornton's quotation (1810) of a Scottish doctor who reported that he had dosed two epileptics with peony root and claimed "that one of them received a temporary advantage from its use." That damning with faint praise may well have been the swan song of the peony in medicine.

But its magic power was still potent in the minds of simple people. Necklaces made of beads of turned peony root were hung about the necks of babies until the closing years of the nineteenth century. Latterly, of course, they were no more than teething rings. Science had spoken, and their value as preventive magic was gone. Gone except, one can feel quite sure, that here and there a grandmother clasped the beads about a baby's neck with a vague memory of their protective power that she had learned from her own grandmother. Dimly remembered magic or teething rings, their line of descent is clear all the way back to prehistoric Greece.

Peonies had a rather short career in the kitchen, but it is fascinating to discover that, while they began their culinary history as a seasoning of the food and drink of poor men, they reached an ultimate dignity as the fare of kings.

Glutton, the personification of one of the seven deadly sins in *Piers Plowman,* the fourteenth-century poem by William Langland, started out for church one Sunday reeking with good intentions. On his way he passed a tavern where Betsy the Brewstere hailed him and inquired where he was bound.

> "To holi church," quod he, "for to here masse,
> And sithen I wil be shryuen and synne na more."

Betsy suggests that instead he come in and try her good ale. Glutton puts up a feeble resistance by demanding to know whether or not she has any "hote spices" to season the drink. The reply is prompt and definite:

> "I haue peper and piones," quod she, "and a pound of garlic. . . ."

Whereupon Glutton enters the inn as morally weak-kneed as he leaves it physically many hours later.

That peony seed served along with pepper and garlic and other spices to season the fare of the poor is made clear by the company Glutton finds when he enters the tavern. There was Cecely the shoe-seller, Wat the warrener with his wife, Tim the tinker with his two apprentices, Hick a hackneyman, Hugh a tailor, Clarice of Cock Lane who, judging by her address, was no better than she should have been, a fiddler, a ditch-digger, a ratcatcher, and various other contemporary working people, ending up with "upholsterers an hepe."

As a seasoning the peony seed must have been much cheaper than Betsy's pepper that had made the long and hazardous voyage from the Far East. But the roots of peony as a food could hardly have served as a staple for the common man. Only the very rich could afford the roots of an exotic perennial of notoriously slow growth. It is only on the tables of kings, nobles and prelates that we meet up with the peony served as a food.

When the Duke of Lancaster gave a banquet for Richard II in 1387 a hundred dozen peony roots were among the provisions laid in along with "the pigges and the maribones, the thousand egges and the Appelles." "Peionys" were served at the wedding breakfast of the Earl of Devonshire in 1389. "Pyionys" were one of the dishes in the third course of the coronation banquet of Henry IV in 1399, and "peiouns" appeared at the banquet given after his second marriage in 1404. "Pyions" were on the menu of the feast that celebrated the induction of John Stafford as Bishop of Bath and Wells in 1425, and at about the same date "pyiouns" were mentioned among the dishes served at a banquet for one John Chaundeler.

We know that at Richard's feast the peonies were served "rosted," perhaps with a sauce. At any rate, at a slightly later date we get a receipt for "A Sauce for peiouns: Take percely, oynouns, garleke, and salt and mynce smal the percely and the oynouns and grynde the garleke, and temper it with vynegre y-now: and mynce the rostid peiouns and cast the sauce thereon aboute, and serue it forth."

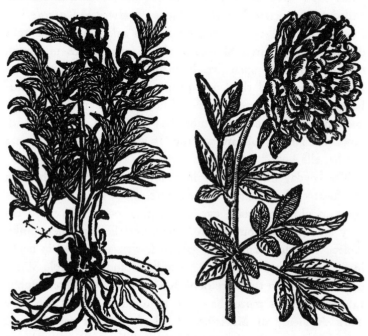

Two varieties of peony shown in Dodoens' *Pemptades*. (*Horticultural Society of New York*)

Peonies appear in a receipt which is a good sample of the lengths to which medieval cooking could go in the way of ingredients and time-consuming methods. *Mammenye Bastarde* dates from about 1430.

To make this dish one pound each of peony root, raisins, saunders (powdered sandalwood), pepper and an unspecified amount of cinnamon were put on the fire in two gallons of wine or ale to which was added a "potelle" of clarified honey. Meantime three pounds of almonds had been set to steep in a gallon each of wine and vinegar, for how long we do not know. Then these were strained out and the nut-flavored liquor was added to the original mixture. Since *Mammenye Bastarde* was intended to be "styf" a modern cook is aghast at the thought of the time required to reduce those four gallons of liquid, especially over an open fire. Eventually that result must have been achieved and then, lest pepper (a whole pound remember!), cinnamon, sandalwood and honey failed to give the dish enough flavor, one was admonished to "sesyn it uppe" with powdered ginger, salt and saffron. It was served "alle flat on a dysshe, alle hote."

The heyday of the peony in cooking seems to have been in the fourteenth and fifteenth centuries. There are no cross references in old cookbooks, even those that boast indices, so the only way to find out where, when and how peonies, pinks, violets, calendulas and other garden flowers were used in cooking is to read cookbooks. The delightful and invaluable Whitney Collection in the Rare Book Room at the New York Public Library contains more than two hundred items. At the New York Academy of Medicine, of all places, is a collection of something over six thousand! One quails at the thought of going on from there to other libraries in this country, not to mention those abroad.

As a postscript to peonies in cooking I should add that I have tried them. I did not have the courage to make a *Mammenye Bastarde* but I "rosted" some roots along with a loin of pork. The taste was acrid and not unpleasant. Judging, however, from its texture, the true function of peony roots is to be made into beads on which babies can cut their teeth.

Peony

In general, these flower histories have been held to the Western world, but when it comes to the peony China has to be taken into account, for the peony is practically the national flower of China. The tree peony is the great flower there and herbaceous peonies are only slightly less beloved. The story of the part peonies have played in Chinese legend and history, medicine and diet should not be entirely disregarded, but where can a Westerner begin—and with what?

Poetry offered a suggestion. Except for Shakespeare's "pioned" banks in *The Tempest,* no English or American poet seems to have been moved to lyric expression by the peony, but anyone who has read translations from the Chinese will remember that peonies figure fairly often in poetry. A mere handful of books provided a rich haul: Eunice Tietjens' anthology *Poetry of the Orient,* Amy Lowell and Florence Ayscough's *Fir-Flower Tablets,* Arthur Waley's *107 Chinese Poems,* and L. Cranmer-Byng's *Lute of Jade.* These not only celebrated the peony in verse but linked it by legend, history and romance to the golden age of Chinese poetry and to the most famous of Chinese love stories.

The tale concerns Ming Huang, an emperor of the T'ang Dynasty (A.D. 712–756). He was not a great ruler but he was, Cranmer-Byng said, a "poet and sportsman, mystic and man of this world, a great polo player and the passionate lover of one beautiful woman whose ill-starred fate inspired Po Chu-i, the tenderest of all their singers."

When the empress and Ming Huang's favorite mistress had both died, a young concubine was brought to the emperor's attention. Yang Kuei-fei was beautiful—"a reed in motion and a rose in flame." A great love flowered between these two, but China was seething with misery and unrest.

We are sadly aware that the modern tragedy of China may

surpass the ancient one, but Arthur Waley, writing in 1917, has said that Ming Huang's was the most tragic period in Chinese history. A rebellion developed into a civil war that took thirty million Chinese lives.

When the first flare-up came, the soldiers surrounding the emperor refused to defend him unless he permitted them to execute Yang Kuei-fei, whose extravagance and follies they considered responsible for all their troubles. Ming Huang was faced with a cruel choice between what he believed best for his country and the woman he loved. Brokenhearted himself he sent her forth,

> lily pale
> Between tall avenues of spears to die.

But Yang Kuei-fei lives on—and will as long as Chinese literature endures. For not only Po Chu-i has written of her but Li Po as well, and they are generally considered the two greatest of Chinese poets.

One of Li Po's lyrics celebrates the Feast of Peonies during the happy time the lovers were together before the rebellion broke out. They were living in a fabulous Chinese city whose triple walls were marked here and there with tall drum towers and bell towers. The palace where the lovers lived was surrounded by gardens crosshatched by canals and bounded by lakes. Near one of these lakes was a pavilion where, during the Feast of Peonies, the emperor and Yang Kuei-fei used to go at sunset to admire the great flowers growing between the balustrade of the pavilion and the water.

It was in this setting that the emperor sent for Li Po and bade him immortalize his mistress. One version of the tale contends that Li Po was so drunk when he arrived that court ladies had to steady his tablet and Yang Kuei-fei herself held his block of ink. But drunk or sober it does not matter. The

Peony

great poet has set the emperor's lady before us and she lives for the Chinese immemorially when peonies scent the twilight in their season.

> She is the flowering branch of the peony
> Richly-laden with honey dew.

Le Floriste François

Cest L'Amour seul qui me Cultiue,
Et Phœbus enrichit mes fleurs
D'un nombre infini de couleurs
Lune brune l'autre plus viiue
Prenant le pur des Elements
Pour composer mes ornements

Docquet fecit

A ROVEN Chez Louis du Mesnil dans la Cour du Palais 1658

Title page of *La Floriste François*, 1654, by de La Chesnée Monstereul, possibly the first horticultural monograph ever published. (*Rare Book Room, New York Public Library*)

Tulip

"Tulipa, or the Dalmatian Cup, is a strange and forrein floure. . . ." And indeed it was when John Gerard wrote in 1597. It had then been in England for only a score of years. Gerard goes on to say that his "loving friend, James Garret, a curious searcher of Simples and learned Apothecarie of London," had been trying for twenty years to find out all the different kinds, but each year brought so many new colors and varieties from abroad that to record them was like "trying to roll Sisiphus stone, or number the sands." The problem, Gerard thought, would have to wait for "some that meane to write of Tupila a particular volume."

A good many particular volumes on the tulip have been published since Gerard's day but no one of them offers any explanation of the mysterious silence that shrouds its early history. Sir A. Daniel Hall, generally conceded to be the most eminent of modern authorities on the tulip, notes that it is "somewhat remarkable that neither Theophrastus, Dioscorides nor Pliny should have noticed so conspicuous a plant of which several species are indigenous and not uncommon in Greece and Ionia." He adds that tulips do not appear in Italian painting until the middle of the sixteenth century nor was he able to trace them in Persian art any earlier. Together with other modern writers on the tulip, Sir Daniel places the first recorded tulips as those described by de Busbecq in Turkey in 1556.

Somewhere between the years 2200 and 1600 B.C., however, a Bronze Age craftsman turned out a black pottery jar on which he had silhouetted tulips in white—tulips "like those," said

Sir Arthur Evans, "that grow wild in the glen of Juktas today."

At least three thousand years of complete silence stretches between those Minoan tulips and the ones that de Busbecq brought to Europe from Constantinople. Ordinarily one expects to find a conspicuous common flower in ancient myth and legend, in primitive magic and early medicine. But the tulip presents only an enigma.

Modern students of Biblical botany tend now to identify the Rose of Sharon in the Song of Songs and the "rose" in Ecclesiastes with a mountain tulip. If this is true, tulips make a brief appearance in Jewish literature. But there is no certainty about it.

The "Saturion" in the Greek herbal of Dioscorides has been identified as various orchids and even, Dr. Gunther adds, as a tulip. That "even" makes it so improbable that the Saturion was a tulip that it would not be worth noting were it not that some Renaissance herbalists, Gerard and Parkinson among them, believed this to be the case. It may have been wishful thinking on their parts because the Saturion possessed the desirable property of being able to "stir up courage in ye conjugation."

These, then, are all the shreds and patches of evidence we have that the tulip was even noticed in antiquity. The Minoan jar alone offers us any concrete evidence. Its silent testimony that someone in that far distant time once looked at tulips and admired them only serves to deepen the mystery. Why was a flower that was particularly handsome and very conspicuous ignored for three thousand years?

We now turn to the man who is known to have introduced the tulip into Europe. In 1556 Ogier Ghiselin de Busbecq wrote to his friend Nicolas Michault from Constantinople that not far from Adrianople he had seen "quantities of flowers—

Minoan jar with tulip designs. From *The Palace of Minos* by Arthur Evans. (*Used by permission of the estate of Sir Arthur Evans and of the publisher, Macmillan & Co., Ltd., London*)

narcissi, hyacinths, and tulipans, as the Turks call them." He goes on to say that the tulip "has little or no scent, but is admired for its beauty and the variety of its colours."

Later, as the writings of Clusius and others bear witness, de Busbecq had quantities of tulips, both bulbs and seed, sent to Europe and before the end of the century tulips had become the most exciting novelties in the garden.

In addition to tulips, de Busbecq is also credited with the introduction of lilacs, mock oranges and horse chestnuts into Europe. On horticultural grounds alone he deserves our gratitude. But botanists, too, honor him as the discoverer and preserver of one of the greatest documents in the history of botany —the earliest and most beautiful copy of the Greek herbal of Dioscorides. Nor were these the sum of his achievements. In any age less glittering with great personalities he would have been famous.

Born the natural son of Georges Ghiselin, Sieur de Busbecq, in 1522, this scholar and gentleman of the Renaissance was given his early education at the University of Louvain and then allowed several *Wanderjahren* at various European universities. He must have had charm and fine manners to add to his brilliant mind, for in 1554 he was chosen a member of the embassy that was sent to England by the Emperor Ferdinand to represent the Holy Roman Empire at the marriage of Mary Tudor to Philip of Spain. Immediately thereafter Ferdinand entrusted him with the difficult and dangerous assignment of going to Constantinople as his ambassador.

That his task was dangerous is witnessed by the fact that de Busbecq's predecessor came back to Europe to die as a result of the ill-treatment he had suffered in a Turkish prison. That it was difficult is obvious when we realize that he was expected to employ some sort of diplomatic magic that would curb the aggressive tendencies of the most powerful ruler in the world who happened also to be a military genius. Not content with the possession of all of Asia Minor, the entire Balkan Peninsula and a large part of North Africa, Suleiman the Magnificent had conquered the greater part of Hungary and had even besieged Vienna. The Holy Roman Empire had been badly mauled by the Turkish raids and it was de Busbecq's duty to try to obtain a desperately needed breathing spell.

By some miracle he succeeded. To his contemporaries he could hardly have been noted as a man who brought new plants and old manuscripts to Europe. He brought something much more valuable—peace, peace for a short time at any rate, although other factors than de Busbecq's diplomacy contributed to that happy end.

All the while he was picking his way along a diplomatic path bristling with obstacles and ambushes de Busbecq kept his eyes open and his mind alert, not only in the interest of his mission but also to see and to enjoy and, when possible, to collect all the objects his wide-ranging Renaissance curiosity considered worth while.

He discovered an important Latin inscription, made a valuable addition to the study of languages, and collected classical coins. He regretted that part of his contribution to European zoology, "a remarkably handsome weasel of a species called sable," died on the journey home, but apparently several thoroughbred horses and six female camels survived the trip. He reported triumphantly to his friend Michault that he had "whole wagon-loads, whole ship-loads of Greek manuscripts. . . . Many of them are quite ordinary, but some are not to be despised. I hunted them out from all sorts of corners, so as to make, as it were, a final gleaning of all merchandise of this kind."

The final gleaning he mentioned referred to one of those great pendulum sweeps of history. Almost exactly a hundred years before de Busbecq reached Constantinople the city had fallen to the Turks. About a thousand years before, Rome had been sacked by northern barbarians. When Rome fell her scholars tucked their treasured manuscripts under their arms, figuratively speaking, and fled to Constantinople. When Constantinople fell in its turn, the tide reversed itself. Scholars with their books fled to Europe. The wealth of manuscripts they carried, coinciding as it did with the invention of printing, sparked the Renaissance of classical learning. But not all men were lucky enough to save themselves and their treasures. For generations after the Turks were established in Constantinople visiting Europeans tried to salvage whatever could still be found from classical times. De Busbecq was one of these gleaners and one of the luckiest, for it was his good fortune to find and preserve for future botanists a fifth-century manuscript of the *De Materia Medica* of Dioscorides.

The Latin title and the Greek name of the author make the book sound impressively erudite. But since this copy is known to have belonged to a woman, it is entirely possible that this was originally no more than a book of household medicine. Its owner was the Princess Juliana Anicia, of the royal house in Constantinople, so the copy of Dioscorides given her was a very fine one indeed. And the Princess Juliana may have had much need of it, for she lived in a period of great violence. Today her book is a priceless treasure valued by all students of botanical and medical history.

It is in this book that we find the Saturion that Parkinson and other herbalists of the time decided was the tulip.

In the letter to Michault in which de Busbecq boasts of his shiploads of manuscripts he continues: "One treasure I left behind me in Constantinople, a manuscript of Dioscorides, extremely ancient and written in majuscules, with drawings of the plants. . . . I should like to have bought it, but the price frightened me; for a hundred ducats was named, a sum which would suit the Emperor's purse better than mine. . . . This manuscript owing to its age, is in a bad state, being externally so worm-eaten that scarcely anyone, if he saw it lying in the road, would bother to pick it up."

Two varieties of tulip from Dodoens' *Pemptades*. (*Horticultural Society of New York*)

But de Busbecq bothered—bothered until he had persuaded the emperor to buy it. Thus the *Codex Juliana*, as it is called, went to the Imperial Library in Vienna.

Eventually, of course, lilacs, mock oranges, horse chestnuts and tulips would have reached Europe without de Busbecq's help. But this colorful and cultivated man who had the wit to

provide future scholars with a valuable document is worth remembering. Every gardener who plants a tulip bulb is no less
in his debt.

Although the tulip was greeted in England with the same
enthusiasm it had aroused on the Continent, it remained a
"forrein floure." It was welcomed to the gardens of the great
country estates and displayed with passionate pride, but it was
still foreign in the sense that it had no place outside of gardens.
It was too new and strange to have any significance in folklore.
Its lack of scent kept it out of the containers on ladies' toilet
tables. Herbalists found no important medical use for it. Except
for a brief experimental stage in the kitchens of the seventeenth
century and a wild excursion into finance it remained entirely
in the realm of ornamental horticulture.

The culinary career of the tulip might have been longer if
tulips had not cost so much. An exotic bulb that commanded
fantastic prices could hardly hope to become a common staple.
But the "curious" men of the seventeenth century could not
rest until they had tried it out as a food.

John Parkinson led off with the assurance that tulip bulbs
were nourishing. This had been proved, he claimed, by various
people who had cooked them by mistake for onions. He goes on
to say that he tried some out preserved in sugar and found
them "to be almost as pleasant as Eringus rootes, being firm and
sound and fit to be presented to the curious. . . ."

William Coles thought that "boyled and buttered [they]
make a rare dish."

It was chiefly the bulb of the tulip that found its way to the
kitchen but before the experiments were over the seed had
joined it.

Sir Kenelm Digby, who records the receipt, could have invented it himself. Or he may have collected it on the Continent, to which he made frequent journeys in the interest of the Catholic intrigues designed to keep Charles I on the throne of England. The big burly man who had "a wonderful graceful behavior, a flowing courtesy and civility, and such a volubility of language as surprised and delighted," was forever poking his nose into his own and other people's kitchens. He was a *bon viveur* in the grand manner who never allowed his interest in politics, religion and science to interfere with his enjoyment of the good things of this world. It is he who offers us

Peas of the Seedy Buds of Tulips

In the Spring (about the beginning of May) the flowry leaves of Tulips do fall away, and there remains within them the end of the stalk, which in time will turn to seed. Take that seedy end (then very tender) and pick from it the little excresscencies about it, and cut it into short pieces, and boil them and dress them as you would do Pease; and they will taste like Pease, and be very savoury.

They be indeed. I can testify, for I have tried them, but I found the flavor more like that of asparagus than peas.

At the very end of the century John Evelyn declared that "'the fresh Bulbs are sweet and high of taste," and then apparently tulips disappeared from the kitchen until our own time.

They reappeared in a minor role in a great tragedy. When the people of Holland were starving under the German occupation during World War II tulip bulbs became a common article of diet. Barges piled high with bulbs moved along the canals and drew up at city and village docks.

"Then you ran," a Dutch friend told me. "You had to run to get your share." You paid, she continued, more per bulb than you would have paid to buy them for your garden.

Modern Hollanders would not back William Coles's claim

that tulip bulbs made a rare dish. "In wartime," my Dutch friend continued, "we had no butter and found the bulbs almost intolerable. We had been warned that it was injudicious for anyone to eat more than six bulbs at a meal. But, hungry as we were, most people were never able to manage more than four. The first two or three mouthfuls tasted not unpleasant and rather sweet," she added, "but for all that your stomach craved food you could not get as many as six down. We tried every way we could think of to make them palatable. We boiled them and we baked them. We even pulled the layers of the bulbs apart and dried them in the oven to make a brown chiplike substance. But we could hardly force them down."

Obviously, tulip bulbs have no place on modern tables except as a last desperate resource for emergency rations.

The part played by the tulip in high finance is almost too well known to bear repeating. Yet in any record of the tulip in history it must at least be sketched in. For a more detailed account the reader is referred to Wilfrid Blunt's delightful *Tulipomania* published in the King Penguin Series.

The early seventeenth century in Holland presented exactly the sort of atmosphere in which speculation flourishes. The Dutch overseas trade was expanding. An active class of merchants pursued their business in a keen and energetic fashion. Optimism reigned and a fantastic boom was born. Its course was as brief as it was spectacular. For within less than three years the crash had come and the tulip mania was over.

Up to 1633 or the beginning of 1634 the trade in tulip bulbs was still in the hands of the professional growers, and it was pretty much a luxury trade. Only the very wealthy could afford the prices a rare bulb commanded and few bulbs were really cheap. In 1624 a single bulb of *Semper Augustus* sold for 1,200 florins, which comes as near $1,200 as makes no difference.

But by 1633 poor men had begun to buy bulbs—probably not those in the same bracket as *Semper Augustus* but good bulbs that could be raised to sell at a profit. Their cultivation was easy to learn. The buying and selling of such a commodity was something that even men of limited intelligence could grasp. The butcher, the baker, the candlestick maker, cobblers and tailors, spinners and weavers began raising bulbs in their back yards to make a bit of extra money. By the end of 1634 there was active nonprofessional buying and selling.

By the middle of 1635 prices had risen steeply. Often, too, buying was done on credit or by payment in kind. Trade in futures began, in the number of offsets a bulb would produce. From that it was only a step to wild speculation. Mr. Blunt quotes an authority who says that a nobleman might buy 2,000 florins' worth of bulbs from a chimney sweep who did not have any and would then sell them to a farmer who did not want any, but who planned to sell them in turn to someone else.

And so it went. Prices continued to skyrocket. A single bulb of the tulip *Victory* was paid for in kind as follows: "2 loads of wheat; 4 loads of rye; 4 fat oxen; 8 fat pigs; 12 fat sheep; 2 hogsheads of wine; 4 barrels of 8-florin beer; 2 barrels of butter; 1000 lbs of cheese; a complete bed; a suit of clothes and a silver beaker—the whole valued at 2500 florins."

At the peak of the excitement one bulb of *Semper Augustus* again went for nearly $5,000 with a carriage and pair thrown in.

Here was a classic example of a boom. Much of the speculating was being done by people of small means who had no control over or knowledge of the market. Many of them knew little or nothing about the commodity in which they dealt. The whole structure rested on the general business optimism of the time.

How familiar all this sounds to those who remember 1929! When the first doubts arose, when the first uneasiness about the limitless profits to be made on the futures of tulip bulbs was spoken aloud, the whole crazy financial bubble burst. Within two or three days the collapse was complete.

At this point the professional growers stepped in even ahead of the government. Gradually order was brought out of the chaos, and in the long run the growers profited greatly. For the story of Holland's tulip mania had advertised the flower all over Europe better than even a modern advertising campaign could have done.

Old English tulips have recently returned to our bulb catalogues. For a number of years now collectors have been scouring the English countryside, especially the cottage gardens, for specimens of the nineteenth-century florists' flowers. The Old English tulip is among the survivors thus gathered.

The revival of interest in these special flowers would be a matter of purely horticultural interest if it were not for the amazing story of the florists themselves. For several centuries the word "florist" meant a specialist, as it does today, though a very different kind of specialist. For the early florist bred flowers, from seed, cuttings or offsets. Great gentlemen of the seventeenth and eighteenth century were proud to be florists, and the flavor of the happy world in which they lived permeates *The Garden Book of Sir Thomas Hanmer* which describes his gardening adventures in the 1650's. ". . . now the Florists fly about to see and examine and take the chiefe pleasure of gardens, admiring the new varieties that Spring produces."

These florists were rich men, country gentlemen with great estates who frequently bought their original stocks from abroad. They had gardeners and gardeners' boys to help them.

But toward the middle of the eighteenth century quantities of new plants began to reach England from America and other parts of the world. Then such men lost interest in breeding and hybridizing. They ceased to be florists and became instead collectors of strange and exotic plants.

In their place a new race of florists arose—poor men, factory workers, coal miners, petty tradesmen and artisans. From the latter part of the eighteenth century up to about 1860 it was these men who created the flowers now known as "florists' flowers."

Of all the florists' flowers tulips and pinks were the most popular. The other flowers in which these men specialized were various kinds of primula, especially auricula and polyanthus, ranunculus, pansies, dahlias and a number of others.

A delightful introduction to florists' flowers is to be found in Henry Phillips' book *Flora Historica,* published in 1824. There, in writing of *Dianthus,* he says, "It has been observed that the Pink has lost its powerful attraction for the nobility of this country, and is degenerated into a mechanic's flower, because its cultivation is so carefully and successfully attended to in manufacturing districts." He goes on to give a glowing description of the English cottager admiring his plants of a Sunday morning, surrounded by his neatly clad family. "Give the cottager," he continues, "a garden, and you bar up the ale-houses; for the mind of the most illiterate will occupy itself in leisure, and when domestic employ is not found to amuse, idle politics are sure to attract to the chequered post," that is, the local pub.

"Mechanics" when Phillips was writing meant factory work-ers, and the manufacturing districts he mentions were largely those of the textile mills throughout the English Midlands. In spite of the pretty picture Phillips drew of the cottager surrounded by his neatly clad family, it is a matter of historical record that there was not much that was pretty about the beginnings of the Industrial Revolution. For working people this was a terrible period.

The cottager of Phillips' smug description was to become a rare bird in the industrial sections of England. The greater number of the new mill hands, deprived of their livelihood in the centuries-old hand-weaving trade, had poured into the towns from the country districts. Their general living conditions in the mill towns were almost beyond belief.

Writing of the period between 1820 and 1848, a modern historian said: "At no time, probably, in the history of England has there been more misery among the mass of the people. . . ." And he goes on to point out: "This poverty-stricken, sordid life was not that of the poorest, the most improvident, and the most unfortunate of the community, but was characteristic of the great body of substantial, hard-working laboring population, only a fortunate few rising above it."

Yet among the men whose lives were spent under the stress of a ninety-hour work week and almost intolerable living conditions some had the energy and spirit to become florists. Ill-housed, ill-clothed and often half-starved, they tramped to work in the gray dawn in order to be at bench or shaft by seven o'clock and often were still there at eight or nine at night. How they managed to find the time for gardening is a mystery. They lived crowded in squalid rooms, often in damp, unventilated cellars, but some of them were able to get the use of small bits of land on the outskirts of the town for their gardens. Here some of these "mechanics" raised vegetables and some bred fruits that were to be as famous as the gooseberries grown by the Lancaster artisans. Other men—out of a need for color and beauty—grew flowers. If it were not for the fact that every

Tulip

writer on florists' flowers assures us that factory workers and coal miners were breeders of fine tulips, pinks, primroses and the rest, it would be hard to believe it possible.

Along with the joy of growing flowers went the only social life most of these men knew. They banded together to form florists' clubs or societies which held meetings, gave exhibitions at the proper seasons, and laid down rigid rules as to the points a flower had to have to qualify for exhibit.

Tulips were divided into three classes: roses, byblomen, bizarres. A rose tulip had white petals marked with some shade of red or pink. A byblomen was like it except that the color was purple, lilac or lavender. A bizarre had a yellow ground with markings in any color. These classes were again subdivided into flamed or feathered flowers. A flamed rose tulip had a flame-shaped red or pink mark that did not quite reach to the edge of the petal; a feathered byblomen was feather-stitched in lavender or lilac all around each white petal; and there were flowers which were both flamed and feathered.

The self-color breeders were of no interest to the old florists, or rather they were of no interest until they "broke." We now know that stripes and blotches, the feathers and the flames, come from a virus disease of the bulbs. Once a tulip bulb is infected, nothing will cure it and it continues to produce the marked flowers which were such a delight to the florists.

Since they had no idea what caused a breeder to break, the florists resorted to fantastic expedients to bring about the desired result. Some tried starving their tulips. Others fed them on composts fearfully and wonderfully made. One such compost took "4 barrowfuls of loam, steeped in night soil and urine; 2 barrowfuls of goose dung, mixed with blood; 2 barrowfuls of sugar-baker's scum [a mixture of blood, lime-water and oily matter]; and 2 pecks of sea sand." This unsavory mess had to be ripened for two years, and turned once a month with a fork.

The compost receipts alone would show that the florists never spared themselves hard labor in behalf of their flowers. As tulips tend to fade under a strong sun, the florists protected their blooms with little caps or shades made of circular pieces of cartridge paper treated with a mixture of equal parts of turpentine and boiled and raw linseed oil to make them waterproof. A cap went over every tulip or a frame was built around the whole bed and roofed with canvas. Those who could afford it made themselves chests of drawers or partitioned boxes so that when the bulbs were dug up the different kinds and colors could be kept separated.

It takes from five to seven years to grow tulips from seed. Obviously the workingmen florists were in no position to buy expensive bulbs, so they raised them, at what cost to themselves we can only guess. There is the story of one Dulwich florist who covered his bulbs one frosty night with the blankets from his own bed, according to *The Horticultural Magazine* for June, 1847. While the report does not state that he died of the cold, the report does suggest that his early death was not unconnected with his passionate care of his tulips.

In cottage gardens, on bits of land around town houses, on the plots assigned by towns to working people, poor men grew flowers. The petty tradesmen and artisans of the time may have been a little more prosperous than the factory workers but they, too, lived lives of long hours and hard work. Anyone today fortunate enough to own an Old English byblomen, the rarest of the survivors of the florists' tulips, or one of the lovely feathered and flamed "roses" should know something of the men who bred them so lovingly. What it must have meant to a man who had nursed seed for six years, first into bulb, then into bloom, to see it finally standing there, triumphant as only a tulip can be in all its flamed and feathered splendor!

The tulip is no longer a strange and foreign flower. Four hundred years in Western gardens have made it as familiar a part of spring as our own arbutus or bloodroot—a familiar magnificence that few gardeners would be without.

Crocus designs in faïence on votive garments of the Minoan goddess, Britomartis, from temple repositories. *The Palace of Minos* by Arthur Evans. (*Used by permission of the estate of Sir Arthur Evans and of the publisher, Macmillan & Co., Ltd., London*)

Saffron Crocus

Spring comes to our gardens with the crocus—purple and white and gold. It appears as if by magic from the winter earth in the first warmth of spring sunshine. Too few people realize that the spring crocus has a cousin which blooms in the fall, a gay small flower which has a history, a story that takes us back into a remote past where dates are uncertain and records scant. But still it can be traced, for the crocus is a part, however tiny, of the story of civilization.

Usually, in telling the story of a flower and how man has used it, it is possible to do so only by considering the genus as a whole. But in the case of the crocus we are concerned with only one of the seventy-odd species that make up the genus—with the purple or lavender autumn crocus from which saffron is made. *Not* colchicum, the meadow saffron sometimes called autumn crocus, but *C. sativus*, a variety of true crocus that is close kin to our small heralds of spring. Undoubtedly saffron has occasionally been made from other species and varieties, but it was the autumn crocus that was cultivated for practical purposes long before flowers were appreciated for their beauty alone.

Saffron has played a part in man's religion and has served him as a medicine, a dyestuff, a flavor and a perfume. It is known factually so far in the past that one is tempted to venture even further back in time and picture that vivid yellow dyeing priestly hands before it dyed priestly garments; when its pleasantly astringent perfume was an offering to the gods before man's widening mental horizon allowed him to dare to use it for himself. But, speculation aside, we can place saffron almost as far back as we can find evidences of civilization.

More than four thousand years ago human hands fashioned a spouted pottery jug, decorated it with pairs of red and white crocus, fired it and turned it over to a Bronze Age housewife to use for water, wine or oil. This jug was found in Crete, where Sir Arthur Evans, while exploring the culture of the Minoans, found the first evidence of many of our common flowers. On a wall in the palace of the Kings of Minos there is a fresco in which we find our crocus again. *The Blue Boy Picking Crocus* was painted at a slightly later date than the jug was made. His is a strange, elongated figure, clad only in a loincloth and painted a blue-gray. Stretched at an awkward diagonal across a rocky field, he is gathering crocus and putting them into bowls scattered among the rocks. The artist was so anxious that there be no doubt whatever about the flowers that he exaggerated the swelling curves of the petals and turned the conspicuous stigma and stamens into something very like a fringe. As the crocus was one of the Minoans' sacred flowers, Evans thinks this picture may have had a religious significance.

Later still we find the crocus definitely associated with Minoan religion when it appears on the votive robes dedicated to the great Minoan goddess, Britomartis.

No woman, unless dead to all feminine instincts, can be indifferent to the clothes worn by the Bronze Age ladies of Crete. Pocahontas in her very best buckskins would never seem elegant to us, nor would the best-dressed modern Eskimo. But Minoan women of thirty-five hundred years ago had chic. Their skirts were full and wide below tight-waisted bodices, with elbow-length sleeves, which were cut low to expose the entire breasts. With the exception of that slightly startling difference, these dresses would be smart today. They have that indefinable something we call "style."

Saffron Crocus

It is such a frivolous something, so sophisticated and so worldly that it is almost shocking to find their revered goddess flaunting these sprightly garments. Yet there she is for all to see, a debonair little figure modeled in faïence. On faïence votive robes cut to the same pattern and hung in her temples we find the sacred crocus—sometimes on a flat panel down the front of a dress, sometimes decorating the edges of the large ruffles that form a skirt.

It is very probable that this goddess presided over the production of saffron, a flourishing industry on which a goodly part of the wealth of the Kings of Minos must have been based. Since Crete was an island with an overseas trade—a sort of early Mediterranean version of Great Britain—it is interesting, though somewhat fantastic, to speculate about the problems involved.

"Processing" and "distribution" are words so steeped in associations with twentieth-century mass production that it is hard to think of them as applied to a prehistoric business. Yet the stigma of the crocus must be gathered by hand, dried and pressed to make saffron. That is surely "processing." "Distribution" we know nothing about but we do know that Crete carried on trade around the entire Mediterranean. Saffron would have been a luxury item in that trade, restricted to royalty or the very rich. It takes over four thousand flowers to produce an ounce of saffron and the price has always been correspondingly high. A pound of saffron today costs $152.

The mystery of the Minoan writing has only recently been unraveled. Once the long slow job of deciphering all the texts is completed we shall know more about saffron and its importance to Crete. For even before the texts could be read one could see in them, repeated again and again, a symbol that is unmistakably the crocus.

In Egypt there are no crocus to be seen on pottery or on frescoed wall, but we can read about them, because in the

Flower Chronicles

Papyrus Ebers the herb *snwtt* has been identified, on much sounder grounds than is usual in ancient descriptions, as the saffron crocus. On the strength of that identification, we have a good excuse for taking a look at this remarkable medical work, one of the oldest complete books in the world.

In the winter of 1872 Georg Ebers, a German Egyptologist, was excavating near Thebes when he was approached by a

Various forms of hieroglyphic signs for saffron and bee. *The Palace of Minos* by Arthur Evans. *(Used by permission of the estate of Sir Arthur Evans and of the publisher, Macmillan & Co., Ltd., London)*

native who had something to sell. Packed in a metal case, wrapped in old mummy cloths, was an object that must have taken Ebers' breath away. It was a rolled manuscript, in perfect condition, its ink—black for the text, red for the rubrics—as sharp and bright as when a scribe had used it nearly thirty-five hundred years before. The document was sixty-eight feet long, twelve inches wide.

Ebers could not afford the price demanded by the Egyptian, but a compatriot, a Herr Gunther, came to the rescue and bought the manuscript, which was eventually given to the University of Leipzig.

The Papyrus Ebers was written out at about the same time that the glazed clay figures of the Minoan goddess were made, around 1550 B.C., but modern scholars believe that it is a copy of a much older medical work, and that possibly the original from which the Papyrus Ebers derives was compiled as long ago as 2650 B.C., about the time Cheops built his pyramid at Giza. If this is true, the use of saffron in Egypt would predate anything we know about it in Crete.

Along with saffron, which is supposed to have been imported into the country, and such native plants as dates, raisins, papyrus and lotus, the Papyrus Ebers contains as strange an assortment of drugs as one would encounter in all the strange medicines of antiquity. The toes-of-a-dog, human brain, scribe's excrement, worms' blood, and an-old-book-boiled-in-oil are among the components used in prescriptions for all manner of ills.

When taking some of these gruesome remedies, it was doubtless comforting to the patient to preface his dose with a prayer, one of which reads: "Oh Isis, thou great magician, heal me and save me from all wicked, frightful and red things, from demoniac and deadly diseases and illnesses of every kind. Oh Ra. Oh Isis."

Saffron was one of the drugs used to "remove rheumatism in the sacral region." If rubbed on there, the pain was supposed to disappear immediately. Eating crocus seed on bread would have the same effect. Saffron was also good for paralysis—though only on the right side of the body. Crocus-from-the-hills and crocus-from-the-delta, along with various other herbs, made a medicine "to force out urine." In sweet beer, it "strengthened the teeth." It was used in a plaster for gumboils and again with other herbs in a poultice to apply to the abdomen when there was an obstruction.

Grotesque as all this sounds, it has been pointed out that the priests, who were also the physicians of Egypt, were not mere "magicians contending with a demon-infested world." They were, naturally, men of their time, so both prayers and spells appear in the Papyrus Ebers. But it is clear that these early doctors also reasoned about their treatments. Medicine was administered orally for internal troubles; pain was generally treated with poultices; ointment was used for skin diseases; and for eye infections, then as now a major problem in Egypt, medicine was dropped into the eye.

We have traced the crocus into such far reaches of antiquity that before we come to it in classical times it will seem that we are stepping onto familiar ground when we enter the garden presumably laid out by Solomon in the tenth century before Christ:

"Until the day break, and the shadows flee away, I will get me to the mountain of myrrh, and to the hill of frankencense. . . . Thy plants are an orchard of pomegranites, with pleasant fruits; camphire, with spikenard, spikenard and saffron; calamus and cinnamon with all the trees of frankencense; myrrh and aloes with all the chief spices."

In Greece dawn "spread her saffron robe" over the world as early as the time of Homer. One Greek myth tells us that the crocus sprang from the ground where Zeus had lain with Hera. Another says that it was named after a baby tragically killed, while a third gives it the name of a youth who died for love of the shepherdess Smilax.

The garments of gods and goddesses, nymphs and nereids, were often described as saffron-hued, so the crocus as a dyestuff probably reached Greece very early, quite possibly from Crete. Its fame as an aromatic perfume may have come from the Orient. Theophrastus lists it among the plants so used, but by and large it is most often referred to in Greek literature as a color.

The Romans followed the Greeks in their enthusiasm for the color and perfume of saffron, but in the decadent days of Rome the heritage of moderation derived from the temperate Greeks went by the board, with saffron as with everything else. Theaters and banquet halls were drenched with a scent most of us would find distinctive and not exactly unpleasant, but certainly not worth the fabulous cost. Between courses of a banquet given in Nero's time slaves sprinkled the floor with sawdust mixed with saffron, vermilion and powdered mica—perfume, color and glitter all in one packet.

At the same banquet, described in *The Satyricon of Petronius Arbiter*, cakes were served in the form of apples and other fruits. "We applied ourselves wholeheartedly to this dessert and our joviality was suddenly revived by a fresh diversion, for at the slightest pressure all the cakes and fruits would squirt a saffron sauce upon us, and even spurted unpleasantly in our faces."

The story of the crocus in antiquity would necessarily include its use in cookery, as a perfume, as a dye and in medicine, but the most interesting aspect would be to trace it as a commercial commodity catering to these uses, because it was one of the most lucrative and romantic commercial activities in the early history of man.

All through the Middle Ages and down to about a hundred fifty years ago saffron continued to be a profitable article of commerce—so valuable that a few pounds of crocus bulbs could be offered as security for a loan in lieu of gold or jewels; so important that in fifteenth-century Nuremberg three men were buried alive for adulterating it.

There is evidence that the saffron crocus may be the one flower that owed its arrival in England to the Crusades though it was a pilgrim rather than a Crusader who brought it home. The story originated with Richard Hakluyt, a sixteenth-century geographer whose enthusiasm for the history of discovery has preserved valuable narratives for us, some not entirely free of tall tales. If this story about the crocus is a tall tale it is still worth the telling if only to emphasize the value put upon saffron at the time.

"At Algiers a pilgrim stole beads [corms] of saffron and hid them in his Palmer's staff which he had made hollow before of purpose, and so he brought this root to this realm, with venture of his life; for if he had been taken, by law of the country from whence it came, he had died for the fact. . . ."

From other sources the coming of the crocus to England is usually placed in the reign of Edward III, 1327–1377. In any case it began to be cultivated there early in the fourteenth century. As it takes over sixty thousand flowers to make a pound of saffron, it is clear that, once a cultivator of the precious stuff had obtained his bulbs, his principal expense was labor. That, in those benighted days, was no large item in any farmer's or businessman's budget. Once the ground was cleared, cultivation was fairly simple. With a tool known delightfully in Middle English as a "dybbyl":

> Three ynches depe they most sette be
> And thus seyde mayster Ion Gardener to me.

Profits were high but the small amount of saffron yielded by thousands of flowers kept the supply from exceeding the demand. Perhaps, too, saffron was not such a sure-fire crop as it might have seemed. There is an old English folk saying that sums up bad luck: "You set saffron and there comes up wolfsbane."

In spite of that discouraging adage farmers considered saffron a good investment. In 1557 Thomas Tusser included it in his *Hundredth Good Pointes of Husbandrie,* a most engaging agricultural treatise all in rhyme.

Saffron Crocus

Two versions of crocus from early herbals, *Hortus Sanitatis* of Mainz and
The Grete Herball. (*The Pierpont Morgan Library*)

> Pare saffron plot
> Forget him not;
> His dwelling made trim
>   look shortly for him.
> When harvest is gone
>   then saffron comes on;
> A little of ground
>   brings saffron a pound.

About a century later saffron still had importance as a
profitable crop. Robert Turner, an herbalist of the time of
James II, was a royalist whose loyalty to the House of Stuart

made him only too happy to catch the Calvinist Roundheads in an inconsistency. Strict observance of Sunday was one of the tenets of their faith, so Turner pointed out gleefully that the saffron crop "must be gathered as soon as it is blown, or else it is lost; so that Jack Presbyter for covetousness of the profit can reach his Sabbatarian conscience to gather it on Sunday."

Individual farmers throughout England obviously found saffron worth cultivating but the major production centered around Saffron-Walden, a town in Essex which took its name from its chief product. Writing about the middle of the seventeenth century, John Evelyn tells of paying a visit to Audley End, one of the great houses of England, "in Saffron-Walden parish, famous for that useful plant with which all the country is covered." Saffron growers were often called "croakers."

For more than four hundred years saffron continued to be cultivated in England as an important commodity. It was an ingredient in innumerable medical prescriptions; it was indispensable to a kitchen of any pretensions whatever; it was an important dyestuff; and it had a number of minor uses as a perfume and aromatic, besides being used as a substitute for gold leaf on illuminated manuscripts.

By 1800 all but its medical uses had declined to a point where saffron no longer had industrial importance. Yet what a story it is! Unless all the indications in Crete deceive us, here is a luxury item that has been in production for at least three and a half millennia.

Saffron as a drug is still in our official pharmacopoeia. Made into a tea it is sometimes used in the treatment of measles. Its property of provoking perspiration tends to bring out the rash and combat the fever. As modern chemistry turns out more "miracle drugs," the life expectancy of the crocus as a medicine is probably short, but no other flower has a longer documented record.

It is a vastly confused, contradictory and often absurd record. Actually, as one reads herbals and medical books from the first to the nineteenth century one has a despairing impression that saffron went into *all* the medicines described.

Saffron did figure in a preposterous number of medicines, especially those designed to raise the spirits of men. Perhaps the cheerful color of saffron connected it with gaiety even in its medical history. Several herbalists mention that it moved men to laughter and Francis Bacon remarked that "it maketh the English sprightly." Be that as it may, in classical times saffron had been noted medically as having a relationship to women and wine, though not concerned with song. Dioscorides said that "it stirs up also to venerie."

According to Pliny, saffron in wine will relieve or cure the more unpleasant results of overindulgence in alcohol, but "chaplets, too, made of saffron and worn on the head, tend to dispell the fumes of wine." It is venturing on specialists' ground to suggest it, but the chaplet is a circle, and the circle connotes remote and primitive magic. It is just possible that Pliny's remedy for drunkenness stems from a far past, when man first began to struggle with a problem which is still with us.

Echoes of the use of saffron for coping with alcoholism are to be found in various herbals up to the Renaissance, when the great sixteenth-century botanist William Turner dismissed the matter with the biting remark that saffron was "good for weak braynes that cannot well beare drinke." William, one somehow feels sure, had a good hard head and carried his liquor, if not with grace, at least with dignity.

The medical history of saffron is far too complicated for any layman to unravel. But if we turn to the domestic medicine of the stillroom books we can get a good idea of the ways it was used—for obstructions, "meazels," plague, "Vapours of the Spleen and fits of ye Mother," consumption, as a wound salve, and especially in cordials for jaundice.

The use of saffron for treating jaundice is of course obvious. Long before the sixteenth-century Swiss physician Paracelsus publicized the Doctrine of Signatures, the theory was being put into practice. The Doctrine of Signatures held that a resemblance between the external characters of a disease and some physical agent (as that between the red skin of scarlet fever and a piece of red flannel) was supposed to indicate the agent in the treatment of the disease.

The association of ideas in saffron—yellow—jaundice is obvious, but earthworms do puzzle us. It is not clear how they, along with saffron, came to be used for jaundice, but Elizabeth Grey, the seventeenth-century Countess of Kent, begins a prescription for jaundice quite simply with "Take earth Wormes . . ." Later prescriptions tend to be more explicit. Nine earthworms split and cleaned, with a handful of "Sallendine" and a pennyworth of saffron in ale was "Mrs. Skillins Rect. for the Yellow Jaundice," according to a receipt in *A Book of Simples*. Another, very long and complicated, adds a peck of snails to a quart of earthworms and a whole ounce of saffron, along with quantities of herbs.

Finally, there is a straightforward receipt within the reach of all but the very poor, which probably saw frequent use:

Take a handful of earth wormes and put them awhile in salt and water to cleanse themselves then put them into a quart of white wine and steep well until they dissolve then strain them out then put to the strained liquor four penny worth of english saffron and let that steep well in it also and let the party grieved take of this liquor thus prepered a quarter of a pint first in the morning and at four a clock in the afternoon and last at night. Probatum est.

Saffron Crocus

The cordials of the herbals and stillroom books were designed to combat melancholy and to lift the spirits of suffering men. In this negative form the classical idea of saffron as conducive to gaiety may have finally taken shape. Even though saffron was used constantly for both melancholy and jaundice, no clear thread for its usage can be traced in its medical history. But that history, confused as it is, is impressively long.

Saffron is far from unknown in our American kitchens today. Two world wars that have revolutionized our whole economy have almost exterminated the genus *cook*. The band of amateurs who have, willy-nilly, taken over diversify the drudgery of daily meals by exploring the cuisines of foreign countries in search of interesting and nourishing foods. From Spain and Portgual come many a dish colored and flavored with saffron. In fact chicken and rice so flavored and colored has almost ceased to be exotic. Bouillabaisse from Marseilles is another saffron-flavored dish that is far from unfamiliar.

In contrast to our tentative experiments, saffron was ubiquitous in English and European kitchens throughout the Middle Ages. *The Forme of Cury*, 1390, was the first cookbook in the English language and was compiled by some of the two thousand cooks in the kitchen of Richard II. Its appearance probably inspired other eager souls belonging to that vast fraternity which is perennially interested in the welfare of the inner man. So a number of other collections of receipts were forthwith written down and a few have survived, among them one listed in the British Museum catalogue as "Harl. 279." It is from this that the following receipts were taken.

Cokyntryce

Take a Capoun, and skald hym, and draw hem clene, and smite hem in the waste across; take a Pigge, and skald hym and draw hym in

the same maner, and smyte hem also in the waste; take a nedyl and
a threde, and sewe the fore party of the Capoun to the After parti
of the Pygge; and the fore partye of the Pigge to the hynder party
of the Capoun, & than stuffe hem as thou stuffest a Pigge; putte hem
on a spete, and Roste hym; and whan he is y-now [enough], gild
hem with yolkes of Eyroun, and pouder Gyngere and Safroun, thenne
wyth the Jus of Percely withowte; and than serve it forth for a ryal
[royal] mete.

Smal Cofyns

Take fayre Floure, Safroun, Sugre & Salt, & make ther-of a past;
than make smal cofyns; then take yolkys of Eyron, & separate hem
fro the whyte & lat the yolkes be al hole, & not to-broke, & lay iii
or iv in a cofyn; and than take marow of boyne, ii or iii gobettys,
& cowche in the cofynn; than take pouder Gyngere, Sugre, Pasonys, &
caste a-bove; & than cover the cofyn with the same past, & bake hem,
& frye hem in fayre grece, & serve forth.

It is difficult to keep within bounds when it comes to quoting
old receipts. Surely almost anyone would like to know how
"To Make A Fayre Garbage" (chicken giblets, feet, etc., with
many seasonings) or how to handle "Smal Byrdys Y-Stwyde"
or "Oystyrys in Gravy Bastarde." But we cannot linger indefinitely over such appetizing delights. The point about saffron
in cooking is that from being used in practically all dishes it
gradually disappeared from English kitchens entirely and from
most Western cooking except the Hispanic. Now in our own
time it may make a comeback but it is too early to say just how
popular it will prove so far as taste is concerned. But certainly
it is one of the most delightful coloring substances in all
cookery.

A number of our familiar flowers have served as religious
symbols in some of the earliest civilizations we know. Still more
have histories as medicine reaching back over several thousand

years. The crocus belongs to both groups. That should be, heaven knows, distinction enough for any flower but the crocus is unique in its relationship to man. Besides its religious and medical aspects we find clear indications that it had been used as a dye and a perfume for so long a time that Bronze Age Crete had a flourishing industry based on the production of saffron. A pleasant smell and a pretty color must have been among the earliest amenities that mankind knew. Such amenities played their part in leading man out of savagery into civilization. The role the crocus played in that great drama must have been a tiny one, but who can deny that the flower was on the stage?

Drawing from an engraving in *The Floral Telegraph or Affection's Signals* by "Capt. Marryat, R.N.," 1850. The numbers refer to a code for the Language of Flowers. (*Rare Book Room, New York Public Library*)

Daisy

*T*here are two kinds of Dases/one with a reed floure which grows in the gardines/and another which groweth abroade in euery grene and hygh way."

So without apology and with no less authority than that of William Turner, the father of English botany, this is the story of two different genera under a single title. "*Bellis perennis,* common daisy . . . Europe including Britain. Asia Minor." "*Chrysanthemum leucanthemum,* ox-eyed daisy . . . Europe including Britain. N. America . . . a weed of old pastures. Useful for cutting." Thus the Royal Horticultural Society's *Dictionary of Gardening* describes the two typical species with which we are concerned.

We Americans reverse the definitions and have slightly changed one name. For us the oxeye is the common daisy and the "reed floure" is the English daisy. The latter comes to our gardens as a double variety but it, too, has a single type which was probably its primitive form. In ancient literature and early medical writing it is often unclear which flower is meant. In any case, their stories are so interwoven that it would be difficult, if not impossible, to untangle them.

The clinching argument for considering the two daisies together is, however, an emotional one. Reared as we all have been on English poetry, Ophelia's daisy, which is thought to have been *C. leucanthemum,* Milton's "daisies pied," Burns's "wee modest crimson tipped flow'r," and Wordsworth's "unassuming commonplace" are all daisies, no matter what the botanists may say.

Flower Chronicles

The daisies of prehistoric times and of antiquity are of questionable authenticity thanks to the numerous members of the composite family that look like daisies. The most earnest student could hardly hope to classify them with any certainty. But it does seem that *bellis* and a number of species of chrysanthemum were native to the Near East and the Mediterranean area. So perhaps we may dare to take a look at certain ancient daisies with the feeling that they are truly our own—although it is always possible that they may only be kin.

Beautiful gold hairpins, each ending in a daisylike ornament, were found when the Minoan palace was excavated. They are believed to be more than four thousand years old. Later, by about five hundred years, is a game board around which Minoan courtiers must have gathered to play. It is a handsome affair, gay with color, and it is bordered by a design of yellow and white conventionalized daisies. The young Sennacherib, later to be infamous as the "Assyrian wolf," must often have looked up at the portraits of his father and various officials, done in tile on the wall of the palace and framed in a border of yellow and white rosettes that seem plainly inspired by a daisy. Numerous daisies are to be found on ceramics in Egypt as well as elsewhere throughout the Middle East.

It looked for a time as if it were going to be possible to find daisies firmly planted in very ancient medicine. Since their appearance and disappearance there illustrate the difficulties of identification in the remote past, we might pause for a moment to take a look at Assyrian medicine which may date back to 2000 B.C.

The late R. Campbell Thompson was a botanist who specialized in Assyrian medical plants. He did not list any daisies in his definitive work, *A Dictionary of Assyrian Botany*, yet as a young man he had identified *bellis* in a number of Assyrian medical prescriptions that he translated from the cuneiform texts in which he found them. He himself would have been the first to admit the uncertainties of any such identifications.

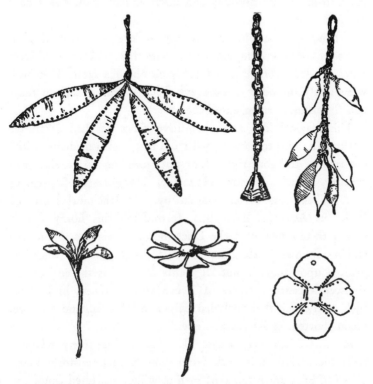

Floral and foliate gold jewelry from Minoan tombs. From *The Palace of Minos* by Arthur Evans. (*Used by permission of the estate of Sir Arthur Evans and of the publisher, Macmillan & Co., Ltd., London*)

Medicine men in remote antiquity simply put down the local name for herbs so well known as to need no descriptions. Thus almost insuperable problems were posed for those as yet un-dreamed-of men like Dr. Thompson who, millennia later, developed such a strange curiosity about what plant was intended.

So, even though Dr. Thompson's final decision was that *bellis* was not among Assyrian herbs, it seems not unfair to turn back to his earlier findings and discover daisies used as a cure for eye trouble.

A daisy, or a daisylike flower, has an "eye" just as its English name of *day's eye* suggests and primitive medical men were quick to draw conclusions from such obvious facts. This herb was plainly intended to cure eye troubles just as saffron must benefit sufferers from jaundice.

This magical idea from primitive times has had a strange history. It seems to have passed from magic into medicine without fanfare and gone right along until sometime in the sixteenth century. Then a curious character, Theophrastus Bombastus von Hohenheim, better known by his alchemical name of Philippus Aureolus Paracelsus, formulated this hoary notion into a theory he called the Doctrine of Signatures. Paracelsus and his followers held that "God's Hieroglyphickes" were imprinted upon most if not all plants. As late as the end of the eighteenth century traces of it can still be found in herbals, such as the one that included daisies in "A Medicine for sore, blood-shotten, & Rheumatic eyes."

It is not, however, a case like that of the peony where a traceable thread runs back from modern to prehistoric times. This is simply an instance of men in widely scattered times and places who leaped independently to what was for them an obvious conclusion—an "eye" for an eye.

According to Dr. Thompson's own early findings, Assyrians were among these men. In his *Assyrian Medical Texts* he placed two asterisks before the name of a plant whose identification he doubted. When he felt quite sure of one with "a very slight doubt as to the exact species" he used one asterisk.

"For sick eyes:—**Ricinus thou shalt bray, cook in beer . . .

Daisy

[the hiatus is in the text] Pour in his eyes; thou shalt bray *bellis, bind on."

That is a typical sample of the various eye prescriptions, but it is typical, too, that medicine at that time was not considered enough. Charms had to be recited when the dose was taken. "Whom shall I send to the daughters of Anu that they may bring me their ewers of *halalu*, their basins of bright lapis that they may gather [the waters] and bring [them] to the failing eyes, the painful and troubled eyes." Another ends with the cry, "O, Gula. Quicken recovery." Something of the urgency of that physical pain comes to us across the centuries.

The daisy of those far-off times was not only an answer to pain in the eyes. Modern "beauticians" might experiment to see if there is any foundation for its cosmetic use—though the Assyrians apparently thought there was. "To turn grey hair black . . . thou shalt bray *bellis. Anoint in oil."

If daisies are impossible to identify with any certainty in the medicine of antiquity, they are somewhat more easily placed in classical times, though confusion still exists. Dioscorides gives a few commonplace uses for a couple of species identified as chrysanthemums, but Pliny, while almost certainly indicating *bellis*, leaves the reader baffled as to what complaint the flower will cure. The sum total of the 13th chapter of the XXVIIth book of his *Natural History* reads:

"Bellis is the name of a plant that grows in the fields, with a white flower somewhat inclining to red; if this is applied with artemisia, it is said, the remedy is still more efficacious."

It was not only in remote antiquity that the daisy was associated with magic charms in medicine. In Anglo-Saxon times "if a man is in the water elf disease then are the nails of his hand livid, and the eyes tearful and he will look downward." Daisies, along with many other herbs, cure this condition if

you pour ale and holy water over them and sing a charm designed to ensure that the "baneful sores"

> neither burn nor burst,
> nor find their way further,
> nor turn foul and fallow,
> nor thump and throb on,
> nor be wicked wounds
> nor dig deeply down.

There is a dreadful precision about that description. The holy
water is obviously a bit of Christian trimming superimposed
upon primitive British medical practice that could easily have
been current in Beowulf's time.

It was, however, later that daisies came into their own in
medicine. Mrs. Maud Grieve puts it in the fourteenth century,
when, she says in her *Modern Herbal,* they were much used for
wounds, gout and fevers. That is quite true, but before we consider them at that time it would be well to note them as one of
the herbs most often used by the physicians of Myddvai. The
first of this extraordinary family of Welsh medical men practiced during the early part of the thirteenth century and
founded a dynasty of doctors whose story is fabulous and
fascinating.

Rhiwallon of Myddvai was house physician to Rhys ab
Gruffydd (Rhys the Hoarse), Lord of Dinevor—a Welsh nobleman who was married in 1219 and died in 1233. Rhiwallon was
the son of a poor cowherd and the Lady of Llyn-y-Van-Vach.
This local Lady of the Lake was a miraculously beautiful girl
who, after various coy appearances on, and disappearances into,
the lake which was her home, abandoned it and settled down
on dry land with her cowherd husband to whom she brought
great wealth. Her father had, however, stipulated that she
would have to return to the lake should her husband strike her

Daisy

without anger three times. Since the couple were deeply in love, the husband was very careful but, over a period of years, a playful slap with a pair of gloves and two equally innocuous gestures finally cost him his wife. She had in the meantime borne him three sons of whom Rhiwallon was the eldest. The boys had been told of their mother's origin, so they used to go to the lake where she lived and wander about its shore in the hope of seeing her. One day she did appear to Rhiwallon and told him that he was destined to benefit mankind by relieving pain and curing illness. She pointed out various herbs to him and explained their healing virtues. Thus Rhiwallon received his early medical training.

This charming story was probably the local explanation of how the son of a peasant actually became physician to the lord of the manor. As such Rhiwallon enjoyed certain rights and privileges laid down by law and modeled on the regulations governing the feudal status of a royal doctor. Rhys gave him the estate called Myddvai, but the physician was a member of the nobleman's household—twelfth in rank. He sat not far from his lord at table; paid no taxes on his land; was provided with a horse and his clothing—his woolen clothes being given him by the lord, his linen by the lady of the castle. If ordered abroad to tend the sick he was entitled to an armed escort though he could never leave the castle without his lord's permission. Within the castle he treated everyone free of charge, and when Rhys rode forth to war Rhiwallon accompanied the troops.

It is not often that we get so vivid a picture of life in early feudal times and in this case the picture is sharpened by the personal flavor of some popular proverbs which were based on medical maxims that originated with Rhiwallon or his descendants. "He who goes to bed supperless will have no need of Rhiwallon of Myddvai." "A light dinner, less supper, sound sleep, long life." "The bread of yesterday, the meat of today, the wine of last year will produce health." "Drink water like an ox, wine like a king." "God will send food to washed hands."

That last proverb leaps to the eye. Even the most casual reader of the Myddvai medicine is struck by the repeated admonitions to cleanliness. "Whatever sex you be, wash your face and hands, etc., with cold water every morning . . . ; wash your back and the nape of your neck once a week also."

Medieval medicine contains few if any other places where cleanliness is even mentioned, let alone stressed. Occasionally there is instruction to take a clean vessel, or some such casual direction, but the physicians of Myddvai quite evidently thought the matter worth emphasis.

It is possible that this extraordinary bias in favor of cleanliness helped to account for the success of the physicians of Myddvai. Rhiwallon's son followed him as a local doctor and, in due time, his son's son—and then his son, literally for centuries. On May 12, 1842, Rice Williams, M.D., died at the age of eighty-five, "the last, although not the least eminent, of the physicians descended from the mysterious Lady of Llyn-y-Van-Vach." Six hundred years of medical practice in one family is certainly a proud and extraordinary record.

Two manuscripts embodying the medicine of the early physicians of Myddvai have come down to us. While both date from the fifteenth century, there is no doubt whatever that much of the medicine in them is far older. Charms and spells that must have been in use long before Rhiwallon's time also are included. The predominance of such flowers native to Wales as daisy, primrose, foxglove and violet indicates that this was very old local medicine indeed.

And thus we return to the daisy, which was copiously used by the physicians of Myddvai.

"Warts: to Remove. Whosoever would remove warts, let

him apply a daisy bruised in dog's urine thereto and they will all disappear."

"Insanity: to Cure. When a man becomes insane, take daisy, field southernwood, and sage, digest it in wine, and let the patient drink it for fifteen days."

"When a Man is affected with Plague or Black Pox [malignant small pox], take white ox-eye (when the centre has become black), tormentil, rue, and if you like add a leaf of bay; wash these carefully, bruise with water, and administer to the patient in strong ale as hot as he can take it. Let this be done while the patient is in bed between sheets, and near a good fire, so that he may perspire freely. By God's help the eruption will be transferred to the sheets."

"An Ointment to Clear the Eye" is more complicated, taking a number of herbs including daisy, which are pounded in butter, allowed to stand for a week, then strained through a clean cloth and put in a glass vessel. A bit of this ointment about the size of a grain of wheat is put into the eye for three days and nights "in order to remove opacity, web, or membrane" and thereafter the eye "will be clear and bright. It is proven."

The feeling the early Myddvai doctors had about the curative power of daisies was so strong that the flowers were incorporated into medicines to heal tumors, jaundice, erysipelas, boils, scrofula and "All Kindes of Hurtful Aches in Whatsoever Way They Come."

This latter use accounts for such old English common names for the daisy as "Bruisewort" or "Banewort." Banewort, or possibly sometimes "bonewort," has also a special meaning explained by William Turner, who said that "the Northern men call this herbe a Banwort because it helps bones to knyt agayne."

Useful as the daisy was to the physicians of Myddvai, it had still another virtue of even greater importance to them. It could tell a doctor whether his patient would live or die. "Take the

flower of the daisy and pound it well with wine, giving it to
the patient to drink; if he vomits it he will die of the disease,
if not he will live and this has been proven."

After this majestic beginning in early British medicine and
such uses as Mrs. Grieve mentions in the fourteenth century, the
curative properties of daisies received less attention from medical men until herbal medicine itself gradually disappeared. Just
once rather briefly, as the centuries rolled by, did the daisy again
assume any pharmaceutical importance. That was after Paracelsus had expounded the Doctrine of Signatures and daisies received more emphasis in prescriptions for eye remedies, not only
in formal medicine but also in the instructions for home care of
the sick that one finds in the stillroom books.

In *A Choice Manual, or Rare and Select SECRETS IN
PHYSICK & CHIRURGERY* (1659) there are four prescriptions for eye medicines that require daisies.

"The Right Honourable, the Countesse of Kente," who "Collected and practiced" the SECRETS was no mere village herb
woman who had, by some miracle, married a nobleman. Elizabeth Grey was an aristocrat by birth. Her mother was Mary
Cavendish, daughter of that formidable Bess of Harwick who
had built Chatsworth, Worksop, Blosover and Harwick Hall.
After the three gentlemen who successively married the fabulous
Bess had passed to what must have been a welcome repose, that
redoubtable lady bestowed her hand upon the widowed Earl
of Shrewsbury and the pair served for years as jailers of Mary,
Queen of Scots. Gilbert Talbot, the eldest son of the earl by
his first wife, married his stepmother's daughter Mary, and
these were the parents of our countess.

Like all great ladies of her time, the Countess of Kent had
to know about domestic medicine and practice it in her home.
In fact she was so interested in this branch of her household
duties that she was herself the inventor of a medicine, "The

Bellis maior from Dodoens' *Pemptades*. (*Horti-cultural Society of New York*)

Countess of Kents pouder, good against all malignant and pestilent Diseases; French pox [syphilis]. Small Pox, Measells, Plague," etc. This stooped to nothing so lowly as the daisy but included such expensive drugs as pearls, gold, coral, jet and other ingredients beyond the reach of common sufferers.

When it came to eye remedies, however, as well as "A Drink for one that hath a Rupture" and "A Medicine to cure Garget in the Throat," Elizabeth Grey had recourse to daisies and other simple herbs that anyone could find. Wild daisy roots, twice distilled in wine along with other herbs, were good to preserve the sight. And she also used daisies in a prescription for making a water with which to treat sore eyes. But "a Pin or Web in the Eye" seems to have been her specialty, since she had three remedies for this condition.

The juice of the petals of the English daisy, strained through "a linnen cloath" was one, and another took such additions as egg white, hazel bark and woman's milk. But one wonders why anyone bothered with daisies and troublesome formulas when the countess had a third remedy which was simplicity itself.

"Take two or three Lice out of one's head, and put them alive into the eye that is grieved and so close it up, and most assuredly the Lice will suck out the Web in the eye and will cure it, and come forth without any hurt." Whereupon, presumably, they could be returned to the head to await further need. This wife of one earl and stepdaughter of another was also a daughter of her time, and it was not a squeamish one.

Daisies have been used rather often in heraldry and there is no mystery as to why. Marguerite, the French word for daisy, is derived from a Greek word meaning "pearl."

When Francis I called his sister Marguerite of Marguerites his meaning was clear, and naturally the lady used the daisy as her device. So, too, did many another Margaret—Margaret of Anjou, wife of Henry VI, Margaret, Countess of Richmond, and Margaret Beaufort, mother of Henry VII, among others.

The Lady Margaret Beaufort may or may not have had a daisy on her coat of arms, but the flower was definitely her badge. The badge, which may possibly have predated coats of arms, was an emblem rather informally adopted although it was rarely worn by its owner. It served as a sort of trademark on objects belonging to its owner and was usually worn by his or her servants and retainers. When Henry VII built his chapel in Westminster Abbey, sometime between 1485 and 1509, he had his mother's badge of three daisies, beautifully carved, set among the sculptured ornaments.

St. Louis is said to have had a daisy engraved on a ring he wore. Along with it was a fleur-de-lis and a crucifix. This ring, the king claimed, represented all he held most dear: religion, France, and his wife.

Not only the Margarets but the English family surnamed Daisy used it as their heraldic device, for obvious reasons. So, for some unknown reason, did a gentleman named Sir Richard Quain who rejoiced in arms that included "a rock covered with daisies proper."

Of all the topics connected with flowers, folklore has had the most attention paid to it and is the easiest to look up. So, these stories have concentrated on other subjects in which flowers were concerned. But in the case of the daisy some bits from the large collection of folklore on the flower are so beguiling that they are included here.

First of all, since every one of us has shared that bit of flower magic, is the familiar chant

He loves me, he loves me not.

Flower Chronicles

There is an old English saying that spring has not come until you can set your foot on twelve daisies—which presupposes the bounties of nature not only in flowers but in the size of good country feet. The traditional English milkmaid, as well as all her kind, hung her shoes out of her window and put daisy roots under her pillow when she hoped to dream of her lover. As for dreaming of daisies themselves—that was good luck if it happened in spring or summer; bad luck if in fall or winter. You must put your foot on the first daisy you see in spring unless you want daisies to grow on your grave or that of someone dear to you before the year is out.

Students of folklore may trace these superstitions back to some ancient magic but they could be rather simple rustic fantasies springing from a desire to give significance to a beloved commonplace. Out of what country memories did Shakespeare put into the mouth of Lucius, in *Cymbeline*, the words:

> The boy hath taught us manly duties. Let us
> Find out the prettiest daisied plot we can
> And make him with our pikes and partisans
> A grave.

A much more elaborate bit of folklore about daisies comes from an old Celtic legend. According to this, the spirits of children who died at birth scattered new and lovely flowers on earth to cheer their sorrowing parents. One infant was responsible for the appearance of a flower "with a golden disc surrounded by silver leaves . . . and the flower of thy bosom, oh Malvina, has given a new flower to the hills of Morven."

Whether because of that last legend or because, as one author puts it, the daisy is "one of the earliest floral amusements of infancy," it symbolized "innocence" in that Victorian extravaganza known as the language of flowers.

Daisy

"Florigraphy" reached the height of its absurdity in Victoria's time, but actually this "science of sweet things" had its beginning in the preceding century. It blossomed, oddly enough, from seed sown by that brilliant, courageous and unsentimental woman, Lady Mary Wortley Montagu.

Edward Wortley Montagu was appointed ambassador to Turkey early in the eighteenth century and his wife went with him to Constantinople. The same intellectual curiosity that made Lady Mary investigate the Turkish practice of inoculation against smallpox (which she adopted for her own family and later introduced into England) made her interested in all sorts of local customs. One of these was the way in which the Turks used symbols to convey a message. Lady Mary described this in a letter to a friend at home. "There is no colour, no flower, no weed, no fruit, herb, pebble or feather, that has not a verse belonging to it; and you may quarrel, reproach, or send letters of passion, friendship, or civility, or even news without ever inking your fingers." She enclosed a sample message which included, among other symbolic objects, a rose and a jonquil.

This communication caused no furor whatever, but when Lady Mary's letters were published in 1763, a year after her death, the idea that flowers could form a "language" was born in England, though it did not come of age until half a century later.

La Mottraie, the companion of Charles XII, who left Turkey two years before the Wortley Montagus arrived, originally brought the Turkish idea of a language of flowers to Europe. The English development along those lines may have owed something to him as well as to Lady Mary. At any rate, it is clear that the French went in for a "langue des fleurs" with enthusiasm. If this seems uncharacteristic of a people noted for their devotion to reason and clear thinking, one must remember that we tend to judge any country by its best literature and art. Anyone whose youthful education was burdened with *Les Malheurs de Sophie* is aware that the French at their bourgeois worst could be as stuffy and sentimental as any Victorian Englishman or period-of-Grant American.

Whatever its origin, once the idea took hold it was pursued with a sort of dreadful solemnity. Books appeared by the dozen expounding the "grammar" of the new language. One author writes: "Every professor, ay, every student of this gentle art, may introduce new and varied combinations into its simple laws; but there are a few rudimentary rules that should not be neglected. When a flower is presented in its natural position, a sentiment is understood affirmatively; when reversed, negatively." What, one wonders, would have been the reaction at a Victorian tea table had a young girl appeared wearing daisies with their heads hanging down, since daisies, in the language of flowers, mean "innocence"?

The daisy played a prominent part in this "science" and reached dignity in helping to demonstrate Shakespeare's "taste and judgment" as he displayed these attributes in the "coronal wreath of the lovely maniac, Ophelia," crowflowers, nettles, daisies and long purples.

The crowflowers were firmly identified as a species of lychnis often called The Fair Maid of France. Daisies represented "the purity or spring-tide of life." Long purples were an arum sometimes called "dead men's fingers." Nettles speak for themselves. So, according to this author, you get

Crowflowers	Nettles	Daisies	Long Purples
Fair maid	stung to the quick	youthful bloom	the cold hand of death

And this should be read: A fair maid stung to the quick; her youthful bloom under the cold hand of death. Which proves, according to this enthusiast, that Shakespeare was acquainted with the science of florigraphy.

Daisy

No one would have been more surprised than Shakespeare, nor more amused, for, as those who know their *Hamlet* will remember, he had another and far more indelicate interpretation for long purples.

These books pass from exuberance to exuberance. It would take a talented gardener indeed to bring to bloom all in one season the flowers intended to convey to some bewildered girl that they were "the interpreters of love," lilies, tulips, carnations, jonquils, hollyhocks and crown imperial! But some, like a mother's message to her child, were more within the bounds of possibility. Moss signified maternal love; juniper, protection; primrose, youth; and the daisy, again, innocence. A bouquet of these oddly assorted members of the vegetable kingdom would then convey to the young the assurance that "maternal love will protect your youth in innocence and joy."

This fantasia was not confined to England and France. An American book on the subject was published anonymously in Philadelphia as early as 1835. This gives a very different meaning to the daisy: "I will think of it." "In the time of chivalry, when a lady would neither accept nor reject the vows of her lover, she ornamented her forehead with a wreath of field daisies, which expressed, *I will think of it*." It was all very confusing. How could the gentleman in question be perfectly sure whether his lady proposed to consider his suit or whether, depending on the way the flowers were worn, she wished him to know that she was innocent or the contrary?

The twentieth century, inured to less fanciful "science," takes its daisies more simply—either with the "great affecioun" Chaucer felt for them or straightforwardly as Wordsworth's unassuming—and beloved—commonplace.

Opium poppy. Goodyer's translation of *The Greek Herbal of Dioscorides,*
edited by R. T. Gunther. (*Used by permission of the estate of Dr. R. T.
Gunther and of the publisher, The University Press, Oxford*)

Poppy

or all its flimsy texture the poppy has flickered through human history like a little flame. Like the flame that both warms and burns, it runs to extremes. It has brought countless men a destructive habit that has wrecked their lives; to countless others it has brought sleep and ease from pain. Long before Iago mentioned "all the drowsy syrups of the world," opium had been their mainstay. Fra Bartholomaeus Anglicus, the thirteenth-century monk who wrote philosophy as if it were poetry, called the poppy "a slepi herbe."

Only a handful of our common garden flowers, all once so valued in medicine, are to be found in drugstores today, but among them the poppy is important. Morphine and codeine are two of the more familiar drugs made from the plant and few people get through life without being grateful, at one time or another, for the freedom from pain that they can bring. Modern techniques present us with little white pills that seem worlds removed from the crude opium of their origin. It may have been as early as Neolithic times that man began to be aware of the potent qualities latent in the seed pod of the fragile flower that shed its petals on every breeze. Whatever the date, the evidence of ancient medicine in Egypt and Assyria, and of mythology in Greece, all points to an early understanding of the narcotic and soporific properties of the poppy.

To stop children from crying immoderately "a mixture of the pods-of-poppu-plant with fly-dirt-from-the-wall is recommended."

Disgust is any modern parent's instant reaction to such a prescription. But if one can forget the remedy for a moment, a bridge is thrown between one human being and another. Across the gulf of all the differences that separate the twentieth century from ancient Egypt a span is made of nothing more tangible than the echo of a sound—the sound of a baby crying. Without difficulty any modern parent can reach back through most of history to sympathize with those Egyptians who were worried because their child was crying immoderately. Their version of a soothing syrup is thirty-five hundred years old, and could conceivably be older

Poppies appear also in a prescription "to clear out the body," in a "stinging" remedy for pain in the abdomen (a counterirritant?), and in a medicine to heal diseased toes. The last-named includes eighteen ingredients, sixteen of which, a modern commentator points out, could have been advantageously discarded. Had the diseased toes been washed in "Water-from-the-Rain-of-Heaven" and anointed with fresh olive oil, the rest of the drugs, poppy included, might have been unnecessary.

When scholars claim that the Papyrus Ebers, from which these prescriptions were taken, is only a copy, made about 1580 B.C., of a much older medical manuscript they may well have in mind Ra's headache medicine. This was prepared for the god by the goddess Isis and thus links some rather sophisticated medicine to prehistoric mythology.

A poppy seed pod, coriander, wormwood, juniper and the-Berry-of-the-Sames-plant were incorporated in honey. This was smeared on the temples of the god, and it is reported that he was instantly cured. If so, the poppy was responsible, since nothing else in the prescription would have had any effect.

In Assyrian medicine the poppy had many uses, oddly enough another stomach remedy and one for the feet. This time it was the sole of the foot that needed attention. For "broken" soles opium was mixed with fat and bound on.

The Assyrians seem to have been the only people who ever used the root of the poppy. They prescribed it to "encourage a man when he has approached his wife and . . . towards his wife his heart is not lifted up. . . ."

Ein andere Art eines Diſtillierofens/mit einem irdinen Helm/ vnd küpfferin Külkeſſelin/faſt bräuchlich/den man auch mit Holtz anwärmen mag.

Still for the production of herbal medicines, from Lanitzer's *Kreuterbuch*.
(*Horticultural Society of New York*)

A variation of this idea was taken over by the Babylonians after they had conquered the Assyrians. There is a tablet which gives a list of the plants that grew in the garden of the Babylonian king, Merodach-baladan. The poppy was among them but evidently represented fruitfulness rather than sleep.

Merodach, incidentally, was the king who sent an embassy to Hezekiah about 720 B.C., ostensibly to congratulate the Israelite king on his recovery from an illness, but actually to suggest an alliance.

Classical Greek medicine used the poppy but without much

reference to its narcotic or soporific qualities. Hippocrates lists it among the strengthening and nourishing items of diet, but it is very doubtful that he even knew of opium. Theophrastus, after giving an unusually clear description of the plant, merely remarked that "it purges downward."

It is strange that the peculiar properties of the poppy should not have been mentioned in Greek medicine, because long before Hippocrates' time the Greeks knew the effects that opium had on man. For, if Greek medicine ignored the potent aspects of the poppy, Greek mythology defined them.

Demeter, so runs the myth, created the poppy for the express purpose of getting some sleep after the loss of her daughter Persephone. The twin brothers Hypnos and Thanatos (Sleep and Death) were represented as crowned with poppies or carrying poppies in their hands. Clearly the Greeks were aware that a merciful sleep induced by opium might easily lead to death.

By the beginning of our own era the dangerous properties of the poppy were known and admitted. Pliny could in one breath give a careful description of how to collect raw opium and in the next issue a warning that "taken in too large quantities [it] is productive of sleep unto death even."

Dioscorides said bluntly that "being drunk too much . . . it kills."

Since the poppy is still in the pharmacopoeia, its medical history is so long and so technical that only a specialist should handle it. But there is one aspect of it that even an amateur can undertake blithely. Anyone can see with what alacrity the poppy would lend itself to quack medicine. Opium was made to order for quacks. So, this is an excellent chance to explore that shady corner of the story of medicine.

However, before abandoning orthodox medicine entirely, one use of the poppy in the Middle Ages well worth lingering over.

Poppy

In a fourteenth-century medical manuscript there is a prescription for making a sleeping draught called "dwale." This was a well-known remedy for insomnia in Chaucer's time and he mentioned it casually in *The Reeve's Tale:*

Doctor preparing medicine. From *The Grete Herball.* (*The Pierpont Morgan Library*)

> Ther was na more, hem neded no dwale
> This miller hath so wisly bidded ale,
> That as an hors he snorteth in his sleep . . .

But in the medical manuscript dwale was described as a drink "to make a man slepen-en whyle men kerve hym." Equal quantities of hemlock, bryony, lettuce, henbane and poppy were boiled a "litil" in the gall of a boar. (If the patient was a woman, it had to be the gall of a spayed sow!) When the operation was about to take place "hym that schal ben carven" was made to drink this concoction in wine or ale until he fell asleep. "And thanne men may safly kerven hym." Directions follow for waking the patient once the butchery was over.

It seems amazing that recourse to opium was not in common use. At that time the only other way to deaden a man's consciousness while men "kerve" him was to get him into a drunken stupor. Yet it was not the dangers inherent in opium that deterred the early medical men. They used digitalis, belladonna and many another poisonous herb without a qualm. Nor could the patient have objected. Surgery before anesthetics and aseptics presented such dangers that it was often a death sentence. If the patient survived the horror itself he was very liable to die later. This would then have been considered an act of God, but we would put it down to shock, loss of blood or septicemia. The possibility of dying from an overdose of opium was halcyon by comparison. It is really puzzling why it was not generally used.

Since there seems to have been only this one lone genius, it would be pleasant to know the name of the doctor who, some six hundred years ago, worked out this idea for an anesthetic. For his is a name that should be honored especially at this point, before we turn to consider his less reputable professional brethren—the quacks.

". . . for quieting the cries of starving children by throwing them into a forced sleep" Godfrey's Cordial was much used. At least Elizabeth Kent said so in *Flora Domestica*. "The use of these stimulants and narcotics," she continues, "especially in children, without proper care, is highly to be deprecated and," Miss Kent goes on with gentle restraint, "lays in their little frames the foundations of many disorders, besides putting numbers to their last sleep."

She was writing in 1823, during the early days of the Industrial Revolution. Godfrey's Cordial had already enjoyed about fifty years of popularity but this was probably a new use for it. Men thrown out of work by the chaotic conditions of the infant industries found opium cheaper than food. A few coppers would buy the "cordial" that kept hungry children quiet when those same coppers were insufficient to buy bread and meat.

Godfrey, father of the infamous "cordial," belonged not only to the race of quacks but to the period when quackery flourished. Tincture of opium was the only effective ingredient in the nostrum, which was widely used from its invention late in the eighteenth century right down into the twentieth. A. C. Wootten, whose *Chronicles of Pharmacy* were published in 1910, speaks of "the still popular Godfrey!" It took the pure food and drug laws of a later day to remove dangerous narcotics from patent medicines.

There always have been quacks—there probably always will be. But there was a period when these gentlemen reached the fine flower of quackery.

When the Puritans governed England a specter stalked the land. Conscience, a grim tyrant, was pointed out to every waverer, to every feeble spirit who yearned for the fleshpots. But Conscience withdrew into obscurity when the genial Charles Stuart returned to his kingdom. The lid was off the fleshpots then. Along with the very human longing for a little color and gaiety in life went a weak craving for luxury, a greedy grasping for wealth. In such an atmosphere quacks came into their own—successful, impudent, flamboyant. So, beginning with the Restoration and trailing off into drabness only a little more than a century later, the great quacks of English medicine developed and flourished.

The list is a long one and a catalogue of names, dates and nostrums would make dull reading. Also it would take us too far afield from the poppy, since opium was only one of the mainstays of quackdom. It will not only be more to the point but more interesting to find out how these gentry worked in the person of one William Salmon.

"The Power and Vertue of this Medicine flies like Lightening through the whole Body; for it is no sooner received into the Stomach but it presently refreshes the Spirits, chears the Heart, and gives ease and relief in any pain, in what part of the Body soever . . . Allays Grief, procures a quietness of Mind, and causes pleasant Sleep and Rest, restoring Nature to its Pristine State, and repairing the decayed strength . . . giving relief to [an interminable list of ailments that include practically everything one can think of as pathological] after a miraculous manner, and this sometimes after all hopes are past."

This description—or rather part of a description—of the virtues of a tincture of opium appears in Salmon's *Botanologia, The English Herbal.* Similar effusions made up into handbills were passed out on the streets of London and helped to make Salmon a comparatively rich man.

Laudanum also flies through the body like lightning "and appeases all perturbations of the Mind and intestines . . ."; again "restores Nature to its Pristine State" in such fashion that "Unthought of Health comes on, with a violent Career, and takes possession of its ancient Habitation, exterminating in All Ages and Sexes, the roots of bitterness, and the Seminalities of Pain and Disease."

Nowhere in Salmon's lyric descriptions of the virtues of the poppy is there any indication that it is a dangerous drug. Yet it is unlikely that Salmon did not know it. At the time of his death he was reputed to have a library of three thousand books and surely a large proportion of them dealt with medicine. Reputable herbalists and doctors from classical times to his own had carefully pointed out the dangers of opium. It is preposterous to suppose that Salmon had not read what such men as Dioscorides, Pliny and scores of others had written about opium. He knew how deadly it was.

When Salmon wrote his herbal he had reached respectability. At least he was a solid citizen of London, possessed of a good library and a comfortable fortune. He was born in 1644 and had made a long and fantastic journey to reach such security.

Salmon's travels began in his extreme youth when he acted as a zany to a mountebank. The job was as colorful as the phrase. The seventeenth-century mountebank was a walking translation of the word—a man who mounted a bank or bench and cried his wares. An old ballad describes these as

> Promiscuous sweeps of Druggist shops
> Made into Plaisters, Pills and slops,
> All mix't, as you'll hereafter see,
> Up with *Infallibility.*

His zany, or Merry Andrew, dressed in the diapered particolored garments of a fool, was his comic relief—roaring with pretended pain one moment, turning handsprings the next, and mocking his master's gravity by making faces behind his back.

After wandering as a zany here and there about England Salmon next traveled to New England. That he went there and returned is all we know. It is a pity he left no record of that trip, for whatever Salmon's ethics he was no fool. It would have been interesting to read his impressions of the raw new country—of the thin string of clearings along the coast that the first English colonists had made against the great backdrop of primeval forest—of the little village that was going to be the city of Boston—of the scattered hamlets that made up the total settlement of the Massachusetts Bay Colony.

Back in England Salmon set himself up to practice medicine.

There is no indication that he had any formal training. Only the fact that he collected a large library suggests that he did some reading on the subject.

For a while Salmon seems to have carried on an ordinary practice. But he soon discovered that he could make more money by writing and by selling the nostrums he invented.

Another famous quack was "Spot" Ward—so called because of a birthmark on his face—a protégé of George II. He had first been introduced to his sovereign when that dull and lethargic gentleman was suffering from a dislocated thumb. Ward gave the thumb a quick jerk and was rewarded by a royal kick in the shins. Ignoring the kick, Ward respectfully suggested that his Majesty try to move the thumb. This King George could do without pain for the first time since the malady had seized him. He was so overjoyed by this "miraculous" cure that Ward's fortune was made. Honors and gifts were heaped upon him. Presumably his practice had hitherto been a rather shabby one but now it included such glittering names as those of Lord Chesterfield, Fielding and Gibbon. But not all English men of letters were taken in by Ward's slick methods. Samuel Johnson told Boswell that Ward was the dullest man he had ever met; and Pope directed one of his barbed couplets in Ward's direction:

> Of late without the least pretense to skill
> Ward's grown a famed physician by a pill.

In addition to the famous pill Ward was noted for his "sweating powder," which consisted chiefly of ipecac and opium, together with a number of other and ineffectual drugs.

Some said that Ward was the brother of a respectable dry-salter. Others had a more colorful story, to the effect that he had originally been footman to an English nobleman. According to the latter version, it was while traveling with his master in Europe he had collected prescriptions from various monks he met.

In any case, Ward rose from humble origins to a dizzy height, and heights went to his head. He left a request in his will that he be buried in Westminster Abbey "as near the high altar as is convenient." Fortunately for the honor of English medicine and English common sense this preposterous demand was ignored.

That Ward might well have gathered prescriptions from monks on the Continent is amply upheld by descriptions of some of the drugs they manufactured. *Baume Tranquille*, for instance, was well laced with opium, though a number of other herbs went into it as it was originally prepared by a Capuchin monk called Père Tranquille. A fellow monk, one Père Rousseau, added "as many large live frogs as there are pounds of oil. These are to be boiled in oil until they are almost burnt. Their juice and fat combines with the oil and greatly augments the excellence of the remedy."

This particular "medicine" was so highly prized that Madame de Sévigné, writing to her daughter on the 16th of December, 1684, could say, "I am sending you the most precious treasure I have; my half bottle of Baume Tranquille. I could not send a full; the Capucines have no more."

Those were the days when a large dollop of opium could be added to practically anything to bring "miraculous" relief to the sick and suffering. Unscrupulous men disregarded the clear warnings of danger given by doctors and herbalists before them. The quacks were out after easy money and plenty of it. Opium was made to order for them and they took full advantage of it.

Thus it seems likely that it was the quacks from the Restoration period through the eighteenth century who popularized opium. For by the beginning of the nineteenth century the tincture of opium called laudanum was as casually bought and used as aspirin is today. Every druggist carried it and undoubtedly some were more patronized than others because of the strength of the tincture they sold. Laudanum consisted simply of opium dissolved in alcohol to which water, distilled or not, might or might not be added.

Since a number of well-known poets and writers have been opium addicts, and since laudanum was the form in which they all took opium, it may be worth while to pause for a moment over this particular drug that owes its origin to the poppy.

Laudanum was originally given to the world by Paracelsus, who rechristened himself modestly "a greater than Celsus," and is still a controversial figure. Some believe that he made notable contributions to medicine; others dismiss him as a charlatan. But for our purpose he was chiefly the inventor of laudanum, which began its existence as a very expensive medicine that was suspected of containing opium. The mid-sixteenth century had not yet learned to take opium casually. As a matter of fact, Paracelsus' prescription called for "a quarter of its weight in opium to which was added henbane juice, mummy, salts of pearls and corals, the bone of the heart of a stag, bezoar stone, amber, musk, unicorn and some spices, with a few drops of many of the essential oils."

Gradually laudanum lost such costly trimmings as mummy and unicorn. Suspicion that opium was involved gave way to acceptance of the fact that opium was the backbone of the remedy. By the beginning of the nineteenth century the cheap and simple tincture known as laudanum was not only acknowledged as the most popular painkiller but had begun to present itself as a social problem as well. The same Miss Kent whose comments on Godfrey's Cordial have already been quoted speaks of laudanum as being "so much used instead of tea by the poorer class of females in Manchester and other manufacturing towns and not unknown to the same class in London as a gentle sedative and the inducer of oblivious delirium from the cares of life."

Literary men, as well as the poor, turned to laudanum as an "inducer of delicious delirium." George Crabbe, Samuel Taylor Coleridge and Thomas De Quincey, to take them in the order of their birth dates, 1754, 1772 and 1785, were all opium addicts, as was Francis Thompson, who was born the year De Quincey died, 1859. At the beginning of *Confessions of an English Opium Eater* De Quincey tells of walking the streets of London nearly crazy from neuralgic pains in his head and face. He happened to meet a former fellow student at Oxford who suggested that he take some laudanum to deaden the pain. De Quincey bought some tincture of opium on his way home and took a dose immediately. ". . . and in an hour, O heavens! . . . what a resurrection! what an apocalypse of the world within me! That my pains had vanished was now a trifle . . . swallowed up in the immensity . . . of divine enjoyment thus suddenly revealed . . . here was the secret of happiness . . . happiness might now be bought for a penny and carried in the waistcoat-pocket. . . ."

It was, of course, not so simple as all that, though De Quincey took opium moderately for years before he began to feel its ill-effects. But his lyric eulogy has, one gathers, brought disappointment to a number of people—especially to those who thought that if they just took some opium they would be able to write as well as a De Quincey or a Coleridge. Apparently one gets out of opium what one takes to it! At any rate, it seems to be pretty well established that men such as Coleridge and De Quincey, with delicate and highly organized sensory apparatus, had dreams full of sound and color and light, and this seems to have followed with the two lesser poets. But the average person, not so well endowed with sensitivity, soon discovers that opium dreams do not stimulate his imagination as he had hoped they would. One gathers that when they come at all those dreams are rather dull.

Leaving aside the moral as well as the medical problems posed by opium, it is still obvious that addiction itself is an evil—something that is bad for the individual personally, and thus hurts society through him. Yet we owe *Kubla Kahn* to this evil, and possibly much of the color and imagery of *The Ancient Mariner*. Inevitably one is drawn to the futile speculation as to whether or not Coleridge would have been a better poet had he not taken opium. No one can answer that one, but we do know that he took to opium a high degree of poetic talent. All the others mentioned here were lesser artists and perhaps had no more to give the world, opium or not, than what Thompson had to offer in his poem to *The Poppy:*

> All that the world of me esteems,
> My wither'd dreams, my wither'd dreams.

It is hard to realize how anything so gay and so charming as some of our garden poppies could be literally the cause of a war. Yet our peony-flowered poppies and the fringed carnation-flowered poppies are simply cultivated varieties of the opium poppy. And the opium poppy was quite literally the cause of a war.

In November, 1839, the British declared war against China and in August, 1842, China surrendered and signed a dictated peace.

As everyone who reads history knows, there are always two causes of a war—the underlying cause and some immediately provocative incident. Opium was concerned in this case with both.

The underlying cause of the Opium War was England's determination to get China to open its doors to ordinary commercial traffic by means of a trade treaty. France, Holland and

the United States were almost equally eager to establish commercial relations. But China was determined to have nothing
to do with the "barbarians," though she was not averse to
making money out of them so long as that could be done without recognizing any official equality. In 1798 Lord Macartney,
at the head of an embassy sent to China to try to negotiate
such a treaty, met the same reception that had already been
accorded several Dutch missions. He was obliged to take part
in "the ancient Confucian masquerade in which the Son of
Heaven, as Lord of the World, received tribute from Outer
Barbarians come from the darkness to worship the light." The
masque was produced with such exquisite taste that there was
no sting in it; but neither was any treaty forthcoming. Apparently the only profit from Macartney's mission was the rose
that bears his name.

Meantime events in India affected the situation. The East
India Company was faced with the problem of opium. For
centuries opium had been grown and processed in Bengal and
under British dominion the cultivation of poppies increased.
But the East India Company realized that to dispose of its opium
to its potential labor supply was a shortsighted policy. Its pernicious effects would swiftly deplete even India's vast backlog
of unskilled labor. So why not sell to China?

Why not indeed? True, there was a Chinese law against the
importation of "Foreign Mud" but the trade could be managed—and it was. The East India Company kept its own skirts
clean by having no official connection with the traffic. It
auctioned off the opium crop to "country firms," that is, independent merchants who hired ships and ran the contraband
into Canton, which was the only port in which "barbarian"
ships were permitted.

At Canton business was done, legal and illegal business alike,
with the hong merchants, who were a monopolistic group that

had no support from the Chinese government in dealing with foreigners. They handed out vast sums to "fix" government authorities who might ask inconvenient questions. The buying and distributing of opium, a completely illegal operation, required a complicated and widespread organization. Individually, many of the hong merchants were pleasant and attractive men, but it was they who fastened upon their fellow countrymen a destructive and pernicious habit. Only their co-operation made the opium trade possible. On an international scale it was rather like the rackets of some of our own great cities.

The "barbarians"—British, American, French and Dutch— doing business at Canton worked under galling conditions. Whether they traded illegally in opium or legally exchanged woolens, cottons, furs and spices for tea, silk and porcelain they were subjected to insulting regulations. No "barbarian" merchant might bring his wife and children and set up house-keeping in Canton. Their inferiority was stressed by forbidding them to go boating on the river for pleasure or to use sedan chairs. They had no protection from national consuls or trade officials and were completely at the mercy of the edicts issued by the hong merchants.

So it was that, while the traffic in opium grew by leaps and bounds, the difficulties of doing business with the Chinese also increased. The highhanded and insulting regulations laid down by the hong merchants became more and more intolerable. England and the Dutch before her had really tried to arrange for orderly and recognized commercial relations. Both countries had been blandly rebuffed. But now England, with Waterloo behind her and conscious of her great increase in power, felt that the situation was no longer to be borne. War was the obvious answer, and England sent several men-of-war to escort some of the opium ships putting in at Canton. The Chinese fired on these ships. The men-of-war returned the fire. Thus the Opium War began.

It lasted nearly three years. At the peace table the Chinese ceded Hong Kong to the British crown and opened the five treaty ports of Canton, Amoy, Foochow, Ningpo and Shanghai to trade with the West. Opium was not mentioned in the peace treaty, so it was still contraband and the illegal traffic therein continued until 1908.

It is an ugly story, that of the Opium War. But it should be remembered to the credit of Great Britain that all Englishmen did not subscribe to the action of their commercial interests and their government. A vote of censure was proposed and debated in Commons. Lord Macaulay, the historian, made a chauvinistic speech defending the government and boasting of the British flag waving in glory over Canton. But Gladstone, just beginning his career in the House, had the moral courage not only to vote for censure but to speak eloquently for it. In sober, quiet words he summed up what the flag meant to him and then thundered that it had become no more than "a pirate flag to protect an infamous traffic." Brave words those, and the only incident in the whole sordid affair worth remembering.

On Memorial Day the American Legion sells its scarlet poppies. Young people who buy them know that the funds so raised go to help wounded veterans, and "veterans" to them are those from World War II and Korea. Only the older generation associates the poppies quite literally with Flanders Field and World War I.

Cause of one war, symbol of another; associated always in men's minds with sleep and death—yet, valiant and undaunted, the poppy is the gayest flower in the garden.

NAMES.

A.

G. Kvar &c.

J. Cyanus minor.

I. Fior campese.

G. Korn - blume.

F. Barbeau, Bluet-
   Fleur.

J. Coronilla
   Yesba.

D. Blaauwe
   Koren-
   blom.

CORN
BLUE BOTTLE.

PARTS USED.

The Herb and
Flowers.

PREPARATIONS.

In the Shops
none.

PLACE.)

In Corn
Fields

TIME.

June and
July.

VIRTUES.)

The distill'd Water of the Flowers is sometimes used for inflamed and sore Eyes.

T. Sheldrake delin.

C.H. Hemerich sculp.

One of "the exquisite Drawings of the late Ingenious T. Sheldrake" from
an eighteenth-century herbal, *Botanicum Medicinale.*

Cornflower

ne day in early spring a boy died in Egypt. Although he was an unimportant young king who did not live to see his twenties he was buried with such magnificence that the discovery of his tomb thousands of years later was the sensation of a whole generation. The wealth that surrounded Tutankhamen in death gives us some measure of what must have been lavished on a Thutmosis or a Ramesses. Their tombs, of course, as well as all those that have been found so far of the royal and princely families of Egypt, have long since been plundered down to the last glass bead. The peasants of Egypt rarely live much above a subsistence level, and often on the edge of starvation. Naturally enough, they have looted the treasure their fathers and forefathers helped to create. Buried underground, it could benefit no one. The logic if not the morals of this argument is understandable, but the loss to archaeology is beyond counting.

The greatness of that loss is apparent when one reads Howard Carter's account of the contents of the tomb of Tutankhamen. The perfectly normal human interest in buried treasure is exhausted long before one has finished the two-volume book. One grows literally sick and tired of treasure. Jewelry, alabaster vases and cups, statues carved in all sizes and many materials, weapons, textiles, furniture and gold—gold everywhere. And in the midst of all this splendor, cornflowers!—shriveled and brittle, but still blue and still recognizable.

Fastened to the gold cobra that juts from the forehead of the king's effigy on his second sarcophagus was a tiny wreath made as carefully as any piece of jewelry. A twig had been bound together to form a circle about six inches across. Over the twig olive leaves had been folded, first the dark-green shiny side up, then the silvery underside, and so on around the circle. These leaves served as clips alternately for cornflowers and the blue petals of water lilies. The whole was woven firmly together by threadlike strips of papyrus.

According to P. E. Newberry, who discussed the plants identified in the tomb, this was probably the king's "Wreath of Justification" to which a chapter is devoted in the ancient Egyptian *Book of the Dead*. But even though the little wreath may have fitted into the traditional funeral formula of the time, Mr. Carter felt that it had a special significance. In those exciting early days when the tomb and its treasures were being explored, in spite of all the strange and valuable objects to be examined and catalogued, Mr. Carter seems to have been very conscious of the unseen human factor. In an alabaster wishing cup and the little wreath of cornflowers, across all those centuries, he sensed poignantly the personal sorrow that followed the young king in death.

And it may well have been so. On the back of the throne that was part of the furnishing of the tomb is a picture of Tutankhamen and his girl queen. He stands dressed for some official function while she seems to be anointing him with oil or perfume. This picture, beaten into the sheet gold that covers the throne, was the work of an artist still under the influence of the freer forms and treatment that flourished during the reign of Tutankhamen's predecessor, who was probably also his father-in-law, Amenophis IV, that brilliant and tragic heretic who had tried to persuade his people that there was but one god. Under his liberalizing influence the rigidity of Egyptian art had given place to something fresh and naturalistic, almost informal. From this golden picture comes a suggestion of youth happily and affectionately at ease. It is not difficult to share Mr. Carter's belief that the young king and queen loved each other and that whatever may have been the ritual significance of the wishing cup and the tiny wreath they also expressed the girl's grief for her young husband.

One day in June, 1918, nearly three thousand five hundred years after Tutankhamen died, a girl was married in a suburb

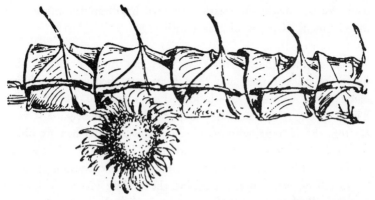

Cornflower (*C. depressa*) in an Egyptian funerary wreath. From *Die Gartenpflanzen in Älten Ägypten* by Ludwig Keimer. (*Hoffman und Campe, Hamburg*)

of Baltimore. She married one of the young officers France had sent to this country to help train American soldiers for combat overseas in World War I. One of the presents that was sent this American bride came in a letter from a cousin on a ranch in far-off British Columbia. The cousin's husband was off to war and there was not much money on the ranch for wedding presents. But there was no lack of imagination and generosity, for the present enclosed in that letter was something its owner valued—a cornflower.

"Donald found this flower growing on the edge of his trench," the cousin wrote her young kinswoman, "and put it in a letter he was writing to me. Every bride should have something blue and I thought that if you put this in one of your slippers you might like to feel that you were standing on a little bit of France when you are being married."

Almost the whole span of recorded time stretches between that funeral in Egypt and that wedding in America. And yet the story of the cornflower has remained very little changed over the centuries—its relation to man has been far more one of sentiment than of practical utility.

It is curious that cornflowers were not more firmly established in ancient medicine than they were because they have come down to us in Greek legend as a specific for wounds. Their very generic name ties them to the legend because it was Chiron, the centaur, who called them panacea after healing himself with cornflowers of a wound made by an arrow poisoned in the blood of the hydra. It was Chiron, Greek mythology goes on to tell us, who taught mankind the healing virtues of herbs. But for all that, the cornflower as a healing herb, much less a panacea, somehow did not stick. Almost certainly its virtues were early confused with those of the centaury, also named for the centaur. The centaury is a pink gentian and the cornflower is a blue composite, but in the days of man's botanical innocence distinctions based on form or habit of growth were minor points compared to a similarity of names.

Dioscorides, it is true, specifies fourteen or fifteen ailments for which the cornflower was useful, but the identification in the English edition is a modern one and the early herbalists could hardly have been entirely certain what flower he intended. So over the years the cornflower slipped almost entirely out of use until the Doctrine of Signatures brought it back into medicine as an eye remedy.

In the case of the daisy the Doctrine of Signatures had

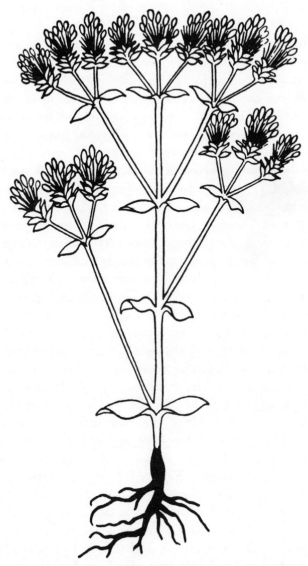

The centauria. Goodyer's translation of *The Greek Herbal of Dioscorides*, edited by R. T. Gunther. (*Used by permission of the estate of Dr. R. T. Gunther and of the publisher, The University Press, Oxford*)

pointed out that the eye of the flower must be valuable for the eye of man. That was rather more elaborate reasoning than was usual with this doctrine. For actually the whole solemn rigmarole was nothing more than simple association of ideas. If you have anything so obvious as saffron—yellow—jaundice, why not cornflower—blue—eyes? Why not indeed, and into inflamed and painful eyes went cornflowers.

By the end of the sixteenth century the cornflower was firmly established as an eye medicine. Turner, Gerard, Parkinson, Dodoens, Nicholas Culpeper and many other herbalists mention it as such and by the early eighteenth century it was so firmly fixed in the pharmacopoeia that William Salmon had no less than five prescriptions in which cornflowers were used to cure ailing eyes. Since William was a quack, he seized upon any accepted thing and elaborated it to his own glory—or so he hoped. *The Spiritous Tincture of the Flowers*, made with common brandy, was "a secret for sor or running Eyes." *The Cataplasm of the Flowers* was especially for "Eyes afflicted with hot Rheum." A "wonderful water for the Eyes, and their Diseases" was made—so Salmon says—of cornflowers macerated in "Snow water" though he does not vouchsafe the method by which a midsummer flower and snow could be brought together. *The Essence of the Juice of the Leaves and Flowers* "helps in the Dropsie . . . and is peculiar against the poison of Scorpions, Phalangium, Viper, Mad Dog and Plague" besides cooling inflamed and painful eyes. Finally there was *The Collyrium, or Eye-Water*. To make this you take as many cornflowers as strikes your fancy, add them to the dough of rye bread, bake and then distill the result "in a glass body in a Bain Marie." This product will not only cure any diseased condition of the eye but so strengthens them that "People for which reason are pleased to call it *Break-Spectacle Water* since those who use it

can discard their spectacles." The French called a similar concoction *Eau de Casselunettes.*

As a result of this long-drawn-out fervor about cornflowers
and eyes, an official drug made from the flowers continued in
use right down into the early part of the twentieth century.

In a most out-of-the-way and unexpected field cornflowers
have played a part in the erudite realm of comparative mythology.

The story of the lady who cherished the head of her lover,
whom her brothers had killed, hidden in the earth under a
potted basil plant was first told in the West by Boccaccio. Most
of us know it best from Rossetti as "Isabella and the Pot of
Basil."

Now, there is a rather—to the lay mind—far-fetched similarity between this legend which originated in Sicily and a Russian folk legend which concerns the "basilek," which is the Russian name for cornflower. However, there are a whole series
of Sicilian legends which correspond to a Russian series, so that
this one about the basil-cornflower is simply an extra scrap of
evidence that the Russian and Sicilian legends are related. In
each case local circumstances determined the plants and other
details of the stories but their general similarity suggests a
common source, which is found in Byzantine legends. To quote
the enthusiastic comment of a French scholar, it would be "ex-
cessively interesting to establish a new legendary parallel between the Greco-Italian *basilic* (basil) and the Greco-Russian
(*basilek*) (cornflower) and thus enlarge, by a precious new
detail, the circle of comparative mythology."

A word should be said about that old English name for cornflower—bluebottle. Various writers have been scornful about it
or puzzled by it. Several have tried to find some other derivation

than "bottle" for the word because they could see no possible connection between the shape of the flowers and a bottle. Yet there should be no question about it. As late as the middle of the seventeenth century William Coles could recognize them as bottles. Some seeds, he said, "grow in knaps like Bottles, as Knapweed, which some call Darbottle, Blewbottle, great Centaury &." If the bottles to which Coles refers were in use in his time they stretched all the way back to the Biblical Joshua to whom the Gideonites went in disguise, in old shoes and old garments, and they carried old sacks and wine bottles, *old and rent and bound up*. The bottles to which Coles refers are blood brothers to the bottles of the Old Testament—just skins, or rather pouches made of skin, to hold liquids. The symbol used in heraldry for a bottle is obviously based on the skin rather than on any utensil of pottery or glass and shows clearly where the cornflower got its name.

Another old English name for the cornflower shows plainly that the sentiment inspired by the flower was not always a happy one. "Hurtsickle" they used to call it. Any plant capable of inflicting damage on one of those cumbersome ancient sickles is worthy of note on that score alone. Clumsy as they were, medieval sickles probably made their way crisply enough through the gold of ripe wheat. But when they came up against the slim silver stem of the cornflower there was trouble. The primitive iron just couldn't take it. So we get the name.

Looking back over the history of the cornflower in relation to man we find only bits and pieces. But, except for those ancient farm laborers who cursed it as American farmers were to curse the daisy, the cornflower has held a rather special place in men's affections if not in their kitchens and pharmacies. So few common objects boast so rare and pure a color. It is easy for that color alone to make the flower the symbol of some personal sentiment. Except for those ancient sickle wielders who had no love for it, the cornflower seems always to have inspired affection. "The chylder," said William Turner with unwonted gentleness, for his own children drove him almost to distraction, "the chylder use to make garlandes of the floures."

Arms of the Earl of Rosebery, whose family name is Primrose. From *The Scots Peerage*, Vol. VII, ed. by Sir James Balfour Paul. (*Messrs. Douglas & Foulis, Ltd., Edinburgh*)

Primrose

The story of the primrose is an English story—as English as Jane Austen. Probably no other flower is so intimately interwoven in the life of a country. Narcissus belonged in much the same way to ancient Greece but we do not now associate it with Greece. Japan, of course, has her chrysanthemums but they came to her from China and are a cultivated taste. The tulips of Holland did not reach Europe until the sixteenth century. The lilies of France are iris, and conventionalized iris at that. And so it goes. But Primulas—primrose, cowslip and oxlip— are native to the British Isles and part of the very fabric of existence there.

When he is transplanted by the needs of business or diplomacy to the far places of the earth, the Englishman who is also a gardener (and a surprisingly large percentage of them are) cultivates with interest the flora of the country to which he was sent. But he is apt to go to a good deal of trouble to raise, among those unfamiliar flowers, some from home. If he can establish a few clumps of English primroses he is happy. A nineteenth-century author who wrote about flowers in a manner as lush in sentiment as it is feeble in grammar observed that "Anglo-Indians, in the midst of all his [sic] Oriental magnificence, deems a root of primrose or a tuft of English violets one of the highest luxuries obtainable."

England displays a rose on the royal coat of arms, but she carries a primrose in her heart.

This identification of the primrose with England is emphasized by the fact that the primrose is a North European plant. The cowslip is native to nearly all of Europe, but it could hardly have been very common in the Mediterranean area in classical times because traces of it are so few there.

A Greek myth tells us that Paralisos, the son of Flora and Priapus, died of grief because of the loss of his betrothed. His body was transformed by his parents into "the rathe primrose that forsaken dies."

Now, this young man's name is obviously that from which the name of the disease derives, and we find primroses often used as a specific for paralysis, though not until we come to the herbals of the Renaissance. Primroses are not mentioned by Theophrastus or Dioscorides, and the single one so identified in Pliny fails to carry conviction: "The leaves of it, seven in number, and very similar to those of the lettuce, spring from a yellow root." It is a pity that identification is so uncertain, for surely Pliny's primrose was not to be despised. "Taken in water, it is a cure, they say, for maladies of every kind."

With that vague picture behind us we can leave the primrose of classical antiquity and turn with British primroses to the land that is not only their physical but also their spiritual home.

Primroses play a minor role in the medicine that has come down to us in the Anglo-Saxon leech-books, but where they do appear it is in the folk medicine that comes from a time so far in the past that only the dimmest traces of that past remain. But as if to label those traces unmistakably British they are marked for us by humor and poetry and primroses.

However deadpan one of these early doctors may have been when prescribing for some harassed husband, one feels sure that there was a twinkle in his eye when he came to record the prescription in his leech-book: "Against a woman's chatter: taste at night fasting a root of radish, that day the chatter cannot harm thee."

Primrose

Another receipt calls for gathering worts for three nights "before summer comes to town" and the charming phrase recurs. Then for heaviness of spirit, radish is to be eaten with salt and vinegar and "soon the mood will be more gay." Chaucer, Shakespeare and Housman need not have been ashamed of those phrases, and all three poets, one feels sure, would have enjoyed them.

Along with the old doctor's twinkle and poetic words, primroses appear in the leech-books. It is their function to cure wens and "the dry disease," which was treated by putting pounded herbs, cowslips and primroses among them, on a hot stone over which water was then poured. The patient was "reeked" in the steam again and again. "It will soon be well with him."

Still later sources show that primroses were a part of British medicine. The medical manuscripts that have survived from the late Middle Ages all show the influence of classical medicine modified by local custom handed down from a remote native past. This was, to a degree, true all over Europe as well as throughout the British Isles.

The great Welsh physicians of Myddvai, for instance, could offer prescriptions for aches and pains in such variety that one could choose classical simplicity or medieval complexity and still have primroses to ease the trouble. To make a precious ointment for all kinds of pains you merely took primroses, root of the red nettle, water hemlock and iris and boiled the lot in butter. If, however, the very ease of this method suggested that it could not be efficacious, the same manuscript would offer you another of soothing complexity:

"Take gander's fat, the fat of a male cat, and red boar's fat and three drams of blue wax, water cress, wornwood, the red strawberry plant and primrose. Boil them in pure spring water. When boiled stuff a gander with them and roast it at a distance from the fire. The grease that issues from it should be carefully kept in a pot. It is a valuable ointment for all kinds of aches in a man's body and is like one that was formerly made by Hippocrates. It is proven."

To the fourteenth-century physician it seemed wholly possible that the juice of "primerose" put into a man's mouth would restore his lost speech; that a potage of primrose, violets, bugloss and water cress would be good for liver troubles; and that primrose distilled along with other herbs would make a "noble watyr for all sekenesses in manys body, and for all the membyrs of mannys body."

After the revival of learning the primrose continued to be used in medical practice in "Cephalicall diseases," but Parkinson was wrong when he said wholly so used. The rediscovery of the Greek myth undoubtedly sent the primrose into prescriptions under the name Paralytica. Its older use for aches and pains was dressed up under the name Arthritica. The newly discovered "cephalic" character made primroses specifics for palsy, "phrensie," vertigo, falling sickness, convulsions and similar ailments. But the older idea that they were valuable for wounds, sores, aches and pains hung on even into modern times. In *The Practical Houskeeper, and Cyclopedia of Domestic Economy, adapted to all classes of Society*, etc., edited by Mrs. Florence K. Stanton and published in Philadelphia in 1898, there is a receipt for making a primrose ointment for burns and ulcers.

Finally, the primrose played a part in combating an affliction not usually dignified as pathological.

According to Robert Burton (1577–1640), in his *Anatomy of Melancholy*, "Rusticus pudor, bashfulness, flushing in the face, high color, ruddiness are common grievances, which much torture many melancholy men, when they meet a man or come in company of their betters." Burton is scornful of one authority, Felix Plater, who claims that if the condition springs from fear or suspicion, there is nothing to be done except "to reject or condemn it." Instead, Burton contends that, if the sufferer anoint his face overnight with hare's blood and wash it off in the morning with strawberry or cowslip water, he will be greatly benefited. One would indeed have had to reach a pathological state of bashfulness to be willing to face such a remedy.

When it comes to the primrose as a cosmetic, "divers Ladies, Gentlewomen and She Citizens whether wives or widows know well enough" that an ointment made of lard and cowslip petals will take away "Spots, Wrinkles, and Sunburnings." At least so said William Coles in *The Art of Simpling*.

Quite probably the cosmetic ointment goes back to the old native leech-books in which ointments containing primroses were considered good for all sorts of aches, pains and "dolours." Sunburn could easily be included among the latter, and then it was only a step from a medicine to a cosmetic. But cowslip water, which must have had a long life among the cosmetics of the stillrooms in England, came from the Continent and owed its power to the process of distillation. It reached England in a book which is one of the landmarks of botany.

"Some weomen springkle yt floures of Cowslip wt whyte wyne and after still it and washe their faces in that water to driue wrinkles away / and to make them fayre in the eyes of the worlde rather than in the eyes of God whom they are not afrayd to offende with the scluttishnes / filthines / and foulnes of the soule."

These harsh words appear in *A New Herball* by William Turner. This was one of the few cosmetic receipts that the great botanist committed to print, but since he was reporting on the virtues of cowslips as he found them in the works of "Tragus / Fuchsius / and Matthiolus," he felt constrained to record this use of the flowers, though he does so in words all his own.

Flower Chronicles

Turner belonged to a goodly company—those sixteenth-century men who laid the foundations for modern botany. These men with inquisitive minds lived in a time when to question and to criticize was not only disadvantageous from a worldly point of view but dangerous. Their courage brought them intellectual rewards that as scholars they valued: freedom to criticize the traditional learning in which they had been reared, to stretch their minds with experiment and personal investigation, and to question authorities sanctioned by time, tradition and the Church.

Among the authorities so sanctioned were classical medical writers whose descriptions of herbs often left much to be desired in so far as identifications were concerned, and thus posed baffling problems. These were further complicated by the fact that the flora of the Mediterranean area, whence came all authoritative medical writing, was quite different from the flora of North Europe.

Turner set himself the task of writing a modern herbal based whenever possible on his own observation of plants, and with this he incorporated a coherent organization of all the information he was able to gather from his fellow workers abroad. It was the first book in English to give detailed and exact descriptions of plants—a monumental job done under immense difficulties.

Turner's difficulties were both political and personal. There was never enough money and always too many children. "My chylder have been fed so long with hope that they are very leane, i wolde fayne have them fatter," he wrote when he was trying to get a church appointment in York. He did get it but after two years was looking for another which would supply him with a house "where i may studie in and have some place to lay my bookes." The quarters in York were either so restricted or else his family was so large that he could not, he complained, "get to my books for ye crying of childer and the noyse yt it made in my chamber." This must have been a truly trying situation for a man who added a preoccupation with botany to his professional duties as a minister. Yet for all his vehemence these were only minor irritations in a life packed with trouble.

A passionate believer in the doctrines of Luther, Turner was naturally pleased when Henry VIII's matrimonial tangles separated England from the Church of Rome. But even the great Tudor compromise was not for him because he was too strict a Protestant. Before he knew it he was exiled because his religious ideas failed to march with those Henry had laid down as *Necessary Doctrine for any Christian Man*. It was during this period that Turner first studied abroad and made his friendships there.

On the accession of Edward VI Turner came back to England only to leave it a short seven years later when the young king died and his older half-sister Mary came to the throne. During her brief, horrible reign Turner worked abroad. For future generations Latimer's cry at the stake, "Play the man, Ridley, we shall this day light such a candle . . ." was to keep bright for Englishmen the great freedoms of mind and conscience. But to Turner, Nicholas Ridley was a friend with whom he had played tennis and read Greek at Cambridge. Ridley's death was a grief to Turner, and another source of the bitterness that so often sharpened his pen.

It was not until Elizabeth became queen that Turner came home for good, but not to honor, ease or affluence. He could not compromise and the mildly ritualistic practices of the Church of England infuriated him. Although he accepted an appointment as dean of Bath and Wells he made "unsemlie" remarks about bishops and was finally suspended for refusing to wear a surplice. He thereupon gave up his long struggle with the Church, retired to London, and died there in 1568.

Primroses appear carefully described in Turner's great herbal, which was published the year he died. It is to be hoped that he lived to see it, and had the taste to appreciate it, for it is a superlative example of fine printing from the hands of Arnold Birckman of Cologne.

Turner would have been horrified to know how many generations of females after him risked their immortal souls to be fair in the eyes of the world—using cowslips as he had suggested to them. But he would have been still more shocked to learn of a more exciting cosmetic use another primula afforded. Parkinson recommended that the mountain primrose, the auricula, serve as rouge. If crushed and laid on the cheek "of any tender skind woman, it will raise an orient red colour."

Turner's primroses, carefully described, appear in the third and last section of his herbal. There, according to the title page, "are contained the herbes / trees / rootes and fruites / whereof is no mention made of Dioscorides / Galen / Pilny and other older Authors." Here he undertook to do for England what Tragus' *Neu Kreuterbuch* had done for Germany: to describe those native plants that did not appear in the herbals of Mediterranean writers and to find for those plants the virtues they must surely possess.

So in the all-English part of the herbal primroses naturally appear, and the sanction of four great botanists kept them in medical practice and cosmetic use for generations to come.

In the kitchens of cottage and castle alike the cowslip held its own for something like four hundred years. A whole cookbook could be written around cowslips alone, for the number and variety of receipts featuring them is amazing.

Both leaves and flowers were eaten by country people as a salad. Cowslips served as potherbs. Mixed with other herbs they were used to stuff meats. The flowers were made into a delicious conserve and were also candied and pickled. There were cowslip tansies and cowslip tarts. Cowslip syrup was made, as was cowslip tea.

Only the most ardent cook would care to follow through all the details but there are many desserts based on cowslips. Two receipts, nearly three hundred years apart, suggest the development of their use.

Primerolle

To make primerolle in pasthe take blanched almonds and flour of primerolle grind it and temper it with swet wyne and good brothe drawinge into the thik mylk put it into a pot with sugar salt and saffron that it have colour like primerolle and boil it that it be stondinge and alay it with flour of rise and serue it as a standinge potage and strawe theron flour of primerolle aboue and ye may diaper it with rape rialle in dressinge of some other sewe.—From a rare MS., *c.* 1470, titled *A Noble Boke off Cookry ffor a Prince Houssolde or any other estately Houssolde.*

Cowslip Pudding

Having got the flowers of a Peck of Cowslips [no mean job, that!], cut them small and pound them with Half a Pound of Naples Biscuits (lady-fingers) grated and three Pints of Cream. Boil them a little; then take them off the Fire, and beat up sixteen Eggs, with a little Cream and a little Rose-water. Sweeten to your Palate. Mix it well together, butter a Dish and pour it in. Bake and when it is enough, throw fine Sugar over and serve it up.—From *The Art of Cookery, made Plain and Easy* . . . By a lady (Hannah Glasse), 1747.

There is also a cowslip cream that stands in the same relation to the pudding that our floating island does to baked custard. Then, of course, the pudding receipt could be poured into pastry shells to make cowslip tarts. The variations on this same theme—of a cowslip custard boiled or baked—seem infinite. Every stillroom book and cookbook carries its personal variations.

Cowslip wine runs through English literature in such a

sprightly fashion that it seems worth while to take a look at how it was made. Again, the number of receipts for making this is vast but John Evelyn's from his *Acetaria; A Discourse of Sallets,* 1699, seems a fair sample. Some, as he says, leave out all the syrup and some add the whites of eggs, but by and large this is how this rather ladylike intoxicant is achieved.

Cowslip Wine

To every Gallon of Water put two pounds of Sugar; boil it an Hour and set it to cool. Then spread a good brown Toast on both sides with Yeast; But before you make use of it, beat some Syrup of Citron with it, an Ounce and a half of Syrup to each Gallon of Liquor: Then put in the Toast while hot, to assist its Fermentation, which will come in two Days; during which time cast in the Cowslip-Flowers (a little bruis'd but not much stamp'd) to the quantity of half a Bushel to ten Gallons (or rather three Pecks), four Limes slic'd, with the Rind and all. Lastly, one Pottle of White or Rhenish wine; and then after two Days tun it up in a sweet Cask. Some leave out all the Syrup.

Few flowers have been so copiously used in cooking as the cowslip.

From the kitchen to the nursery is only a step, as every child knows. So when spring—in Tennyson's phrase—"letters cowslips on the hill," the nursery as well as the kitchen benefits. A toy is made with cowslips and a game played with it. Fifty or sixty flower umbels, nipped off close to the top of the main stem, are hung across a string stretched between two chairs. The flowers are then pressed slowly and carefully together and tied tightly to form a ball—a totsie children call it, and with this they play titsy-totsy.

When flowers and fairies first began their association in English folklore we do not know. But, whenever it was, primroses naturally had a part to play. There are places in England where cowslips are known as the fairy flower or fairy cup because fairies seek shelter in the blossoms when it rains. "In a cowslip's bell I lie."

It is fascinating to discover, on looking into the matter, that fairyland is now believed to be a world-wide country. Its existence, here or there, varies in time. The fairy beliefs of American Indians or Eskimos belong to the present or the very recent past, but the fairy beliefs of Europe are old beyond our imagining. A classical dictionary lists Nereides, Oreades and Naiades, for instance, as "divinities of a lower order" and Andrew Lang refers to them as fairies. Authorities join to underline the modern idea that fairies have descended from pre-Christian minor deities. These deities had a hold on the imaginations, fears or affections of men so that memories of their cults survived, handed down by word of mouth from generation to generation.

Fairies, as they settled down in a locality, seem to have taken on local color. Perhaps the very size of England dictated that of its unseen population, which measured its height in inches. This was a very active community operating, in spite of supernatural powers, along very human lines. From the cruel, evil and frightening elves of early days, whose traces are to be found in Anglo-Saxon literature, English fairies seem to have become almost as civilized as the people among whom they lived. And like those people, English fairies had a passion for flowers.

Shakespeare did not invent Oberon and Titania, Mab or Puck or Ariel. They were ready to his hand in local legend. He probably had for them the affection that any country child of his time must have known for familiar characters, unseen but real, who peopled his world. Santa Claus is our nearest modern equivalent. All Shakespeare had to do was to describe these well-known persons and they lived, as they will live as long as the

Primula veris minor. Dodoens' *Pemptades.* (*Horticultural Society of New York*)

Primrose

English language endures, in such lines as "I am that merry wanderer of the night." Or

> Where the bee sucks, there suck I;
> In a cowslip's bell I lie.

Then there is the fairy who explains to Puck that he serves the Fairy Queen and what his duties are:

> The cowslips tall her pensioners be:
> In their gold coats spots you see;
> These be rubies, fairy favors,
> In those freckles live their savors.
> I must go seek some dewdrops here,
> And hang a pearl in every cowslip's ear.

If Shakespeare's fairies were small enough to creep into the bell of a cowslip, another Elizabethan poet, now almost forgotten, describes them as somewhat larger. William Browne of Tavistock (1588–1643), one of the minor Jacobean poets, grew up near the English-Welsh border where, it seems, fairies were especially active. His Oberon was

> . . . a prince of subtill powers,
> Clad in a suit of speckled gilliflowers.

> * * *

> His ruffe, a daizie, was so neatly trimme,
> As if, of purpose, it had grown for him.

Thus Browne's Oberon must have been about five inches tall. And throughout *Britannia's Pastorals* the proportionate size is kept in mind as Browne describes a fairy feast, the furnishings thereof, the music, the food.

A spruce little elf in a monkshood flower for a hat,

> Brought in his bottles; neater were there none
> And every bottle was a cherry stone.

* * *

The glasses pure, and thinner than we can
See from the sea-betrothed Venetian
Where all of ice, not made to overlast
One supper, and betwixt two cowslips cast,
A prettier fashion hath not yet been told
So neat the glass was, and so feat the moulde.

Of course primroses in folklore are not confined to fairyland. Many local legends and customs in England must include them, as does the May Day festival near Horn Castle in Lincolnshire where the "May gads" are peeled willow wands tied about with cowslips.

This would be true, too, on the Continent and especially in Germany, where a number of legends bear every indication of being very old. These are chiefly concerned with the idea of the cowslip as "the key flower."

A less ancient legend, dating after the conversion to Christianity, gives a gay and delightful explanation as to how the flower came by this name. It seems that St. Peter was informed that certain unregenerate souls were trying to get into heaven by a back door. He was so flustered at the thought that he dropped his keys. They fell to earth, and where they fell a clump of cowslips appeared. Schlüsselblumen the Germans call them. Primroses they call Himmelschlüssel, Keys of Heaven.

In spite of the fact that the primrose is so intimately English it had no national significance until the 1880's, when it blossomed out as Primrose Day. This was a national festival dedicated to the memory of Benjamin Disraeli, the Earl of Beaconsfield.

It is one of the most delightful ironies of political life that the most un-English of English statesmen should be commemorated by the most English of English flowers. Disraeli's devotion to England cannot be questioned but he was the descendant of aristocratic Spanish Jews who had fled to Venice during the persecution of the Spanish Inquisition and he was only one generation removed from influences stemming out of Southern Europe and the Near East. Theatrical, sophisticated, cynical, with a brilliant mind and a rococo turn of phrase, he was as unlikely a person to be represented by the dim little English primrose as could well be imagined. Yet there is an excellent reason why he should have been.

When Disraeli became prime minister in 1868, Queen Victoria had been for years in retirement mourning her husband. The queen was truly grief-stricken by the loss of Prince Albert but one cannot escape the suspicion that that grief was sometimes overshadowed by outrage that anything so dreadful could happen to the Queen of England.

Disraeli brought the queen out of her seclusion. Skillfully, with shameless flattery, he introduced her to a world filled with excitement and glory. When he bought the controlling interest in the Suez Canal for England he wrote the queen as if he were making her a personal present: ". . . you have it, Madam, . . . the entire interest of the Khedive is now yours." He made his sovereign Empress of India and conjured up visions of the grandeur and splendor of her realm. He turned the tiresome business of state and diplomacy into personal matters of glamour and romantic importance. Victoria was his adored royal lady, he her humble and devoted servant.

The queen repaid him in primroses. She and her ladies gathered them in the woods when the court was at Osborne, and they were shipped swiftly to the prime minister in London. They were, Disraeli wrote her, his favorite flowers, ambassadors of spring, "an offering from the Fauns and Dryads of Osborne." Was the fat little queen, aged fifty-six or -seven, a faun or a dryad?

On the last unforgettable page of his *Queen Victoria*, Lytton

Strachey suggests that the mind of the unconscious old woman who lay dying that day in January, 1901, may have held shadowy pictures stretching back and back over her long life-time. A phrase at a time, he sketches scenes that may have stirred the fading memory. Among these is a picture from the queen's middle years, of "the spring woods at Osborne, so full of primroses for Lord Beaconsfield."

The paradox of the primrose and himself could hardly have escaped Disraeli but he must have decided that the irony was too keen for him to stress personally. When Victoria gave him a peerage he did not display primroses on his arms.

They appear, however, on the arms of the Earl of Rosebery, "as was only to be expected," said the authority from whom this piece of information was gleaned, and a reference to Burke's *Peerage* disclosed that the earl's family name was Primrose. His arms, primroses and all, are of the fanciest kind, bescrolled and beplumed in rococo splendor. But another Primrose family, not ennobled until 1903, displays handsome primroses on both crest and shield.

Since a number of primulas are among the most important of rock garden alpines, we should not leave the primrose without mention of the first botanist to explore the European Alps for flowers. We may fittingly take our leave of it among the mountains of the Tibetan-Chinese frontier, where a modern plant hunter gathered a notable harvest.

Charles de L'Ecluse (1526–1609) was not only "the prince of discriptive botanists." He was also a brave and vivid, brilliant and interesting human being. It was he who brought the alpine primula, the auricula, to European gardens. This was only one achievement in a long career which Richardson Wright has described delightfully in his *Gardener's Tribute*. It cannot all concern us here so we may take leave of Clusius with that early

Primrose

rock garden plant and with his epitaph which no one who
mentions him can resist quoting,

> When Clusius knew each herb earth's bosom yields,
> He went aimpling in the Elysian Fields.

Reginald Farrer, born in 1880, was de L'Ecluse's spiritual
descendant. He was taught at home by tutors and at fourteen
built his first rock garden on a cliff near his father's house. As
a grown man he made several trips to the Far East in search of
plants for the Royal Horticultural Society.

In *The Rainbow Bridge* and *On the Eaves of the World*,
Farrer has left us accounts of his plant hunting along the
borders of Tibet and China. These sum up, for the armchair
alpinist, the very breath of excitement that lies in mountain
climbing for plants. If Farrer's adjectives tend to run wild and
his descriptions are regettably prone to purple patches, gardeners
will forgive him because of the undoubted sincerity of his
love of flowers.

The list of newly discovered plants that Farrer sent home is
a long one: asters, columbines, corydalis, delphiniums, gentians,
iris, lilies, roses and primroses were all among them. But in
Farrer's eyes the greatest of these were primroses.

Primroses Farrer could not call by their botanical names.
Since few if any white men had ever looked upon some of those
he found, let alone named, he gave them familiar names for
his own use—the citron primrose, the welcome primrose, the
wood nymph, the rock nymph, the oread, and the grand
violet.

The discovery of the grand violet was one of the high lights
of Farrer's adventures. It happened at the end of a hard but
rewarding day of hunting and climbing. Coming down one of
the mountains in the Satani Alps of western Kansu, Farrer
caught a glimpse of "a new note of purple shining like a dim

spark." It was behind and above him, so he turned and toiled upward to find a hitherto unknown plant—"a grotesque rare glory, with the upper 'petals' lying flat back on the tube like an angry cat's ears, while the lower ones stretched straight forward like an angry child's pout."

Shouting against the roar of a waterfall, Farrer managed to attract the attention of his fellow worker, Purdon, who joined him and together they gathered the treasure. Night was coming on and a thunderstorm threatened. The return to their quarters involved fording an ice-cold river at dangerously high water, rain came in torrents to lash them, and the storm crashed around them. But theirs had been a glorious and successful day.

When Farrer came to die, still a comparatively young man, in the lonely mountains of northeast Burma, let us hope that the malaria that killed him was able to dull his senses to the soggy heat of the rain forest and carry him in a fevered dream up onto the cold ledges of the Satani Alps where he had found so many primroses. They were rare exotics, these alpine primulas, not likely to flourish in British gardens. But still they were primroses—and so a link with home.

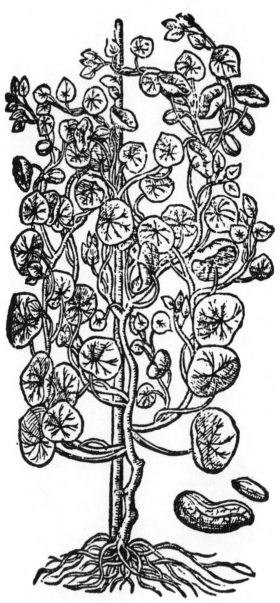

Nasturtium from Dodoens' *Pemptades*. (*Horticultural* Society of New York)

Nasturtium

Nasturtiums, marigolds and sunflowers were the only innocent gold to reach Europe on the floodtide of treasure that poured from the New World into the Old during the years when Spain was looting her American empire with bloody hands. "Golde, Silver, Pearles, Emeraldes, Turkeses," thus Nicolás Monardes begins a list of the kinds of cargo the high-pooped ships brought in. It was plunder on a grand scale, but not even the proudest Indian could have resented the loss of that handful of wrinkled seeds that some seaman or adventurer stowed away in his pouch to take home.

It was a brutal and reckless time, full of the vitality and excitement that ring in the very title of the book which introduced the nasturtium to Englishmen: *Joyfull Newes out of the Newe Founde Worlde*. This book, published in London in 1577, was a translation by one "Jhon [*sic!*] Frampton, Merchaunt" of *La Historia Medicinal de Las Cosas*, 1574, by Monardes, a physician of Seville.

Dr. Monardes was a busy, happy, and very fortunate man. Passionately interested in his profession, he had the incredible luck to be one of the few European doctors who had access to the novel pharmacopoeia that came from the fabulous "Indies." Not content with the seeds, roots and dried herbs that reached him in Seville, Monardes carried on a lively correspondence with various settlers in the new lands and gave the returning adventurers no rest until they had told him all that they knew of how and for what ailments the different plants were used by the natives. Then he wrote it down, making—as was most unusual in his day—careful distinction between what he had been told and what he learned from experience. His was, however, a lavish era and he saw no reason for confining himself to medical matters, so, among other odd items, nasturtiums appear in his book as "Floures of Blood."

"I sowed a seede which thei brought me from the Peru, more to see his fairnesse," he wrote, "than for any Medicinall vertues that it hath." He ends his brief description with satisfaction that his experiment with the exotic seed was rewarded. "It is a flower very beautiful, whiche doeth adornate the gardens."

From Spain the plant made its way into France and Flanders. By 1597 Gerard had it among the "outlandish" flowers in his garden, sent "by my loving friend, John Robin of Paris." (Robin was keeper of the French king's garden.) By 1629 Parkinson could write that it was "very familiar in most Gardens of any curiosity." He thought it a flower "of so great beauty and sweetnesse withall, that my Garden of delight cannot bee unfurnished of it." Besides, he said, it had "a fine small sent, very pleasing, which being placed in the middle of some Carnations or Gilleflowers . . . made a delicate Tussiemussie, as they call it, or Nosegay, both for sight and sent."

Parkinson's description of the flower that he goes on so charmingly to call "yellow lark's heels" brings up an odd discrepancy. It seems to be generally accepted that the "Floure of Blood" that Monardes introduced in 1571 was *T. minus,* the dwarf annual. The larger-flowered trailer, *T. majus,* has been, say both British and American authorities, in cultivation since 1684 or 1686. Now, the plant from which Parkinson, in 1629, picked flowers for his delicate Tussiemussie was no dwarf. It spreads itself, he says, "into very long trayling branches, interlaced one with another very confusedly (yet doth it not winde it selfe with any claspers about either pole or any other thing, but if you will have it abide close thereunto, you must tye it, or else it will lye upon the ground)." Certainly on the strength of Parkinson's account of the plant there is every reason to believe that *T. majus* reached Europe more than half a century before 1686.

Now, nearly four hundred years after its introduction, the nasturtium continues to adornate the gardens, but in the in-

Woodcut of Nicholas Monardes, the first European to publish a description of the nasturtium. From the frontispiece of his *Dos Libros*.

terim it was put to work. The first job it was to do for mankind was to serve in one of those half-desperate, half-pathetic experiments that were being made in an effort to find a cure for scurvy. In an age of unbalanced diet and widespread malnutrition the disease was everywhere prevalent, but its most dramatic and tragic aspects were at sea.

They were brave men, those early transatlantic sailors. Anyone who has ever watched a full gale in winter on the North Atlantic from the deck of a modern liner shudders to think of what a similar experience must have been like on the little wooden ships that made the early crossings. In addition to such acts of God as gale or calm, there were pirates and hostile ships of rival nations. But these melodramatic disasters, if the ship survived at all, were measurable in time by hours or days. Scurvy was a creeping thing of weeks or months. It not only incapacitated a crew physically, but it drained the men of all energy and spirit. Ordinary day-to-day work was inefficiently done or practically came to a standstill. Defense, in case of attack, was sometimes impossible.

A hazy notion arose that some food other than the easily stored salt pork or beef, even something green, might help. For a time nasturtiums were highly valued in the fight against scurvy because, according to John Evelyn, they were thought to be "the most effectual and powerful Agents in conquering and expurging that cruel Enemy." The seed pods were picked when fully grown but still green, and pickled. It must have been quite a business while it lasted, because any gardener can see that even a single barrel of nasturtium seed represented growing on a large scale. It was not until nearly the end of the eighteenth century that it was discovered that either lemons or limes were really "effectual and powerful" against scurvy and in 1795 the Admiralty turned British sailors into "limeys" by decreeing a daily ration of lime juice.

Nasturtium

This brief incursion into preventive medicine could almost be described as the complete medical history of the nasturtium were there not one more note, and a rather amusing one, to add.

Parkinson's "Yellow Lark's heels." (*Horticultural Society of New York*)

Herbalists in general seem to have agreed with John Parkinson that nasturtiums had no curative value, and the flower appears in few if any herbals until we come back to our old friend William Salmon. William recommended nasturtiums for a number of ailments. Practically all of these are the same for which Dioscorides recommended orris root. It really looks very much as if Salmon decided on his own hook to put nasturtiums, hitherto neglected, into medicine. But for what? To answer that question it is not hard to picture him reaching for the nearest herbal on his bookshelves, and it happened to be Dioscorides'. A careful comparison suggests that Salmon may well have lifted a whole series of prescriptions from iris, the first item described by the classical herbalist, and transferred them to a more interesting herb. He did, however, add some eighteenth-century frills. One of these is "the Spirit," distilled from what part of the plant he does not say, but twenty drops to a dram "in some proper Vehicle" is the correct dose. This, among other virtues, "provokes Lust and is good against impotency."

It is clear that nasturtiums did not brighten the physick gardens, but they did have a long if modest sojourn in the kitchen due to John Evelyn's manly effort to bring "Sallets" to the attention of his meat-and-bread-eating fellow countrymen.

John Evelyn is best known as a diarist, although his extremely interesting personal narrative has suffered by comparison with the more sprightly one of his contemporary, Samuel Pepys. But in addition to his famous diary he has left behind him a large collection of writings, many of them concerned with gardens and gardening. Next to his diary in importance is a work titled *Sylva, or A Discourse on Forest Trees*. He liked to write "Discourses" and several are listed among his printed works, none of them more beguiling than *Acetaria; A Discourse of Sallets*. Since nasturtiums are among the "herby ingredients" he suggests for a "sallet," we have an excellent excuse to take a look at what the latter half of the seventeenth century would call a salad.

". . . we are by *Sallet* to understand a Composition of certain Crude and fresh Herbs, such as usually are, or may safely be eaten with some Acetous Juice, Oyl, Salt, &., to give grateful Gust and *Vehicle*." A "sallet" of nasturtiums might contain some or all of "the tender Leaves, *Calices, Cappuchin Capers,* and flowers laudably mixed with the colder Plants." These "herby ingredients" must be "exquisitely cull'd and cleans'd of all worm-eaten, filmy, canker'd, dry, spotted, or anyways vitiated Leaves . . . discreetly sprinkl'd with Spring Water . . . remain a while in the *Cullender* and finally swung together gently in a clean coarse napkin; and so they will be in perfect condition to receive the Intinctus following."

The "Intinctus" consists, in part, of "Oyl . . . without smell or the least touch of rancid; . . . the best Wine Vinegar . . . ; Salt . . . of the brightest Bay gray-salt; Mustard . . . temper'd to the consistence of a pap with vinegar. Note: That the Seeds are pounded in a Mortar; or bruis'd with a polished *Cannon-Bullet,* in a large wooden Bowl-Dish, or, which is preferr'd ground in a Quern contriv'd for this purpose only; Pepper . . . not bruis'd to too small a Dust; the Yolks of fresh and New-laid Eggs, boil'd moderately hard, to be mingl'd and mashed with the *Mustard,* Oyl, and *Vinegar*." This, with various "Strewings and Atomizers" was the basic receipt.

That engaging description of a "sallet" and its dressing will melt the heart of any salad lover today, especially the pepper "not bruis'd to too small a dust." But it is doubtful if many Britishers explored the possibilities Evelyn so alluringly presented to them. Judging from the menus of the time, they must have been few indeed, and nasturtiums from the kitchen garden were used most often as "strewings" of the fresh flowers, or these were pickled as a decorative condiment. The seeds continued to be pickled and used as capers are today.

A more exotic dish, made from a species of *Tropaeolum* may still be in vogue in the high Andes of Peru. The tubers of *T. tuberosum,* which are called *ysamo* there, were cooked and then frozen. Apparently the women of La Paz were especially fond of this dish, which suggests a primitive version of our Birdseye! Another way in which the Peruvian Indian enjoys the same kind of nasturtium is in a farina made from the tubers and mixed with molasses into a sort of jelly.

The French, too, have used *T. tuberosum* as a food, cooking the tubers and serving them as a vegetable.

Other factors tended to keep the nasturtium in the kitchen garden rather than the flower garden until nearly the middle of the nineteenth century. First there was the French influence, which had begun to make itself felt in England and was greatly strengthened after the Restoration of the monarchy in 1660. It really does not matter whether Lenôtre, the great landscape architect of Versailles, came to London or not, as is sometimes debated. His spirit came—there is no doubt of that— and with it such garden furnishings as straight gravel walks, fountains cascading over flights of marble steps, high clipped hedges, and "bosquets" or groves of trees grouped geometrically. The few flower borders permitted only such plants as conformed to the patterned formality and even these were sometimes replaced by "parterres made of clipped box and an intricate design of colored sands."

Then, with almost startling suddenness, the pendulum swung to the other extreme. "Back to nature" was the slogan by the middle of the eighteenth century, although furbelows were added to gardens in the shape of ruined temples, fallen columns, grottoes and suchlike romantic "fabricks." Nature abhors a straight line and never stoops to a geometric curve. Away with the graveled walks and the bosquets so formally planted! Cascades over marble steps disappeared in favor of natural, or naturalized, waterfalls and rapids. Hedges came down and great avenues of trees were razed. But so far as flowers were concerned, there was little to choose between all this and the Versailles school because nature does not go in for well-designed flower borders. Nor would the "natural" landscape of England and the Continent include such exotics as nasturtiums.

If the nasturtium temporarily disappeared from fashionable gardens it could at least lend itself to what passed for scientific investigation in mid-eighteenth century. Elizabeth Linnaeus, daughter of the great botanist, reported to her father that she had noticed before sunrise, and also at twilight, that *T. majus* gave off sparks or flashes of light. ". . . these scintillations were shown to her father and other philosophers, and Mr. Wilcke, a celebrated electrician, believed them to be electric."

Erasmus Darwin, grandfather of Charles, cannot be said to have immortalized this phenomenon in verse, for his *Botanic Garden* is a drearily dull poem, but he has at least recorded this manifestation of "Tropaeo's:"

> O'er her fair form the electric lustre plays,
> And cold she moves amid the lambent blaze.

In Paxton's *Magazine of Botany*, a Mr. Trimmer also reports having seen "scintillations" from nasturtiums.

Fired by all this evidence, a gardener who possessed a long dazzling border of nasturtiums recently made a careful observation of his flowers. He reported that he was afraid he would have to continue to depend on the local electric service corporation, since neither he nor his wife had glimpsed a single spark.

During all this time, of course, the nasturtium had not been entirely banished from gardens. People who did not wish, or could not afford, to follow prevailing fashions kept up their interest in flowers and nasturtiums flourished, as they always have flourished, in the beautiful cottage gardens of England. An item in *The Botanical Magazine* in 1797 reminds us of these facts. The short article pointed out that *T. majus* had so completely superseded *T. minus* that the latter "was entirely lost to our gardens till lately, when it was reintroduced by Dr. J. E. Smith, who by distributing it to his friends and Nurserymen near London, has again rendered it tolerably plentiful."

The Dr. Smith who performed this pleasant small service to horticulture was the James Edward Smith who had a few years earlier performed a much greater service to horticulture and to his country by buying the papers of Linnaeus and founding, in 1788, the Linnaean Society.

In 1804 the Horticultural Society was formed, later to come under the British government as the Royal Horticultural Society. With the Linnaean Society, it gave formal expression to the interest in botany which had never flagged in England, even though flowers, as ornamental garden plants, had not fared too well for a century or more. Plants had long been shipped to individuals in England from all over the world. These now began coming in to the Horticultural Society and, in turn, the Society began sending out trained men to hunt for more. It was a stimulating and exciting period from the point of view of botany and horticulture.

It was at about this time that there appeared the first mention of the nasturtium in American gardens. The nurseryman MacMahon had it in his 1806 catalogue, but nasturtiums did not come into general use until much later in the century. Nor, for that matter, did they in England. Then some of the plant hunters, notably Thomas Lobb, began finding varied and interesting species of *Tropaeolum* in Central and South America. Experiments in breeding were undertaken. A hybrid between *T. minus* and *T. majus* had probably long been in existence and it is said that one of Lobb's finds brought a dark ruby red to the new hybrids. Another supplied the familiar straw color. By 1857 Tom Thumb, the shrubby dwarf annual, in all the glory of the new colors, was on the market, and the nasturtium took the place it deserved in the flower border.

Nasturtium

Now, with a bow to John C. Bolger, who bred the double golden gleam, and to David Burpee, who introduced the multi-colored doubles, I should be able to leave the nasturtium, but the story is not quite told. With all due respect to these two gentlemen, double nasturtiums are not so much of a novelty as the catalogues would lead us to believe. In the *Gardeners Directory*, 1731, Philip Miller lists the last of five varieties as "*Acriviola; maxima, odorata, flora pleno,* the great double nasturtium." And John Hill, in *Eden, or a Complete Body of Gardening*, 1757, remarks of nasturtiums that "when double they become yet more beautiful." But these were more or less common variations of a genus noted for its variability, so we are no less indebted to the two men who recognized a possibility when they saw it and worked so hard to fix the variation so that it might be available to countless gardeners the world over. Mr. Burpee's story of how it was done, especially of his own dramatic telescoping of three generations of plants into a single year, is well worth turning back to the old files of *The Saturday Evening Post*. It is in the issue of March 12, 1936.

There is another little-known story about nasturtiums that may be startling to many gardeners. How many know that there is a blue nasturtium? And what has become of the white nasturtium?

To dispose of the blue nasturtium first, for there is no mystery attached to that—it is a tender climber suitable for the greenhouse only. As *T. azurum*, of course, it is listed in Bailey's *Standard Cyclopedia of Horticulture*, along with the other forty-odd species of *Tropaeolum*. But there is no mention of *T. albiflorum*.

The Frenchman who wrote the first article about *T. albiflorum* (only his initials appear in *Flore des Serres*, Vol. XII, p. 241) describes how he rushed exuberantly to Brussels to see this treasure and how, having seen it, he so coveted it that he cheated Van Houte, the introducer, into selling him some plants. Few gardeners will find it in their hearts to blame him.

The Frenchman first tried to buy some cuttings legitimately, as seeds were not available. But when he admitted that he lived in Paris he was told that the Van Houte establishment had decided to sell only to people living at least three hundred "lieues" distant. (Van Houte had a good thing, he calculated, and he proposed to exploit it.) The Frenchman left the greenhouse in a state of mind which he describes at some length. Then, as luck would have it, he ran into a young German acquaintance. The warmth of the Frenchman's greeting may well have surprised the German, who did not then know that it was occasioned by the clothes he was wearing. This young man, who was himself interested in botany and horticulture, had recently been to Russia. As a result of that trip, he sported fur boots, a "pelisse" (whatever that might have looked like on a man), and a typical Muscovite fur cap. The Frenchman probably invited him to the nearest café, but wherever they did it their plot was hatched.

The young German then took himself off to see the white nasturtium. He, too, asked about buying some cuttings. When queried as to his place of residence, he replied that he was head gardener to "the Grand Vornik de Valachie." To questions as to the whereabouts of Valachie, he replied that it was in Russia, down near the border of Turkey. Such a distance was entirely satisfactory and he acquired three cuttings at the then ruinous rate of fifty francs each. These he promptly turned over to his French friend.

What became of them? They have now apparently vanished from the face of the earth. It is a pity, for the white nasturtium must have been as "rare and faire" as Gerard found his little *T. minus* to be three hundred fifty years ago.

"Cocoxochitl," a species of dahlia. Woodcut from Hernandez' *Thesaurus,* printed in 1651. (*Mackenzie Library of the Horticultural Society of New York*)

Dahlia

The Dahlia you brought to our isle
Your praises for ever shall speak;
Mid gardens as sweet as your smile,
And colour as bright as your cheek.

This bit of husbandly doggerel celebrates the introduction of the dahlia into England by Lady Holland in 1804. Across a century and a half it echoes with the affectionate laughter of two lovers enjoying a happy memory and it gives us an excuse to take a look at this lady whose charms, as well as whose achievement, it proclaims.

Toward the end of the eighteenth century Sir Godfrey Webster was living in Florence with his wife when young Lord Holland came to town. Lady Webster eloped with Holland and in 1796 their first son was born. A year later Sir Godfrey divorced his wife and she and Lord Holland were able to marry. The love affair of a lad of twenty and a girl of twenty-three blossomed into a long and happy marriage, as the "poem" bears witness. For it was written after they had been together nearly twenty years and is the kind of amusing private nonsense a clever man tosses off, half seriously, half in fun, to a beloved woman who is delighted with it but has no illusion that she has been immortalized in deathless verse.

Between 1800 and 1805 the Hollands lived in France and in Spain, where Lady Holland first saw dahlias that had reached Spain from Mexico about fifteen years before. She sent some seed home in 1804 and it is on the strength of that shipment that she is given credit for the introduction of the dahlia into England.

An earlier effort had been made by another Englishwoman. Lady Bute was in Spain when the first dahlias arrived in 1789 and she acquired one of the precious tubers, which she dispatched to England. But this tuber died, so the honor of the introduction has fallen to Lady Holland.

However, it turns out that the distinction was not justly Lady Holland's after all. In *Curtis' Botanical Magazine* there is a picture of a dahlia of a dull brick-red color, looking very like an inferior type of our common annual variety. "Our drawing," says the text, "was taken in June, 1803, at Mr. Fraser's, of Sloane Square, who has the credit of introducing this ornamental plant among us from France."

One is tempted to suppress the unknown Mr. Fraser of Sloane Square in favor of the more colorful Lady Holland but truth must be served. It is not, in any case, a world-shaking matter. Ordinarily, Lady Holland is given the credit and actually it is very probable that the plants produced from the seeds she sent did really start the cultivation of the dahlia in England.

It was, however, a good many years before dahlias graduated out of the class of botanical curiosities. In 1840 *Maund's Botanic Garden* was looking hopefully to a new importation from Mexico from which a race of dwarf dahlias "so much to be desired" might be bred. The plants were then, according to Maund, "excluded from the parterres because of their gigantic size."

Maund knew what he was talking about, but if the dahlia was rejected by the owners of great gardens, it flourished in the hands of those extraordinary amateurs, the workingmen florists. Those factory hands and petty tradesmen who bred the Old English tulips, the fringed and feathered pinks, the gold and silver laced polyanthus, and numerous other lovely flowers were proud of their "Show and Fancy" dahlias some of which are still on the market today.

The dahlia was so late in reaching Europe that by the time it had settled down the "curious" men of the seventeenth and eighteenth centuries, who privately experimented with every novelty in their own kitchens and laboratories, had been gathered to their fathers. Scientific specialists took over. These, however, did take a look at the dahlia as a possible source of food in time of need.

In the early 1840's a disease destroyed the French potato crop. It was hoped that perhaps the dahlia tuber might serve as a substitute, but apparently not all the genius of French chefs could make it palatable. According to a French publication of the time, the tubers had been reported edible. But, the French writer continues sadly, as soon as one had tasted them one refused to concur in this opinion and was content to cultivate the plant for the beauty of its flowers.

Modern specialists have turned to the dahlia for medical reasons and this time not in vain. In the days before insulin was discovered diabetics were often given a substance called Atlantic starch or diabetic sugar made from dahlia tubers. The levulose they yield is no longer fed to diabetics, but it is useful in making clinical tests for the functioning of the liver while inulin, another chemical derived from them, is used in the same way to test the kidneys.

The above collection of odds and ends would hardly make the story of the dahlia outside of our gardens worth the telling were it not for the fact that an exciting and romantic discovery has given the history of the dahlia a special interest.

An Aztec herbal—written in Latin just sixty years after

Flower Chronicles

Columbus discovered the New World—came to light in 1929.

The story of any flower in remote antiquity survives occasionally in myths or as it can sometimes be reconstructed by deduction from the obviously primitive bits of magic embedded in later medicine. That is true at least so far as Europe is concerned. But in the Americas, and specifically in Mexico, which is the native land of the dahlia, conditions were different. An advanced type of culture had developed in Mexico, but its wealth of written records was utterly destroyed in the interest of bringing Christianity to the heathen. The fragments of stone and pottery and the bits of cloth that have survived from Mexico's past offer us no data on the ways in which native flowers were used by Mexicans. So the discovery of an Aztec herbal was a piece of incredible luck not only for the students of the history of medicine but also for botanists.

Dr. Charles Upson Clark was not particularly interested in herbals. He was doing research in a different field for the Smithsonian Institution in the Vatican Library when one day he pulled out, quite casually, a little volume from the farthest corner of a bookshelf. It was a find of the first magnitude, for here in this small vellum book, bound in sixteenth-century crimson velvet and beautifully illustrated in colors that are characteristically Mexican, were medical formulas that were old long before white men reached the New World.

Professor Clark told Dr. William H. Welch of his find. Dr. Welch was the distinguished founder of the Institute of the History of Medicine at Johns Hopkins University. Here was material that belonged in his foundation. He did not rest until he had arranged to have the herbal reproduced in facsimile with a transcription, translation and commentary. Dr. Welch did not live to see the work completed but the costly and difficult job, in the competent hands of Emily Walcott Emmart, was well under way at the time of his death and he knew that it would be finished faithfully and well. As *The Badianus Manu-script* it is available in most big libraries today.

So long before seed or tubers reached Europe, the dahlia ap-

Page from the Badianus Manuscript. The drawing on the right is a species of dahlia, appearing in the only early herbal produced in the New World, translated and edited by Emily Walcott Emmart. (*Johns Hopkins Press*)

peared there mentioned as an ingredient in a purely Mexican medical prescription.

The reason that native Aztec medicine was translated so early into Latin and shipped off to Europe is interesting. There may even be involved some sixteenth-century relationship to our modern publicity methods for raising funds for educational purposes.

Flower Chronicles

The first viceroy Spain sent to Mexico after the conquest was a man of enlightened intelligence. Don Antonio de Mendoza noted with interest the success of a school the Franciscan friars were conducting in their monastery of San Diego next to the Church of Santiago de Tlaltelolco. The pupils were all the sons of Aztec noblemen—caciques—from the capital and nearby towns. The boys did so well that Don Antonio founded a college, the College of Santa Cruz, the first for Indians in the New World. Here, under the instruction of a band of brilliant and devoted Franciscans, these young Indians were taught to write their own language in our alphabet. They also learned to read and write Spanish and Latin. They studied philosophy, logic, arithmetic, music and medicine—native medicine. The fact that it was native medicine should be emphasized, for the Spaniards decided that native herbs and drugs would be more apt to cure native ills than anything they could import from Europe. So Aztec medicine men taught the young students the medical practice of their own people.

Twenty years after the school was founded two of its pupils produced the herbal. Martinus de la Cruz, by that time physician to his alma mater, put down in Aztec the native medicine he had been taught. Juannes Badianus, reader in Latin in the college, translated Martinus' text. De la Cruz is supposed to have done the delightful illustrations.

The herbal is dedicated to the son of Don Antonio, Don Francisco, who according to the dedication asked "so earnestly for this little book of herbs and medicaments for no other reason than to commend us Indians, even though unworthy, to His Holy Caesarian Catholic Royal Majesty." It may be that Don Francisco's request was made on purely disinterested grounds but the modern mind, inured to publicity methods, is suspicious. Can it be that he was less generous than his father? Might he have hoped that this enchanting little book as a sample of Indian intelligence might inspire financial support for his father's college?

At any rate, thanks to kindlier Spanish officials who followed the Conquistadores, two Mexicans have preserved for us in this herbal traces of a still earlier Mexico. So out of a remote American past the dahlia comes to play its part in a remedy to combat epilepsy.

For a recently-developed epilepsy will prevail the stones found in the intestines of the hawks, the small birds *huactli* and the rooster, the root *quetzalatzonyatl,* a stag's horn, whitish incense, white incense, a hair of a corpse, the burned flesh of a mole shut up in a jar, which then are to be well ground in hot water. The epileptic is to drink the liquor so that he will vomit, and before this it will not be useless for him to drink the juice of the shrub called *tlahtlacotic;* the root is to be ground up.

Observe the time, when the epilepsy is about to come, for at that very moment the epileptic is to be set upright and his ribs and sides are to pricked. When coming to himself, he should drink dog's bile, and at the same time his head is to be moistened with a poultice made of the leaves of *quetzalatzonyatl* and *tetzitzilin* and the herb or shrub *acocohxihuitl* ground in water. He is to eat the brain of a fox and a weasel, cooked. He is then to be fumigated or perfumed with the good odor of a mouse nest burned on a bed of coals, of whitish incense, and of feathers of the bird *cozcaquauhtli* [vulture].

None of the above herbs has been identified except *acocohxihuitl,* which, literally translated, means "water gullet plant" and has been identified as a species of dahlia.

Until modern science came along the methods used in primitive medicine changed slowly from magic-religious practices into herbal remedies with no sharply marked dividing line between the two. So, together with such exotic substances as the hair of a corpse, the burned flesh of a mole, the cooked brain of a fox, and the good odor of a mouse nest burned, the dahlia takes its place among the medicines used in Mexico long before a Spaniard set foot in the land.

All this is not important in itself. It is not even important in the Aztec herbal. But it is important if you are interested in the history of the dahlia, for it confirms the suspicion that in befeathered, colorful, primitive Mexico, Heaven alone knows how long before the white man came, the story of the dahlia in relation to man had begun.

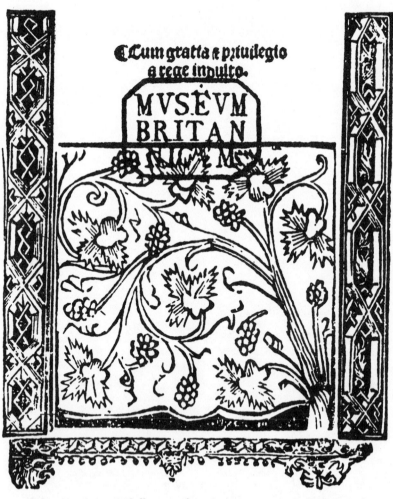

Title page of *An Herball*, 1525, the only known copy of which is in the British Museum. From a facsimile in the *Pierpont Morgan Library*.

Marigold

ome use to make their heyre yelow wyth the floure of this herb / not beynge content with the natural colour which God hath gyven them." Thus said William Turner, as ever stern toward the frivolities of life.

Marigolds have so long a history of sturdy usefulness to man that it is pleasant to start with a frivolity, which seems to be the only one in a story that stretches from antiquity down to World War I.

First, however, we must get clear about the name of this flower. We say "calendula" but it was called "marigold" for centuries before *Tagetes,* a genus of Mexican and South American plants, came to European gardens. There they received such misleading names as French and African marigolds. Now to make everything clear, this is the first, last and only mention of *Tagetes* in this book. The marigolds herein, and especially in this chapter, are all calendulas.

The Assyrian part of the search for the story of marigolds in antiquity is much like that of the daisy and equally disappointing from the point of view of identification. Because again Dr. Thompson mentioned marigolds in his early work and again changed his mind by the time he came to write his *Dictionary of Assyrian Botany.* But *The Assyrian Herbal* and *Assyrian Medical Texts* yield a whole series of prescriptions in which marigolds were used for head ailments—heads itching, scabby, growing gray, etc. It is a pity we cannot be sure about them as marigolds, but since the possibility exists—even though later

Dr. Thompson decided they were actually *Heliotropaeum Europaeum Benth.*—it is at least worth mention.

Another dubious appearance of marigold occurs in the fourth century B.C. in Greece. The "gold flower" of the Greeks was identified in one translation of Theophrastus as *Helichrysum siculum* but a number of other writers refer to the gold flower as marigold. Since identifications in the past are notoriously uncertain, perhaps we may accept the gold flower as a marigold for long enough to be entertained by the irritation it aroused in Theophrastus. It annoyed him that men should be so credulous as to believe that they would derive any medical benefit from crowning themselves with the gaudy flowers sprinkled with an unguent *from a vessel of unfired gold.* This sort of thing, he snapped, proceeds only from "men who desire to glorify their own craft." Promotion techniques were apparently not unknown among the Greek goldsmiths as early as the fourth century B.C.

The Greek scholar who was so scornful of this commercialization of medical practice has already been mentioned as "the father of botany" and the author of *An Inquiry into Plants,* the earliest botanical work we know. Theophrastus was born on the island of Lesbos in 372 B.C. As a young man he went to Athens and became a pupil of Aristotle. Not only a pupil but a friend, for when Aristotle died he made Theophrastus guardian of his children and bequeathed to him his library and his own original manuscripts. Theophrastus carried on the Lyceum, the school in which Aristotle had taught. In fact, he carried it on so successfully that at one time there were said to be more than two thousand students. When Theophrastus died, in 287 B.C., he left his house and garden to the school. Athens, ever ready to honor the highest attributes of the human spirit, gave this scholar and teacher a public funeral—

Marigold

"the whole population of Athens, honouring him greatly, followed him to the grave."

By the time we reach the Romans no more doubt about the plant remains. Our generic name for it comes from the Roman calends, the first day of every Roman month, and the claim was made that these yellow or orange flowers were in bloom on every calends throughout the year, which would be entirely possible in southern Italy. They were cultivated both as garden ornaments and as medicinal herbs which would "help mightily ye scorpion-bitten."

"Sow Marygolds and Spinach at the end of this week" (the first week in April), wrote Sir John Hill in *Eden, or, A Compleat Body of Gardening*, 1757.

Sir John did not have his subject matter confused. He was writing of the kitchen garden which had, long before his time, included marigolds. "Goldes" were among the herbs for pottage listed at the beginning of a fifteenth-century manuscript cited by Baroness Cecil and "Goldez" were among the flavorings used for possets and other drinks.

Marigolds, along with marjoram, parsley and thyme, were used to make a white broth either for "Capon, Mutton or Chickin" in *The Good Houswiues Treasurie, Beeing a verye necessarie Booke instructing to the dressing of meates*. "Beeing" likewise the jewel of the fine collection of cookbooks willed to the New York Public Library by the late Helen Hay Whitney.

Cookbooks, like almanacs and children's books, take a beating. Few housewives have bothered to save that use-scarred volume with the grease stain on page 78 and the spatter of chocolate on page 136. A bigger and better cookbook appears and the old one is jettisoned. As a result of this all too prevalent attitude the tiny *Treasurie* was far more of a treasure than Edward Allde dreamed when he printed it in London in 1588.

(Before or after the Armada, one wonders.) There is a copy in the British Museum, but aside from these two no copy has survived.

A similar broth, which includes marigolds among the herbs used for seasoning, appears in another Elizabethan cookbook as one in which to "stue Sparrows or Larkes." You "parboyle the Larkes before; and then boyle them in the same broth and lay them upon Sops."

Gerard testified as to how widespread was this use of marigolds. "The yellow leaves of the floures are dried and kept throughout Dutchland against Winter, to put into brothe, in Physical potions, and for divers other purposes, in such quantity, that in some Grocers or Spice-sellers houses are to be found barrels filled with them, and retailed by the penny more or lesse, insomuch as no broths are well made without dried Marigoldes."

Sir Kenelm Digby gives receipts for "A Plain Savory English Pottage" and a beef stew that both call for marigolds, among other herbs.

The eighteenth-century Duke of Bolton may have been, as Jonathan Swift said he was, a great booby, but his grace at least knew how to eat well even on fast days. His cook, John Nott, had "An Olio for Days of Abstinence" that is substantial enough to replace any meat dish:

"Put fresh broth and good Pea Soup into a Pot with Borage, Endive, Marigold, Sorrel or other Sweet Herbs grossly shred and some Spinage whole, likewise Turnips, Carrots, Onions, and Cabbage cut in pieeces, a little Saffron, cloves, mace and nutmegs, etc. Add bottoms of Artichokes and Chestnuts (boiled and blanched) with a couple of Collyflowers. Let them boil together as long as is requisite. Add Yolks of eggs and then serve your olio with seppets of bread and garnish as you please."

This same John Nott gives a receipt for pottage which is

Marigold

worth quoting because most of us know the word without ever having stopped to think how the dish was made. Receipts varied, of course, over the years but this seems to be a fair sample:

"Mince several sorts of sweet herbs very fine—Spinache, Parsley, Marigold flowers, Succory, Strawberry and Violet leaves. Pound them with oatmeal in a Mortar. Boil your oatmeal and herbs in broth and serve."

Puddings with marigolds as a flavor were popular. John Evelyn tells how to make one that can be boiled in a floured bag, or baked, as you prefer. Helen M. Fox, in her introduction to the modern edition of *Acetaria*, says that pudding flavored with the petals of marigold is excellent. Marigold dumplings, although *The Compleat Cook* of 1655 did not call them that, also sound good. "Take a penny loafe of stale bread. Grate it put to it halfe a pound of Beef suet shred very small, then take sweet herbs, the most of them Marigolds, shred the herbs very small mix all well together then take two eggs and work them up together with your hand, and make them into round balls and when the Water boyle put them in, serve them. Rosewater, sugar and butter for sauce."

As a flavoring for drinks, marigolds seem to have been most often used in possets. Here is another familiar word we tend to accept without thought though probably most people do associate it with milk. A typical posset is described in *The art & mystery of cookery. Approved by the fifty five years' experience and industry of Robert May in his attendance on several persons of great honour. 1671.* To make this you take a "fair scoured skellet" into which you put some milk and marigold petals. After this has been boiled you strain out the marigolds and add beer or ale with or without sugar!

Marigold wine was made by the usual method of adding toast, spread with yeast, to a sugar and water syrup. The flower petals were put in after the mixture had worked for a couple of days, and one contemplates with respect the thought that a peck of the petals went into each gallon of liquid. A pint of white wine per gallon topped it off and it was ready for the cask.

Like other flowers of strong color and taste, marigolds were pickled and candied in various ways but, by and large, their usefulness in the kitchen was that of a commonplace staple. Although the lily was once described on a fifteenth-century list for the kitchen garden as an herb to be used for pottage, it must far oftener have played the other role assigned to it by the same list—that of an herb "for Savour and beaute." "Goldes" belonged to no such lofty category. They were then, and continued to be throughout their culinary career, concerned strictly with such everyday matters as pottage and posset and pudding.

Marigolds tended to play as humdrum a part in folklore as they did in the kitchen, mostly as an ingredient in various love potions. But at least once, in the sixteenth century, they were used in a fashion that lifts them out of the commonplace as if on wings. They play an important part in a receipt "To enable one to see the Fairies"!

"Take a pint of sallet oyle and put it into a vial glasse; and first wash it with rose-water and marygolde water; the flowers to be gathered toward the east. Wash it till the oyle becomes white, then put into the glasse, and then put thereto the budds of hollyhocks, the flowers of marygolds the flowers or toppes of wild thyme, the budds of young hazle, and the thyme must be gathered neare the side of a hill where fairies use to be; and take the grasse of a fairy throne; then all these put into the oyle in the glasse and sette it to dissolve three dayes in the sunne and then keep it for thy use." Wouldn't it be wonderful if it worked!

Marigold

Ordinarily, however, marigolds turn up in very average love magic. According to Sir James G. Frazer, Balkan peasant girls dig the earth from the footprints of their sweethearts and use it to pot up a marigold which represents to them the symbol of enduring love.

In eighteenth-century England marigolds played a part in a love charm which will do well enough as a sample of the kind in which they appeared. This one is to be found in *Mother Bunch's Closet Newly Broke Open*, one of those cheap, flimsy chapbooks with which would-be men of letters earned a meager living.

The miller's servant girl, Margaret, who consulted Mother Bunch, was probably typical of her kind—overworked and underpaid, credulous and ignorant, young and eager for love. To Margaret the marigold receipt and the magic couplet were valuable tools either to achieve a longed-for end or to settle a difficult problem.

Mother Bunch assured Margaret that she would reveal to her "some secrets that are both relative and conductive to love, which I have never yet discovered to the world . . . Let me see, this is St. Luke's Day, which I have found by long experience to be fitter for this purpose than St. Agnes', and the ingredients more excellent.

Take marigold flowers, a sprig of marjoram, thyme and a little wormwood; dry them before a fire, rub them to a powder, then sift it thro' a fine piece of lawn; simmer these with a small quantity of virgin honey in white wine over a slow fire; with this anoint your stomach, breast and lips lying down, and repeat these words thrice:

> St. Luke, St. Luke, be kind to me;
> In dreams let me my true love see!

This said, hasten to sleep, and in the soft slumber of your night's repose, the very man whom you shall marry will appear before you,

The calendula from Dodoens' *Pemptades*. (*Horticultural Society of New York*)

walking to and fro, near your bedside, very plain and visible to be
seen. You shall perfectly behold his visage, stature, and deportment;
and if he be one that will prove a loving husband, he will approach you
with a smile; which, if he does, do not seem to be over fond or peevish,
but receive the same with a mild and modest blush. But if it be one
who after marriage will forsake they bed to wander after strange
women, he will offer to be rude and uncivil with thee.

Doubtless generations of Margarets, wavering between a
choice of suitors, adopted Mother Bunch's method of deciding
which would make the better husband. One hopes, too, that
those eighteenth-century Margarets were able to beg or borrow
a bit of fine lawn if they did not own one. Should they, in
their youthful eagerness, steal one, they were liable to death
by hanging.

Strictly speaking, three rhymes concerning marigolds quoted
hereafter do not belong to folklore and yet a political couplet,
a riddle and an epitaph all based on marigolds indicate how
easily the flower fitted itself into popular thought, especially
into the popular thought of the seventeenth century. All these
verses date from then and two of them stress an aspect of the
flower that lends itself easily to metaphor. As the sun goes
down, the ray flowers of marigold curve inward and when
morning comes dewdrops are found in the half-closed blossom—
"the marigold that goes to bed wi' the sun and with him rises
weeping."

Robert Turner—by no means to be confused with Puritan
William—considered that this aspect of the flower illustrated
the fact that "God hath imprinted upon the plants, herbs and
flowers, as it were Hieroglyphicks, the very signature of their
vertues" and that in the marigold "subjects may learn their
duty to their sovereign, which his sacred Majesty King Charles
the First mentions in his princely meditations, walking in his
garden in the Isle of Wight, in the following words:

'The Marigold observes the Sun
More than my subjects me have done.' "

Only the most ardent Royalist could have found the mournful little couplet worth quoting, but Robert Turner was an ardent Royalist and also such an enthusiastic believer in the Doctrine of Signatures that he was willing for God's "Hieroglyphicks" to indicate political as well as medical virtues.

John Gay, author of *The Beggar's Opera* (1728), had, on the other hand, no metaphor in mind but was just playing with words when he tossed off his riddle:

> What flower is that which bears the Virgin's name,
> The richest metal joined to the same?

Then, from the light touch of the man as gifted with comedy as his name suggests, we turn to an age-old sadness where a twist of the marigold metaphor may have brought some dim comfort to a couple of sorrowing parents. In a Devonshire church is a small tomb bearing this inscription:

Dedicated to the Pretious Memorie of Mary ye deare and only daughter of George Westwood, Pastor of this Church and of Frances his wife; who leaving the vale of miserie for a mansion in Felicitie we heer entered January 31. Anno Domini, 1648. Aetet suae 7.

> This Mary-gold here doth shew
> Mary worth gold lies hear below;
> Cut down by death, ye fair'st gilt flour
> Flourish and fade doth in an hour.
> The Mary-gold in sunshine spread
> When cloudie clos'd doth bow the head,
> This orient plant retains its guise
> With splendid Sol to set and rise—
> Ev'n so this Virgin Marie Rose,
> In life soon nipt, in death fresh grows.

Marigold

Those last odds and ends included under folklore have not nearly so much right to be there as have some other verses that belong to the marigold story. Yet when it came to classifying them there were difficulties. Technically they belong to medicine, since they come from a medieval herbal, but they are so permeated with local folklore and even primitive magic that one hesitates to label them. They are so interesting, however, in their own right that they deserve a section all to themselves, since they belong, strictly speaking, neither to medicine nor to folklore nor to magic but are a brew of all three.

As has already been noted, Odo of Meune wrote a Latin poem about herbs in 1161, "the first independent herbal to be produced in the West in medieval times," according to Charles Singer. Odo knew something about classical medicine and he is thought to have been influenced by the Arabian practice as it reached Europe through the great medical school at Salerno. Interwoven with this orthodox medical material, like a metallic thread in a tapestry, was the local lore of his countryside reaching back into pre-Christian magical practices.

It seems a pity that Odo's name was not associated with his personal contribution to medieval medicine. A very minor Roman poet of Virgil's time, one Aemilius Macer, was supposed to have written a work on plants and either Odo himself, or someone after him, presented Odo's verses with the cachet of Latin authorship. So it was as *Macer's Herbal* that this early European work enjoyed immense popularity, as the large number of surviving manuscripts bear witness.

One of the most famous of these is a rhymed version in Middle English that is now called the Stockholm Manuscript and is in the Royal Library in Sweden.

> Of herbis xxiii
> I wyl ye telle by and by . . .

is the way the section on plants begins, and it goes on to give the properties of these herbs as they could be used in the treatment of a number of ailments, not forgetting many which might now be classified as psychosomatic.

It is this manuscript which belonged to Philippa of Hainault when she married Edward III of England in 1328, and it may well have been one of her wedding presents or else part of "the dress and equipage of such a lady, who was to be queen of England."

One hopes that Philippa had no immediate need of her herbal, for the early days of her married life were strenuous. When she had landed at Dover with all her suite, "her uncle, Sir John de Hainault, conducted her to London, where she was crowned [and presumably married!] and there were great crowds of the nobility, and feastings, tournaments, and sumptious entertainments every day, which lasted for three weeks." Later there is little doubt that Philippa took up her medical duties and the general supervision of her household with great seriousness, for she was a kind woman.

She has come down in history as the queen who saved the burghers of Calais from the hangman. They appeared before her husband bareheaded and barefooted with halters around their necks after Edward had finally agreed to raise the siege of Calais, provided that the six most prominent citizens yielded themselves to him to save the lives of the rest of the townsmen.

"AH, gentle sir, since I have crossed the sea with great danger to see you, I have never asked you for one favor; now I most humbly ask as a gift, for the sake of the Son of the blessed Mary, and for your love to me, that you will be merciful to these six men."

The king looked at her for some time in silence, and then said, "Ah, lady, I wish that you had been anywhere else than here. You have entreated in such a manner that I cannot refuse you. I therefore give them to you, to do as you please with them."

Marigold

The queen conducted the six citizens to her apartments, and had the halters taken from round their necks, after which she new-clothed them, and served them with a plentiful dinner. She then presented each with six nobles and had them escorted out of the camp in safety.

The woman who was so distressed at the plight of half a dozen strangers must often have been concerned by the very human troubles of the people around her. And in many cases she undoubtedly had recourse to marigolds to heal difficulties not generally considered pathological.

That lusty young groom, for instance. He was an excellent servant, willing and faithful, but he was forever in trouble because he could not let the girls and young wives of the household alone. Marigold petals in his drink surely ought to remedy the matter, for Macer had said they would:

> Good is ye lef, so is ye sed,
> To gryndyn and drynky at gret ned,
> It wyll be dronky wt whey or wt ale
> Or wt good reed wyn yat be stale;
> Alle maner veny will it abate
> In manys body early and late.

For that useful tirewoman who, at a difficult time of life, had conceived the idea that everyone was talking against her, the remedy was more complicated. The queen would give her an amulet made of marigold petals and a bit of laurel wrapped around a wolf's tooth. But to be effective the marigolds had to be gathered under rigid conditions: in August, when the moon was in the sign of the Virgin but not while Jupiter was in the ascendant. The person who picked the flowers must be fasting, recently cleansed out of deadly sin, and must, while doing the job, recite three *pater nosters* and three *aves*. Then, to paraphrase the Middle English lines, the tirewoman could be assured that once she wore her amulet,

Man nor woman would have no might
To speak against her any but right.
Friend and foe would now her greet
With words that were both fair and sweet.

The same amulet had many other uses. Carried on a man's person, it would defend him against all perils. Worn about the neck at night, it would cause the wearer to see in a dream the thief who had recently robbed him. And if marital troubles reached almost to the point of divorce, the same amulet, laid somewhere in a church, would by the time the next Mass had been said, clear up all difficulties. It seems likely that Queen Philippa found marigolds very useful in the management of her household.

What we would consider the more strictly medical aspects of marigolds were equally permeated with magic. If you looked "wisely" on gold early in the morning, it would guard you that day from any fever and, though the herbal does not say how, it had the property of being able to draw "wikked" humors out of the head.

If this be medicine, make the most of it—and it is quite certain that the gentle queen of England did.

Somewhat later in the fourteenth century a medical man wrote down a specific way in which marigolds would help cure wicked humors in the head:

For the demye-greyne (megrim or neuralgia)

Take 1 lb seyngrene (houseleek) and I quatron of mary-goulden, and of violettes a gret hanful, and take a pynte mylke of a woman that beryth a knave childe, that is a mayde y-wedded, and late hem be stamped in a faire mortar al to geder ryte smale, and than ley it on the hole side of the hede; and lat the hede be helde to a gode hote fyre with the plastre ther-on into a tyme the plastre be thurwe [thoroughly] hote on his hede, and then with the hete [heat] ly doun and reste hym well, and he shale be hole.

This was a promising beginning but somehow or other marigolds were never very firmly planted in medieval medical practice. Whatever the reason may have been the part marigolds played in medicine before the seventeenth century was far from a prominent one. With the Renaissance herbalists they took on somewhat more importance, but not a great deal more. Their place was that of an average herb that could be used, as could innumerable others, for female complaints; to ease toothache and inflamed eyes; to make cordials for heart troubles; and as an ingredient in medicines given for plague, melancholy and various other ills. In short, the role of the marigold in medicine was not unlike its role in the kitchen—that of a useful run-of-the-mill staple.

If marigold was a commonplace medical herb to Englishmen and Europeans, it has a special interest for Americans. It appears on all the early lists of herbs and flowers brought to this country by the first settlers. Marigolds were seen in the Dutch New Netherlands by 1642 and in Virginia by 1650. In 1672 John Josselyn, Gent., published his *New England's Rarities Discovered*, describing what he had seen when he visited New England in 1638 and when he had lived there from 1663 to 1671.

Many a homesick colonial housewife must have been torn between pleasure and pain as she looked at her marigolds—pain because they stabbed her with memories of home and pleasure that anything so gay could both season her broth and serve her as medicine. Her faith in the medicinal powers of the herb was based on what was for her a firm foundation—the say-so of Nicholas Culpeper.

It may have been Culpeper's politics that made him so popular in New England, for he fought on the side of Parliament in the English civil war. Eventually he settled at Spitalfields, in London, where he practiced medicine and was noted for treating the poor of his neighborhood free of charge. This no doubt accounted for his own precarious financial situation, which he tried to remedy by bringing out an herbal.

Culpeper's herbal proved to be so popular that it was still in print more than a hundred fifty years after the first edition appeared. One of these later editions describes itself as "This, our *English Family Physician* for one humble fee, remains forever in a house, and cures every disorder. The language is easy and familiar, adapted to the meanest capacity, as was that of the original author:

> 'Whose skill and phrases are so ably planned
> That both the weak and wife might understand.' "

Undaunted by the horrid suggestion that the two terms mentioned might be synonymous, the New England housewife was chiefly thankful for the practicality of Culpeper's advice. Marigolds flourished easily in the new land, and marigolds, Culpeper assured her, were hardly less efficacious than saffron for smallpox and measles. Saffron in those early days of New England must have literally been worth its weight in gold.

So much has been made of the fact that Culpeper based his medical theories on astrology that it is only fair to point out that in his day astrology was still a respectable science. There was nothing original in this. We have already seen stars and herbs mingled together in *Macer's Herbal*. But what was original with Culpeper was that he held theories and reasoned about them. He points out in his "Epistle to the Reader," which serves as preface to his book, that neither Gerard nor Parkinson nor any of the other older herbalists ever gave "one wise Reason for what they wrote, and so did nothing else but train up young

Marigold

Novices in Physic in the School of Tradition and teach them as a Parrot is taught." From his own studies—Culpeper was a Cambridge man—he argued at meticulous and wearisome length that astrology offered an explanation on which he could base his ideas. He was wrong and his contemporary, William Coles, was equally wrong when he based his theories on the Doctrine of Signatures. But English medicine took a good stride forward toward a systematic method when these two men advocated reason rather than tradition.

His radical and independent point of view made *Culpeper's English Physician* a not inappropriate companion to the Bible in New England households. If a family owned only two books, the second was practically always Culpeper and all seventeenth- and eighteenth-century American doctors had the book as a matter of course.

By the time this famous and popular herbal had reached the New World in the 1650's marigolds had been at home there for at least a couple of decades. It seems probable, too, that in the very early days of the settlement a co-operative physick garden was established. But as soon as the colonists achieved individual houses of their own the family physick garden—forerunner of our ornamental garden—supplanted the communal one.

We do not know who she was nor the exact date, but on an April morning a girl went out of a house on Cape Cod carrying a small bundle and a heavy spade. She had laid out her garden the week before. Now it only needed a bit more digging to break up any lumps of soil she might have overlooked. Then she could plant the seeds that her mother had sent from home, and among them were the seeds of marigolds—good to flavor a stew, good to make an ointment or cordial, but better still—so gay and golden—to flaunt a bit of color that the Old World had sent to the New.

Flower Chronicles

Marigolds were used in great quantities in army hospitals during the Civil War, according to what an Englishman, Dr. W. T. Fernie, said in his book *Herbal Simples,* published in 1897. "The plant, especially the flowers, was used on a large scale by the American surgeons, to treat wounds and injuries sustained during the last Civil War; and obtained their warmest commendation. It quite prevented all exhaustive suppurative discharges and drainings. *Succus Calendula* [the fresh juice] is the best form, say the American surgeons, in which the Calendula is obtainable for ready practice."

It occurred to me that the fresh juice of marigolds might be among the items sent by the Ladies' Aid Societies that supplied the Sanitary Commission with so much that went into army hospitals. When I learned that the records of the Sanitary Commission—quantities of them—lie almost entirely unopened somewhere underneath the New York Public Library I decided to attack the matter from another angle. *Harper's Weekly* had been to the Civil War what *Life* had been to World War II. There would be stories and pictures in *Harper's Weekly* of groups of women gathered in the local church to sew and knit and pack supplies for the Union men at the front. But ladies, I learned, did not appear in the public prints during Civil War days except in impersonally symbolic fashion. There might be a picture of a soldier's dream featuring his mother or his sweetheart. Or there might be an idealized conception of the home toward which the soldier's thoughts perpetually turned—again with female figures he was presumed to yearn to see. I turned hundreds of those brittle pages of *Harper's* before I acknowledged that this just wasn't a good idea. An appeal for help to a famous pharmaceutical library produced no results.

The second interesting modern use of the marigold was again a wartime one, this time in World War I. "The flowers have long been used as hemostatic and as such Miss Gertrude Jekyll gave over a large part of her noted Sussex garden to the cultivation of the flowers during the Great War, sending innumerable bushels of the flowers to first-aid stations in France to be used as dressings for wounded soldiers."

This statement appeared in a pleasant little book called *Old-Time Herbs* by Minnie Watson Kamm, published in 1938. I wrote to Mrs. Kamm who replied that she was sorry to say she had destroyed all the references used in her book and that she had no recollection of the source of the marigold one. A letter to the very old gentleman, Miss Jekyll's nephew, who had written her biography, brought forth no reply. As a last resort I wrote to Kew. Sir Edward Salisbury promptly replied that he regretted the fact that there were no records at Kew of this interesting use of marigolds by Miss Jekyll. There the trail seems to end. Perhaps someday more solid evidence will be found to back up the truly interesting tale of the marigold in two modern wars.

Activities of the stillroom as shown on the frontispiece of Hannah Woolley's herbal. (*Rare Book Room, New York Public Library*)

Pinks and Carnations

illyfloures, coronations, carnations, cloves, sops-in-wine, picotees, pinks—the very number of names echoes with the affectionate familiarity the Renaissance felt for *dianthus*.

"A most courteous exposition," said Romeo. And Mercutio swept him an ironic bow: "Nay, I am the very pink of courtesy."

By popular consent the flower symbolized the high point civilization had reached. Pinks, as others have noted, were supremely the flowers of the Renaissance. An Italian painter, Benvenuto Tisio, signed his pictures with a gilliflower in one corner and thus won for himself the nickname "Il Garogale." People sat for their portraits with pinks in their hands or, like Holbein's young merchant, George Gysis, had pinks in a vase nearby. There are pinks among the flowers of Botticelli's *Spring*.

Poets, too, welcomed them. There are pinks and gilliflowers and carnations in Shakespeare, while Spenser, who shared the popular delight, included them in lines that make the spirit of that young age sing:

> Youth's folk now flocken everywhere
> To gather May baskets and smelling Brere.
> Then home they hasten the posts to dight
> And all the kirk pillars in day light
> With Hawthorn buds and sweet Eglantine
> And garlands of Roses and Sope-in-Wine.

The crisp firm substance of the flowers, laced, ruffled and fringed; their delicious scent; their variegated and brilliant colors—all these caught the imagination of a time when "the quick pulse of delight" beat high, to borrow a vivid phrase from the English historian Green. Pinks, new come to the gardens, were one of the special delights of a vital and vigorous age.

Why pinks were newcomers to gardens is a mystery. They were not strange and "outlandish" flowers when the Renaissance claimed them as its own. Every European country of warm and temperate climate has its variety of *dianthus*. As far back as the fourth century B.C. Theophrastus had classified a flower he called *dianthe* as an "under shrub" and stated that it was grown as a coronary plant. The fact that it was so named and the name for it—our generic name—means flower of god, or of Zeus, suggests that it had an even more ancient history with a religious significance. But that is mere supposition. The only fact we have about the far past of the pink is that after Theophrastus mentioned it it disappeared from human history for something like sixteen hundred years!

This seems fantastic but it is apparently true. Most of our knowledge of plants before the invention of printing comes to us through medicine. Empires and kingdoms might fall, literature and learning perish, but medical manuscripts were somehow cherished.

Medicine from Greek antiquity to the Renaissance was almost static so far as the use of herbs was concerned. If you knew your Hippocrates, Dioscorides and Galen you had mastered the herbal lore on which the pharmacopoeia of centuries was based. There were, of course, local and personal exceptions here and there, but in the main you were safe in leaning on the masters. No pinks appear in the standard translations of Hippocrates, Dioscorides or Galen, nor were there any in the work of that cheap copyist of Dioscorides, Apuleius, whose medicine, copiously mixed with magic, was so popular during the Middle Ages.

Pinks and Carnations

There are no pinks in the Anglo-Saxon leech-books Cockayne translated nor are there any in *Macer's Herbal* which dates from 1161. There are none in *Bancke's Herbal* published as late as 1525. The one possible reference to pinks in Pliny is very dubious.

Why, over this vast period of time from Greek antiquity to Chaucer, pinks were ignored is bewildering. There was no medical prejudice against sweet-smelling herbs. Roses, violets, lilies were lavishly used. So too, for that matter, were many evil-smelling and vile-tasting plants. *I. foetidissima*, frankly known as "stinking gladwin," slimy duckweed and bitter aloes all played their part in medicine. Dangerous, really deadly drugs such as aconite, belladonna and digitalis were lightheartedly handled by generations of herbalists. Size had nothing to do with it. Tall lilies and little chickweed both found their way into men's stomachs. Why, then, no pinks? So far there seems to be no answer but it would be exceedingly interesting if an explanation could someday be found.

As a matter of fact, though pinks first began to appear in Chaucer's time in England they were still not mentioned medically. They made their debut prosaically in the kitchen garden as a flavor for food and drink. The fourteenth-century poem, *The Pearl*, lists them in that "erber grene" but it should be noted that every herb mentioned with the possible exception of gromwell belonged in the kitchen garden, of which the arbor may have been a part.

Chaucer himself mentions a pink, the "clove gilofre," along with nutmeg to put in ale, unquestionably a common practice at a time when true cloves were fabulously expensive. His reference has all the charm that naïve inaccuracy must hold even for the most rigidly scientific botanist. For Chaucer's hero, Sir Thopas, rides through a Flanders landscape where among the "herbes grete and smale" were not only liquorice and zedoary (possibly valerian), but pinks that grew side by side with nutmegs!

For at least four hundred years pinks continued to be a popular flavoring for beer, ale and wine. An early receipt describes their use in "ypocras," which was a favorite drink all through the Middle Ages, a wine highly seasoned with herbs and spices—pinks combining the virtues of both.

We are indebted for this receipt to one of the two thousand cooks in the kitchen of Richard II. A number of these men collaborated to write *The Forme of Cury, c.* 1390, the first practical cookbook in the English language. That is, if you can call it the English language when the receipt for ypocras begins "Pur fair ypocras" and ends "de toute soit fair powder." The ingredients, which include pepper, ginger, spikenard, cloves, cardamom, marjoram, pinks and various other herbs, are spelled out in the difficult English of the time with the equally difficult French scattered here and there and, possibly in the case of marjoram, a bow in the direction of Italian. Richard apparently kept a cosmopolitan kitchen.

Fashions in drinks changed, but the clove pink as a flavor remained popular until well into the eighteenth century. In the seventeenth, that indefatigable gourmet, Sir Kenelm Digby, used it in a number of the one hundred six receipts he has bequeathed us for "Meathe" and "Metheglin," the latter recently described as "that powerful intoxicant beloved by Queen Elizabeth." Probably at a still earlier date "Meathe" was simply fermented honey and water while "Metheglin" added herbs. By the time Sir Kenelm published his collection of receipts the distinction had been lost. It is quite impossible to find any essential difference between the two, search as one will.

The search, however, is rewarded with odd bits and pieces of contemporary information that are interesting and amusing. It

Pinks and Carnations

was no sinecure making powerful intoxicants for Sir Kenelm Digby. "With clean Arms stripped up, lade it [the honey and water] for two or three hours!" "Beware of infusing Gillyflowers in any vessel of Metal (excepting silver) for all Metals will spoil or dead their color. Glased earth is best." The water was important and the variety was nearly always specified—rain water, spring water, fountain water, conduit water or Hyde Park water, the last-named always used by "Master Webbe who maketh the kings Meathe." Mr. Webbe took forty-three gallons of water to forty-two gallons of honey and Mr. Pierce's "Excellent white Metheglin" was made in a "Copper that conveniently holdeth three hogsheads." Home brewing was done on no niggardly scale.

Gilliflower wine was made with "Ambergreese" and "run through a gelly bag" by "W.M.," cook to Queen Henrietta Maria. It was still being made a hundred years later when Sarah Harrison included it in *The housekeeper's pocket-book*, 1738.

Scattered sparingly through the cookbooks and stillroom books of some four hundred years are a number of receipts that call for pinks in food. They are among the ingredients in a dish called "Cawdelle Ferry" which dates from about 1430 and sounds rather like a version of zabaglione. But the most engaging of them all is one mysteriously labeled "Salomene." It is mysterious because if the fish is intended it is almost the only edible one not mentioned in the receipt.

"Take wyne, an gode pouder [flour], and Brede y-ground, and sugre an boyle it to-gederys; than take Trowtys, Rochys, Perchys, or Carpys or alle these to-gederys, and make hem clene. and aftere roste hem on a Grydelle; than hew hem in gobettys; whan they be boylid, fry hem in oil a lytil. then caste in the brwet; & whan thou dressist it, Maces, Cloves, Quybibes, Gilliflowers, and cast a-bove, and serve forth."

Tansie was another dish, a sort of sweet omelet, colored with pinks. You could make a green tansie with tansie itself or spinach, a purple one with violets, a yellow one with cowslips or marigolds, or a deep-red one with raspberries. At least the inference is clear that these colors survived the cooking. Ordinarily a tansie was fried on both sides but Hannah Woolley said that "a better and easier way" was to pour it into a buttered dish which was "set upon a Pot of boiling water till it be [done] enough." Since her receipt starts with a quart of cream and a dozen eggs, it is obvious that this seventeenth-century version of a double boiler was the easiest method of handling such an unwieldly quantity.

Hannah also made a "sallad" of gilliflowers that was more of a pickle or relish than anything we would call a salad. You make a syrup with sugar, a clove or two and a little white wine. This with the flower petals is put into a pot with some white wine vinegar and a little more sugar and kept for use.

John Nott, cook to the Duke of Bolton, who published his *Receipt Book* in 1723, made a similar concoction which he considered "a very good sauce for Lamb or Mutton." It sounds like a pleasant change from the ubiquitous mint.

Pinks were made into conserves. They were also candied, by dipping into white of egg and powdered sugar, to serve as ornamental sweets.

It is clear that, though pinks were not a staple to be grown in large crops, they had a very definite place in the kitchen garden—a place they kept from the fourteenth through the eighteenth century.

Quite suddenly pinks, ignored for so long and then relegated to the kitchen, blossomed out in Renaissance gardens.

By the time Gerard was writing in 1597 pinks were not only prominent in gardens but so passionately cultivated that he had to apologize for being unable to do them justice. For "a great and large volume would not suffice to write of every one at large and in particular; considering how infinite they are, and how every year, every clymate and country brings forth new sorts, such as have not heretofore been written of."

Parkinson devotes a whole chapter in *Paradisi in Sole* to the cultivation of *dianthus*, "because Carnations and Gilloflowers been the chiefest flowers of account in all our English gardens." His enthusiasm runs to more than five thousand words in a single paragraph! "Put the earth," he writes lovingly, "a little close to the slippe with your finger and thumb . . . but let this *caveat* be a sufficient remembrance unto you, that you neuer water any of these Gilloflowers . . . with cold water such as you have presently drawne out from a pumpe or well, but with such water as hath stood open in the aire in a cisterne, tubbe or pot for one whole day at the least." And he discourses at length on "the Earwicke," that chief pest of pinks and how to cope with these "most infestuous vermine."

Behind the robust enthusiasm of Gerard and Parkinson stands a misty figure whose sole claim to a place in history is due to his love of pinks. We do not know whether Ralph Tuggie was a butcher, baker or candlestick maker who was also an amateur gardener or whether he was a professional herbalist. All that we know of him is his name, that he had a garden in Westminster, that after his death his wife kept that garden flourishing, and that pinks were his passion. Gerard advises lovers of pinks to repair "to the garden of Mistress Tuggie (the wife of my late deceased friend, Mr. Ralph Tuggie) in Westminster, which in the excellence and varieties of these delights exceedeth all that I have seene, as also, he himself, whilst he lived, exceedeth most, if not all, of his time, in his care, industry, and skill in raising, increasing and preserving of these plants."

It is a pity that some species or variety of *dianthus* today does not perpetuate the name of the man so famous in his time that his contemporaries listed in their gardens "Master Tuggie's Princess" and "Master Tuggie his Rose gillowflower" along with "The Lusty Gallant," "Ruffling Robin," the "Feathered Tawny," and all the other enchanting names lavished on this most beloved flower.

With the rediscovery of pinks in the Renaissance they naturally made their way into medicine. It was amusing to discover that their chief medical use was in taking the place of later techniques in psychiatry. "Lady Button's Melancholy Water" lists two species of pinks among its ingredients and they also appear in the Countess of Kent's "comfortable Cordial to chear the Heart" as well as in scores of other prescriptions for the "tranquilizing drugs" of the day.

Melancholy had long been recognized by the medical profession as a baffling ailment. It was early in the seventeenth century that Robert Burton brought out his *Anatomy of Melancholy*, an immense tome which covered all that was then known on the subject. Scattered through the book are remedies quoted from older authorities and which almost invariably feature bugloss and borage, "I borage give courage." These remedies were designed to ease or cure mental manifestations which Burton described as "a perpetual anguish of the soul," "a commotion of the mind," "a dotage without a fever," and in various other ways. But his intention is clear. Lumped under the general term "Melancholy" were all the symptoms of mental illness now diagnosed as manic depression, schizophrenia, paranoia and the rest.

There was nothing very original about the way melancholy was treated after Burton except that pinks were added to the old prescriptions. This was not invariably done but often enough for any student of herbals and stillroom books to note the fact. No one has ever explained this but we can hazard a guess.

Pinks and Carnations

Possibly the explanation lies in the times. Pinks were a discovery and an enthusiasm of the Renaissance. They carried into the grim days of the seventeenth century memories of a comparatively carefree and joyous past. What could be more natural than to add pinks, associated with happiness and cheer, to the older herbs designed to counteract the gloom of melancholy?

John Parkinson's *Paradisi in Sole* was the last glow in the botanical world of the light and color of the Renaissance. In 1629, the very year in which Parkinson's great book appeared, Charles I dissolved Parliament and embarked upon those eleven years of personal despotism that were to culminate in his own execution and the Protectorate of Cromwell.

Interwoven with Charles's determination to establish the divine right of kings were the religious policies of Laud, his Archbishop of Canterbury. To Protestant England, Laud seemed bent on taking the established church back to Rome, or, as the Puritans had it, "to Babylon."

If Laud had gone to work swiftly and radically, it would have been easier on individuals. A man would have known then quickly where he stood. But Laud moved cautiously—a bit of ritual here, a small theological point there, and for the sake of peace many a reasonable man complied at first. But as Laud continued his way each man had to decide for himself just how far he could go along. All over Europe Protestantism was at bay or on the defensive. Englishmen saw themselves as the last outpost of the hard-won freedom of conscience that the Reformation represented. Step by step ordinarily liberal men were pushed to fantastic extremes of Puritan bigotry by what they felt to be their need to defend their faith. It was truly a time of "perpetual anguish of the soul." The combination of political and religious pressures was often disastrous to sensitive minds.

If pinks were used for melancholy because of their associations with Renaissance freedom and joy "Lady Button's Melan-

267

choly Water" and the countess' "comfortable Cordial" are not entirely amusing. It is also touching that pinks should have been added with so much hope to the old prescriptions.

One wonders if even pinks could have been much help to Queen Henrietta Maria after she had lost her throne and her husband his head. But it is more than probable that she was dosed with Dr. Bulter's Cordial Water against Melancholy which her cook, "W.M.," had noted down and afterwards published in his receipt book, *The Queen's Closet Opened*, in 1655.

Various flowers including pinks and clove gilliflowers were infused along with aniseed, nutmeg and saffron in canary wine. This was then distilled in a cold still over a hot fire "hanging at the nose of the Still Ambergreese and Musk, of each one grain." Sugar was added to the liquor thus made and three spoonfuls were given three times a week. "It cureth all Melancholy, fumes and infinitely comforts the spirits."

For lesser mortals there were countless similar prescriptions that must often have been administered desperately to the men and women whose mental balance wavered and sometimes broke under the burdens of their time.

It may not be entirely without significance that Elizabeth Grey, the Countess of Kent, who lived all her adult life in those troubled years, abandoned all the herbs of the older formulas in favor of only pinks and spices in the remedy she has left us in her stillroom book. There was no curative value whatever in the pinks and spices, but who shall say that the very name of her medicine, "a comfortable Cordial to chear the Heart," did not carry its own healing balm?

Another woman of this period, Hannah Woolley, used pinks so lavishly in medicine and cooking that it seems a good idea to take a look at this extraordinary Restoration housewife. For Hannah's energy, interests and intelligence make her, if not a

ELIZABETH
Late Countess of Kent.

The Countess of Kent. Portrait frontispiece of
her herbal, *A Choice Manual*, printed in 1659.
(*Rare Book Room, New York Public Library*)

personage, at least a personality worth more than a passing
glance.

Hannah was so busy a woman that one can understand why
she either invented or seized upon a prescription for "A very
good Cordial Water without the trouble of a Still." This re-

269

quired pinks, but the basic ingredient was two quarts of brandy. Such a short cut, however, was probably only restored to in moments of stress, for Hannah gives several perfectly conventional receipts such as "The Melancholy Water" and "An excellent Cordial Electuary, for to restore one who is weak, or against Melancholy." Both of these required the long slow process of distillation and the former was dressed up with some "Leaf Gold" and two grains of musk. Such expensive ingredients no doubt confirmed the sufferer's conviction that the deepest depression would be lifted by a concoction which also contained "a Pottle of Sack" and all the old herbs, but began refreshingly with four handfuls of gilliflowers.

All housewives of the time had to be experienced in home care of the sick, but Hannah especially needed such skills because her husband was the headmaster of a school in Essex not far from Saffron-Walden. In 1644, when she was twenty-four, Hannah married this schoolmaster whom we know only as Woolley, Wooly or Wolly, depending on Hannah's spelling fancy at the moment. In addition to her duties at home, she practiced medicine professionally, treating many of her neighbors for eight or ten miles around. She attended her husband's pupils whenever they had "mishaps when they were playing" or "fell into distempers; as Agues, Meazels, Small Pox, Consumptions and many other diseases; in all which, unless they were desperately ill, their parents trusted me without the help of any Physician or Chirurgion."

The Woolleys left the school in Essex, moved to London, and shortly thereafter Woolley died. It was about this time that Hannah brought out the first of her six books. In addition to her medical knowledge she was adept at needlework, a prime cook, and an authority on household management. Her books anticipate practically all the subjects covered by women's magazines today and by the newspaper columns of household hints.

She was amply qualified to instruct the female sex, as she invariably called her readers.

You can learn from Hannah how to kill rats; how to manage

Two species of carnation from Dodoens' *Pemptades*. (*Horticultural Society of New York*)

servants—cook, butler, maids, carver, etc.; how to clean gold and silver lace; how to pot meats for a journey; and how to do "transparent work"—a fearful and wonderful affair of colored wires twisted into the shapes of flowers. But her most engaging instructions consist of sample letters given for the benefit of those of the female sex who are not skilled in the art of letter writing: "mother to daughter," "Widow to

Friend," "Gentlewoman to brother at Oxford," and "Wife to Husband (craving pardon)."

In 1683, when Hannah was sixty, she published her last book, *New and Excellent Experiments and Secrets in the Art of Angling*—a notable finale for a lady who had reached what, in those days, was advanced old age.

Where Hannah's religious and political sympathies lay during those troubled years we do not know. She was probably far too extraverted, far too busy to bother with such matters. But her cheerful faith in her herbal remedies and her unimaginative assurance of their efficacy must often have carried conviction that her pinks, leaf gold and herbs would pull anyone out of the blackest despondency. And, as all doctors know, confidence in the cure is more than half the battle. It is no wonder that the Dictionary of National Biography reported that Hannah, along with her other activities, practiced medicine successfully.

Pinks had not reached the stillroom books out of the blue but via competent medical authorities. Over the years trial and error must have made it plain that the cordial quality ascribed to them was not as great as had been claimed. At any rate, for whatever reason, they gradually lost their reputation for cheering the heart and banishing melancholy. By the beginning of the nineteenth century Dr. Robert J. Thornton could write, in *A New Family Herbal* (1810), that the only use for pinks in pharmacy was "to give a pleasant flavour and beautiful colour to an officinal syrup."

It is odd that pinks did not figure more prominently in perfume and cosmetic receipts, for surely few flowers can equal them for sweetness. Occasionally they are listed among those used for perfumed waters but by and large theirs was a rather minor role.

It was, therefore, enchanting to come upon pinks in—of all

places—a receipt for dyeing the hair black. This was in the *Toilet of Flora*, 1784. Why anyone should make the attempt with pinks, in the form of "Clove-July flowers," it is hard to imagine, because the receipt begins quite simply by stating that "The Leaves of the Wild Vine change the hair black, and prevent their falling off." Then, without paragraphing, it goes on to give directions for another very complicated concoction that consists of burnt cork, tree roots, bark, nut shells, leaves and various seeds and berries which "may be boiled in Wine, Vinegar or Rain-water, with the addition of some cephalic Plant as Sage, Marjoram, Balm, Betony, Clove-July flowers, Laurel, etc."

The story of the pink in the boudoir is as short as it is surprising.

Pinks appeared very rarely in heraldry though their rarity is by no means surprising. Flowers—that is, flowers that look like flowers and not conventionalized symbols—are rare in heraldry in any case, and there is a special reason why pinks were seldom used. No less authority than John Guillim has explained this fact. As Rouge Dragon Poursuivant, 1617, he made the first systematic treatment of heraldry from the records then in existence.

Pinks were, Guillim stated, "for *beauty,* varietie of colour, and pleasant *redolencie* to be compared with the choicest attires of the Garden." Yet they were seldom displayed on coats of arms "because such daintiness and affected adornings better befit *Ladies and Gentlewomen,* than *Knights* and men of *valour,* whose worth must be tried in the *Field,* not under a *Rose-bed* or in a *Garden-plot.*"

Yet in spite of this devastating comment a family Guillim calls "Iorney" (could that be Jordan?) bore pinks on their arms. Later a Livingstone displayed gilliflowers—and very sensi-

bly too, for pinks were never drawn more engagingly or real-
istically than they were in their heraldic form.

Pinks, like many other flowers, have been put to some odd
uses in their time. One John Hanlon, in Surrey, held lands and
houses for which he paid as quitrent no more than three clove
gilliflowers on the day of the king's coronation.

A far stranger use for a flower is when the pink was employed
as an instrument of revenge. Stephen Blake's *Compleat Gardeners Practice* (1664) certainly covers every contingency, for
it gives full directions as to how "To be revenged on a person
who steals your tulips." Powdered dry elecampane root is
sprinkled on clove gilliflowers which are then presented to "the
party that you desire to be revenged of, let it be a he or a she,
they will delight in smelling to it, then they will draw this
powder into their nostrils, which will make them fall a sneezing,
and a great trouble to the eyes, and by your leave, will make
the tears run down their thighes."

We are too sophisticated today to think of pinks as valuable
medicine against melancholy. But perhaps we tend to be too
sophisticated. Ours, like the seventeenth century, is a grim and
troubled time. Pinks in our stomachs we know will help us not
at all but we might do well to transfer the herbalists' conclusions into another sphere. More pinks in our gardens might indeed be "very profitable at all times for such as have feeble
spirits." Or better still, to use Gerard's words, that the pink
"wonderfully, above measure doth comfort the heart."

Surely that would be no mean service.

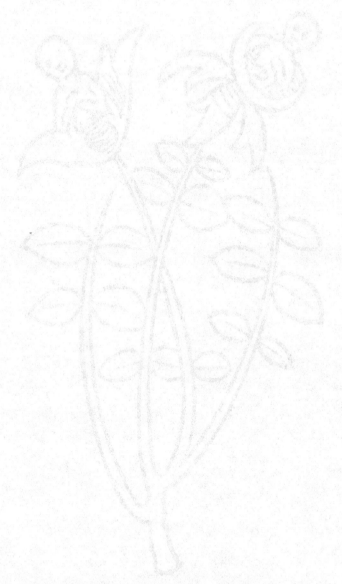

Narcissus. Woodcut from an edition of *Hortus Sanitatis* printed in 1491.
(*Mackenzie Library, Horticultural Society of New York*)

Narcissus

Emelia: This garden has a world of pleasure in't.
          What flower is this?
Servant: 'Tis called Narcissus, madam.
Emelia: That was a fair boy certaine, but a foole
          To love himselfe; were there not maids enough?
          —Beaumont and Fletcher, *Two Noble Kinsmen.*

It would be pleasant to dismiss the narcissus myth, already
worn threadbare, with this Elizabethan wisecrack were it not
for the fact that its very existence has significance in the history
of the narcissus.

The origin of the poetic myth about the beautiful boy so
in love with himself that he was finally drowned while worship-
ing his own image in a mountain pool goes back to a past long
before poetry. It is a common savage belief that a man's shadow
or his reflection is a projection of his soul that can put him in
great peril. Evil spirits in the water, for instance, can drag a
man's reflection down, thus separating him from his soul and
causing his death. Behind the primitive mythmakers who first
began to have a touch of poetic feeling cowered terrified savages frightened by all sorts of commonplace phenomena that
they could not understand.

Another well-known primitive concept may, Edith Hamilton
points out in *Mythology*, account for the identification of the
flower with another beautiful boy. Since seedtime and harvest
are vital necessities of life and life is manifested by blood, some
savages have thought that the fertility of the fields might be

277

ensured by human blood. Later, when a narcissus or other flower sprang up at the place of sacrifice, such flowers might be considered in local legend as the living representatives of the victims. Thus a charming fantasy clothed a brutal deed and the pretty story remained long after its gory origin was forgotten. Narcissus was a handsome youth who died young.

Whichever of these theories may be valid, the point is, if one is interested in the history of the narcissus, that a familiar flower was singled out by prehistoric man in Greece in folk tales that originally had meaning to his primitive mind. Of course prehistoric man saw the flowers around him. For all we know he may have used many of them in his crude religious rites, or as food, or as an ornament for his person. But when we get not proof—for that we can never expect to have—but good evidence that he noticed and used a specific flower in his folklore, a flower that is a familiar and beloved part of our own lives, then that remote ancestor seems much less remote. Beyond the primal needs of food and water and sex something may have stirred within him akin to the pleasure I feel when I lift my eyes from my typewriter to a hillside where hundreds of daffodils are blowing in the April wind.

The fact that primitive man in Greece noticed narcissus is further verified by the appearance of narcissus in some of the earliest Greek literature. They continue to appear in one way or another with an emphasis that shows how truly the flower was a part of Greek life.

There are narcissus, *N. tazetta,* in some of the funeral wreaths found on Egyptian mummies of the Eighteenth Dynasty, but that seems to have been their only appearance in Egypt. Greece was doubly their homeland. A number of species are native to the Greek peninsula and the flower is woven into the myth, legend and early religion of the Greeks—part and parcel of their

Narcissus

physical and spiritual heritage. Donald Culross Peattie points out that the flora of Europe is as intensely national as its peoples and tongues. He speaks, in that connection, of the "plain of Marathon blowing with poet's narcissus."

In one of the earliest pieces of Greek literature, a Homeric hymn of the eighth or seventh century B.C., the narcissus plays a minor role. Pluto, lord of the underworld, had fallen in love with the daughter of Demeter whom he wanted to carry off to his own grim realm. Zeus, in a friendly effort to help his brother god, created a new flower all silver and purple, to tempt Persephone away from her companions with whom she was gathering flowers in a field. Just as Zeus had expected, the silver and purple blossom caught her eye and she went toward it alone. Immediately the earth opened at her feet and the terrible god, in a chariot drawn by coal-black horses, dashed out and swept her away.

Now, the Greek word for the new flower is narcissus and the fact that it was described as silver and purple need not bother us. Virgil and Pliny, both writing some six or seven hundred years later, describe the narcissus as white and "purple." A French botanist who specialized in identifying plants in classical literature accounts for this description by pointing out the crisped red edge of the corona of the poet's narcissus. There is plenty of evidence to show that the ancients never did seem sure in their own minds what was red and what was purple. There is little doubt here as to the flower that was intended. Zeus lured Persephone with a *Narcissus poeticus*.

Toward the end of the fifth century B.C. we get a reference to the narcissus that points to its use in Greek religious ceremonies. In *Oedipus at Colonus* Sophocles speaks of the flower as the crown of the great goddesses. A flower that served as the crown of the great goddesses would naturally fit into Greek religious rites. So, since garlands were hung in the temples as offerings to the gods, it is not surprising to learn that narcissus was a favorite garland flower.

In many of the nineteenth-century books which carry the reference from Sophocles it is quoted as follows: "And ever day by day the Narcissus with its beauteous clusters, the ancient coronet of the mighty goddesses, bursts into bloom by heavens dew." As these lines are certainly unclear and clumsy, it is perhaps tactful that the translator's name is never mentioned. But Sir Richard C. Jebb has rendered them delightfully. In a lovely lyric that the chorus sings to welcome the blind Oedipus to Colonus we find, "Stranger, in this land of goodly steeds thou hast come to earth's fairest home, even to our white Colonus; where the nightingale, a constant guest, trills her clear note in the covert of green glades . . . And fed of heavenly dew, the narcissus blooms morn by morn with fair clusters, crown of the Great Goddesses from of yore."

One of the pleasures of being an amateur researcher is that when one is lured along a byway one can yield to temptation. Not many readers of that chorus would fail to be lured into turning back to the beginning and reading the whole play, a study of the tragedy of old age unequaled even by *King Lear*. Moving and lofty dramatic power reaches one of the great heights when the blind Oedipus, hitherto dependent on help for every step he took, walks off the stage alone, guided only by the inner light, to meet the death he knows is imminent.

To return to Greek mythology, we find the narcissus again in a meadow, this time where "the faire Lady Europa" was gathering flowers with her maidens before she was seduced by Zeus disporting himself in the guise of a bull. Theocritus tells the story in one of his idyls written about 285 B.C., which Gerard says "we may English thus":

Narcissus

But when the Girles were come into
The meadowe flouring all in sight
That Wench with these, this Wench with those
Trim floures, themselves did all delight;
She with Narcisse good in sent,
And she with Hyacinths content.

In the days of the first Elizabeth even a "London Master Chirurgie," who was also a barber, could turn his own translation from the Greek into pretty lines; that is, of course, unless Gerard appropriated some other man's work as he did in so much of the botanical and medical parts of his herbal. No one can really care today and, if the verse is not his own, we can still be thankful for his good taste.

It would be almost a lifework to follow the narcissus through Greek literature. The Greek anthology alone is packed with references. So it is best to leave the matter here with the lines by a late Greek poet, Rufinus—lines that he put into the mouth of a young man, a gay young man with humor and a light touch even in his lovemaking:

I send thee Rhodocleia, this garland, which myself
have twined of fair flowers beneath my hands; here
is lily and rose-chalice and moist anemone, and soft narcissus
and dark-glowing violet; garland thyself with these,
cease to be high-minded; even as the garland thou
doest flower and fall.

Narcissus are poisonous. Although not deadly like aconite, a relatively small amount can cause trouble. There are on record several cases of poisoning from narcissus bulbs eaten by mistake for onions. During World War II, when tulips were a staple article of diet for the population of Holland, the poisonous properties of narcissus kept them off the tables of the

281

Dutch, but cattle were able to tolerate a small amount mixed with the hyacinth bulbs that were their fodder.

Herbs more deadly than narcissus were often used in early herbal medicine, either because their action was not swift enough to identify them as the cause of the trouble or because, as in medieval medicine, so many herbs went into a medication that no one of them could be blamed with certainty if the patient died. But narcissus acted with such speed and vigor that there was no doubt whatever as to its effect. As Dioscorides put it, it "doth move to vomitings."

Thanks to this drastic action narcissus seem to have been pretty well disregarded until the Renaissance. Then the publication of Dioscorides' work reminded herbalists that, even if it was unwise to give narcissus internally, there were a number of external uses for it. Turner was following Dioscorides when he wrote: "The roote broken with a litle hony / maketh the cut synewes to grow together agayn / if it be layd to emplaster wyse. The roote layd to with hony helpeth the ankles out of ioynte / and the old aches of the ioyntes."

In the twilight of the Renaissance in England John Parkinson declared that no one "these dayes" used narcissus medically no matter what Gerard and others may have said. Parkinson felt very modern and, as he so obviously liked to feel, very superior to his older contemparary, Gerard. But Parkinson was wrong. Culpeper, who followed close on his heels, recommended narcissus for both internal and external use and a number of other herbalists followed his example up to the end of the eighteenth century. But by and large the medical history of the narcissus is scant and not very interesting.

In heraldry narcissus occur on the arms of Lambeth, one of the boroughs of London, and on those of Cardiff. But this would

Narcissus

Narcissus from Dodoens' *Pemptades*. (*Horticultural Society of New York*)

be hardly worth mention were it not for the fact that we are
in the midst of a kind of evolutionary change in the heraldic
use of the daffodil, which the College of Arms may someday
have to take into account.

The leek has been the emblem of Wales since the battle of
Agincourt, as Shakespeare has reminded us in *Henry V* when
he made Fluellen say to the King: "The Welshmen did good
service in a garden where leeks did grow, wearing leeks in their
Monmouth caps; which, your majesty know, to this hour is an

honourable badge of the service; and I do believe your majesty takes no scorn to wear the leek upon Saint Tavy's day."

For centuries the leek was the emblem of Wales and was worn as such on St. David's day. Thanks to the Agincourt legend it carries a flavor of romance as well as of onion.

Now, in our own time it has been pointed out that the Celtic word "Cenin" refers both to the leek and to the daffodil. It has also been noted that few leeks grow in northern Wales, while daffodils flourish abundantly. On the basis of this reasoning, and probably from a desire to replace a common vegetable with a pretty flower, daffodils are now often worn instead of leeks on St. David's day. But easier for Americans to see are postage stamps. The current English ones, as well as those of the reign of George VI, carry daffodils along with the English rose, the Scottish thistle and the Irish shamrock.

That sort of semiofficial recognition may well turn the narcissus eventually into a true national emblem.

No flower was ever so appropriately named as *Narcissus poeticus*. For not only is the poet's narcissus a part of Greek poetry but it has caught the imagination of countless poets in our own era.

It has even moved a number of unpoetic men to poetic expression. Mohammed advised those who had no more than two loaves of bread to sell one and buy "a flower of the Narcissus for bread is the food of the body, but Narcissus is the food of the soul." Cataloguing the flowers in his garden at Bettisfield, Sir Thomas Hanmer noted down, "Belle selmane narcissi, right dear ones." And who was the unknown rhymester whose gay couplet we all know so well,

> Daffy-down-dilly that came up to town
> In a yellow petticoat and a green gown?

Narcissus

For the English poets the narcissus was a golden daffodil, but that does not in the least alter the situation. White flower with a shallow red and yellow cup or yellow flower with a large yellow trumpet—and all the related species and varieties—all are narcissus, all have something of the same quality and all seem equally to have caught the imagination of poets.

A great many of the nineteenth-century authors who wrote about flowers and flower lore gave quotations for every flower they mentioned as if the quotation were a *sine qua non* of the subject. They seemed to feel that if they quoted Chaucer on the daisy or Herrick on the daffodil they must find at least one line of poetry for all the other flowers. Now there is no blinking the fact that some familiar flowers have moved few, if any, men to poetic expression in English: the peony, the foxglove and the tulip, to name just a few. So Shakespeare's "pioned banks" in *The Tempest* have been overworked and, failing more Shakespeare, quotations—even mere doggerel—have been combed to find an appropriate line. For that reason this book has shunned "the poets," as writers on flower lore invariably call them. But the narcissus sings as insistently through English poetry as it did through the Greek, so for it an exception is made herewith.

Chaucer spent all his floral "affecioun" on the daisy. At any rate, there is no mention of narcissus, daffodil, affodil or any of the other old names in the glossary. It seems to have been the Elizabethan poets who first brought the narcissus into English literature, not with the excitement about a new-found treasure as they did with the pink, but with the warm delight in something that was at once very familiar and very beautiful.

Shakespeare as usual said it best:

> Daffodils,
> That come before the swallow dares, and take
> The winds of March with beauty.

But he also caught the bucolic flavor that belonged to the wild flower of the English countryside:

> When Daffodils begin to peer,
> With heigh! the doxy o'er the dale
> Why, then comes in the sweet o' the year
> For the red blood reigns in the winter's pale.

A doxy was a beggar's wench and evidently the native flower that grew in such abundance was associated with the love-making of the common people. A contemporary of Shakespeare's, Michael Drayton, has left us an enchanting dialogue between two shepherds, too long to quote here in full but well worth a few words.

Batte, one shepherd, asks his friend Gorbo if he has seen Batte's sweetheart Daffodil as he was coming along. Teasing his friend, Gorbo deliberately misunderstands and persists in describing the flower. Finally Gorbo's native kindness overcomes his mischief and he admits that

> Through yonder vale as I did pass
> Descending from the hill,
> I met a smirking bonny lass;
> They call her Daffodil.

* * *

> And all the shepherds that were nigh
> From top of every hill
> Unto the valleys loud did cry;
> There goes sweet Daffodil!

Milton, of course, had his "daffodillies" that

> fill their cups with tears
> To strew the laureate hearse where Lycid lies.

The joyous gaiety of Elizabethan England was gone and in the grim aftermath that was James even the glowing yellow of the daffodil was associated with death. Herrick, a son of that time, loved his daffodils and used them often to remind himself and his readers that "we have short time to stay as you." Not many lyrics in the English language are lovelier than Herrick's *To Daffodils.*

The romantic poets have gone out of fashion now, but a few of us are still grateful to Wordsworth for his host of golden daffodils,

> Beside the lake, beneath the trees,
> Fluttering and dancing in the breeze.

And, to make an abrupt transition, to Amy Lowell, for her sharp and brittle picture of

> all the daffodils
> Are blowing and the bright blue squills.

But best of all the moderns is Masefield's simple line,

> April's in the west wind, and daffodils.

However, when one thinks of daffodils in poetry one comes back forever to Herrick. There can be no more appropriate ending for the story of the narcissus than the verses that Sir Edmund Gosse sent to a friend written on the flyleaf of a copy of Herrick's poems:

> Fresh with all airs of woodland brooks
>   And scents of showers,
> Take to your haunt of holy books
>   This saint of flowers.

> When meadows burn with budding May,
>   And heaven is blue
> Before his shrine our prayers we say,
>   Saint Robin blue.

Flower Chronicles

Love crowned with thorns is on his staff—
  Thorns of sweet briar;
His benediction is a laugh,
  Birds are his choir.

His sacred robe of white and red
  Unction distills;
He hath a nimbus 'round his head
  Of daffodils.

Narcissus and forget-me-nots in an iron window grill at Lunz, Austria.
(*Horticultural Society of New York*)

Bibliography

Cookbooks and Stillroom Books

Antiquitates Culinariae; or, Curious Tracts Relating to the culinary Affairs of the Old English (Ed. by the Rev. Richard Warner). London, 1791. Listed in *The Whitney Cookery Collection,* by Louis M. Stark. *Bulletin of the New York Public Library,* February, 1946. Second copy in the Helen Hay Whitney Collection, New York Public Library.

Apicius: *Cookery and Dining in Imperial Rome.* For the first time rendered into English by Joseph Dommers Vehling. Chicago: W. M. Hill, 1936.

Avery, Madam Susanna. *A Plain Plantain.* 1688. Reprint by The Herb Grower Press, Falls Village, Conn.

Book of Cookrye, A. Imprinted by Edward Allde at London, 1587.

Book of Fruits and Flowers, A. London, 1653.

Book of Simples, A. (Ed. by H. William Lewer). London: Low Marston & Co., 1908.

Noble Boke off Cookry, A., for a Prynce Houssolde or eny other estately Houssolde (Ed. by Mrs. Alexander Napier). London: E. Stock, 1882.

Digby, Sir Kenelm. *The Closet of Sir Kenelme Digby Knight Opened.* London, 1669. Reprint, Ed. by Philip Lee Warner, London, 1910.

289

Bibliography

Early English Recipes (With an Introduction by Sir Stephen Gaselee). Selected from the Harl. Ms. 279, about 1430. London: De la Mare Press, 1932.

Evelyn, John. *Acetaria; A Discourse of Sallets*. Reprint of 1699 edition by the Women's Auxiliary of the Brooklyn Botanic Garden, 1937.

Fairfax, Arabella. *The Family's Best Friend*. London, 1753.

Glasse, Hannah. *The Art of Cookery made Plain and Easy*. London, 1774. Dublin, 1791. Alexandria, 1805.

Good Hous-wiues Treasurie, The. Imprinted by Edward Allde at London, 1588.

Grey, Elizabeth, Countesse of Kent. *A Choice Manuall*. London, 1653, 1659.

Markham, Gervase. *The English House-Wife*. London, 1683.

Plat, Sir Hugh. *Delightes for Ladies*. London, 1609. Reprinted from the 1627 edition. Collated and ed. by Violet and Hal W. Trovillion. Herrin, Ill., 1939.

Rohde, Eleanour Sinclair. *Rose Recipes*. London: Routledge, 1939.

Two Fifteenth Century Cookery-Books (Ed. by Thomas Austin). London: N. Trübner & Co., 1888.

Woolley, Hannah. *The Queen-like Closet; or, Rich Cabinet* . . . London, 1684.

———— *The Gentlewomans Companion; or, A Guide to the Female Sex*. London, 1682.

Herbals and about Herbals

Arber, Agnes. *Herbals, Their Origin and Evolution* . . . 1470–1670. Cambridge (Eng.): University Press, 1912.

Banckes's Herbal. London: 1525. Second ed., 1526. Only known copy is in the Cambridge University Library. Many subsequent editions.

Bibliography

Brunswicke-Andrewe, Jerome of. *The Vertuose Boke of Distyllacyon.* London. 1527.

A Most Excellent Perfecte Homish Apothecarye . . . Collen Cologne), 1561.

Clarkson, Rosetta E. *Green Enchantment.* New York: Macmillan, 1940.

Cockayne, Thomas Oswald (ed.). *Leechdoms, Wortcunning, and Starcraft of Early England.* Published under the direction of the Master of the Rolls. London, 1864–1866.

Coles, William. *The Art of Simpling.* London, 1657. Reprinted, Milford, Conn., 1938.

Culpeper, Nicholas. *Culpeper's English Physician.* London, 1812 (Ed. by Virtue. London: Kelly, 1860.)

———— *English Physician and Complete Herbal.* Arranged for use as a first aid herbal by Mrs. C. F. Leyel. London: H. Joseph, 1947.

———— *Culpeper's Complete Herbal.* London: W. Foulsham, 1952.

Dioscorides. *The Greek Herbal of Dioscorides.* Englished by John Goodyer, A.D. 1655. Ed. and first printed by Robert T. Gunther, Oxford: University Press, 1933.

Dodoens-Lyte. *A New Herball or Historie of Plants.* London, 1619. This is Henry Lyte's translation of *Historie de plantes* (1557), which is Charles de L'Ecluse's translation into French of Rembert Dodoens' Kruyteboeck (1554).

Emmert, Emily Walcott (ed. and trans.). *The Badianus Manuscript. An Aztec Herbal of 1552.* Baltimore: Johns Hopkins Press, 1940.

Fernie, W. T. *Herbal Simples.* Philadelphia, 1897.

Gerard, John. *The Herball, or Generall Historie of Plantes.* London, 1597.

Gerard's Herball; the essence thereof distilled by Marcus Woodward. London: G. Howe, 1927.

Bibliography

Grieve, Mrs. Maud. *A Modern Herbal.* 2 vols. New York: Harcourt, Brace, 1931.

Leyel, Mrs. C. S. *Herbal Delights.* London: Faber & Faber, 1937.

——— *The Magic of Herbs.* London: J. Cape, 1926.

Lovell, Robert. Πανζωορυκλογια *A Complete History of Animals and Minerals.* Oxford, 1665.

Meyrick, William. *The New Family Herbal.* London, 1790.

Monardes, Nicholás. *Joyfull Newes out of the Newe Founde Worlde* (Trans.). Written in Spanish by Nicolás Monardes, physician of Seville, and Englished by John Frampton, Marchant, 1577. Modern edition published by Constable & Co., London, 1925.

Parkinson, John. *Paradisi in Sole Paradisus Terrestris.* London, 1629.

——— *Theatricum Botanicum:* The Theater of Plants, London, 1640.

Rohde, Eleanour Sinclair. *A Garden of Herbs.* London and Boston: P. L. Warner, 1920. London: H. Jenkins, Ltd., 1926 and 1933. Boston and New York: Hale, Cushman & Flint, 1936.

——— *The Old English Herbals.* London and New York: Longmans, Green & Co., 1922.

Salmon, William. *Botanologia, The English Herbal.* London, 1710.

"The Stockholm Manuscript." *Archaeologie, or Miscellaneous Tracts Relating to Antiquity.* Vol. XXX. Published by the Society of Antiquaries of London, 1844.

Thornton, Robert John. *A New Family Herbal.* London: R. Phillips, 1810.

Turner, Robert. βοτανολόγια. *The Brittish Physician; or, The Nature and Vertues of English Plants.* London, 1664.

Turner, William. *A New Herball. The first and seconde partes of the Herbal of Wm. Turner* Doctor in Physick lately oversene corrected and enlarged with the Third parte lately

Bibliography

gathered and nowe set out . . . Collen (Cologne), 1568. London, 1551–1568.

PHARMACY

Drewitt, F. Dawtrey. *The Romance of the Apothecaries' Garden at Chelsea*. London: Chapman & Dodd, 1922.

Lloyd, John Uri. *History of the Vegetable Drugs of the Pharmacopeia of the United States*. Cincinnati, Ohio: J. U. & C. G. Lloyd, 1911.

—— *Origin and History of all the Pharmacopeial Vegetable Drugs, Chemicals and Preparations*. Cincinnati, Ohio, 1921.

Netter, William. *Ancient Pharmacy and Medicine*. Translated from the German of Hermann Peters. Engelgard (no date).

The Pharmacopoea of the United States. 14th revision, 1950.

Wooten, A. C. *Chronicles of Pharmacy*. London: Macmillan & Co., 1910.

Youngken, Heber W. *A College Textbook of Pharmaceutical Botany*. Philadelphia: P. Blakiston's Son & Co., 1938.

MEDICINE

Browne, Edward G. *Arabian Medicine*. Cambridge (Eng.): University Press, 1921.

Clendening, Logan. *A Source Book of Medical History*. New York: Paul B. Hoeber, 1948.

Hippocrates. *Works* Trans. by Chadwick and Mann. Oxford: Blackwell Scientific Publications, 1950.

—— *Works* Trans. by E. T. Withington. Loeb Classical Library. London: Heinemann; New York: Putnam, 1931.

McKenzie, Dan. *The Infancy of Medicine*. London: Macmillan & Co., 1927.

Bibliography

Medical Works of the Fourteenth Century (Ed. by G. Henslow). London: Chapman & Hall, 1899.

The Papyrus Ebers. Trans. by B. Ebbell. London: H. Milford, 1937. Trans. from the German version by Cyril P. Bryan. New York: D. Appleton & Co., 1931.

The Physicians of Myddvai. Trans. by John Pughe. London, 1861. (A rare book, one copy of which is in the library of the New York Academy of Medicine.)

Sigerist, Henry E. *A History of Medicine.* New York: Oxford University Press, 1951.

Temkin, Owsei. *The Falling Sickness.* Baltimore: Johns Hopkins Press, 1945.

Thompson, C. J. S. *Magic and Healing.* London and New York: Rider, 1947.

Walsh, James J. *Medieval Medicine.* London: A. & C. Black, 1920.

ARCHAEOLOGY AND ANTIQUITY

Cambridge Ancient History (Ed. by J. B. Bury, M.A., F.B.A., S. A. Cook, Litt.D., and F. E. Alcock, M.A.). Cambridge (Eng.): University Press, 1925–1939.

Carter, Howard. *The Tomb of Tut-ankh-Amen.* London and New York, 1923.

Evans, Sir Arthur. *The Earlier Religion of Greece in the Light of Cretan Discoveries.* London: Macmillan & Co., 1931.

——— *The Palace of Minos.* London: Macmillan & Co., 1921–1935.

Moldenke, Harold N., and Alma L. *Plants of the Bible.* Waltham, Mass.: Chronica Botanica Co., 1952.

Olmstead, A. T. *History of Assyria.* New York and London: C. Scribner's Sons, 1923.

Theophrastus. *Enquiry into Plants.* Trans. by Sir Arthur Hort. New York: G. P. Putnam's Sons, 1916.

Bibliography

Thompson, R. Campbell. *The Assyrian Herbal*. London: Luzac & Co., 1924.

―――― *Assyrian Medican Texts*. London and New York: Oxford University Press, 1923.

THE LANGUAGE OF FLOWERS

Adams, H. G. *Flowers, their Moral, Language, and Poetry*. London: Clarke & Co., 1845.

Anon. *The Language of Flowers*. Philadelphia, 1835.

Anon. *The Language of Flowers, poetically expressed, a complete Flora's Album*. New York, 1847.

Bertram, James Glass. *The Language of Flowers: An alphabet of floral emblems*. London: T. Nelson & Sons, 1856.

Dumont, Henrietta. *The Language of Flowers. The Floral Offering*. Philadelphia: Peck & Bliss, 1851.

Ingram, John. *Flora Symbolica; or, The Language and Sentiment of Flowers. Including Floral Poetry, Original and Selected*. London: F. W. Warne & Co., 1869.

La Tour, Mme. Charlotte de. *Le Langage des Fleurs*. Paris, 18(?).

Montagu, Lady Mary Wortley. *Letters and Works*. (Ed. by Lord Wharncliffe). 2 vols. Rev. ed. London: G. Bell & Sons, 1887.

Phillips, Henry. *Floral Emblems*. London: Saunders & Otley, 1831.

Wirt, Mrs. E. W., of Virginia. *Flora's Dictionary*. Baltimore: Lucas Bros., 1855.

FOLKLORE

Allen, Grant. *Flowers and their Pedigrees*. New York: D. Appleton & Co., 1884.

Bibliography

Beals, Katherine. *Flower Lore and Legend*. New York: Henry Holt & Co., 1917.

Black, William George. *Folk-Medicine*. London: E. Stock, 1883.

Brand, John. *Observations on the Popular Antiquities of Great Britain*. London: H. G. Bohn, 1849.

Browne, William, of Tavistock. *Britannia's Pastorals*. 2 vols. London, 1616.

Bryant, Charles. *Flora Diætetica; or, History of Esculent Plants*. London, 1783.

Burnett, M. A. *Plantae Utiliores*. London: Whittaker & Co., 1842–1850.

Folkard, Richard. *Plant Lore, Legends, and Lyrics*. London: Low, Marston, etc., 1884.

Frazer, Sir James George. *The Golden Bough*. Abridged edition. New York, Macmillan, 1922.

Friend, Hilderic. *Flowers and Flower Lore*. London: W. S. Sonnenschein & Co., 1884.

Graves, Robert. *The Greek Myths*. 2 vols. London: Penguin Books, 1955.

Gubernatis, Angelo de. *La Mythologie des Plantes*. Paris: C. Leinwald et Cie, 1878–1882.

Hamilton, Edith. *Mythology*. Boston: Little, Brown & Co., 1942.

Pettigrew, Thomas J. *On Superstitions connected with the Practice of Medicine and Surgery*. Philadelphia: Barrington & Haswell, 1844.

Phillips, Henry. *Flora Historica*. 2 vols. London, 1824.

Standard Dictionary of Folklore, Mythology and Legend. New York: Funk & Wagnalls, 1950.

Thiselton-Dyer, T. F. *The Folk-Lore of Plants*. New York: D. Appleton & Co., 1889.

Thorpe, Benjamin. *Northern Mythology*. 3 vols. London: E. Lumley, 1851–1852.

Bibliography

Cosmetics and Perfumes

Barbe, Simon. *Le Perfumeur Royal*. Paris: A. S. Brunat, 1699.

Bertrand, C. F. *Le Parfumeur Impérial*. Paris: Brunot-Labbe, 1809.

Burbidge, F. W. *The Book of the Scented Garden*. London: J. Lane, 1923.

Lillie, Charles. *The British Perfumer*. London, 1822.

McDonald, Donald. *Sweet-Scented Flowers and Fragrant Leaves*. New York: C. Scribner's Sons, 1895.

Poucher, William A. *Perfumes, Cosmetics and Soaps*. New York: D. Van Nostrand Co., 1942.

Rimmel, Eugene. *The Book of Perfumes*. London: Chapman & Hall, 1867.

Sagarin, Edward. *The Science and Art of Perfumery*. New York: McGraw-Hill Book Co., 1945.

Sawer, J. Charles. *Odorographia, A Natural History of Raw Materials and Drugs used in the Perfume Industry*. London: Gurney & Jackson, 1892–1894.

Thompson, C. J. S. *The Mystery and Lure of Perfume*. Philadelphia: J. B. Lippincott Co., 1927.

Toilet of Flora. A Collection of Simple and Approved Methods of Preparing Perfumes. London, 1779.

Heraldry

Fox-Davies, Arthur Charles. *The Art of Heraldry*. An Encyclopaedia of Armory. London: T. C. and E. C. Jack, 1904.

Guillim, John. *A Display of Heraldrie*. London, 1611.

Lower, Mark Antony. *The Curiosities of Heraldry*. London: J. R. Smith, 1845.

Millington, Ellen J. *Heraldry in History, Poetry, and Romance*. London: Chapman and Hall, 1858.

Bibliography

Scott-Giles, C. Wilfrid. *Boutell's Heraldry*. London and New York: F. Warne, 1950.

———— *The Romance of Heraldry*. London, Dent; New York, Dutton, 1951.

Wade, W. Cecil. *The Symbolisms of Heraldry*. London: G. Redway, 1898.

Plant Hunters

Bartram, William, *Travels*. (Ed. by Mark Van Doren). New York: Barnes & Noble, 1940.

Cox, E. H. M. *Plant-Hunting in China*. London: Collins, 1945.

Darlington, William. *Memorials of John Bertram and Humphry Marshall*. Philadelphia: Lindsay & Blakiston, 1849.

David, Armand. *Abbé David's Diary*. Being an account of the French Naturalist's Journeys and Observations in China in the years 1866 to 1869. Trans. and ed. by Helen M. Fox. Cambridge, Mass.: Harvard Univ. Press, 1949.

Farrer, Reginald. *The Rainbow Bridge*. London: E. Arnold, 1921.

———— *On the Eaves of the World*. 2 vols. London: E. Arnold, 1917.

Fortune, Robert. *Three Years Wanderings in the Northern Provinces of China*. London: J. Murray, 1847.

———— *A Journey to the Tea Country of China*. London, 1852.

———— *Yedo [Tokyo] and Peking*. London, 1863.

Harvey, Athelston G. *Douglas of the Fir*. Cambridge: Harvard Univ. Press, 1947.

Ward, F. Kingdon. *The Romance of Plant Hunting*. London: E. Arnold & Co., 1924.

Wilson, Ernest Henry. *A Naturalist in Western China*. 2 vols. New York: Doubleday, Page & Co., 1913.

———— *Plant Hunters*. Boston: Stratford Co., 1927.

Bibliography

FLOWERS AND GARDENS

Blasdale, Walter C. *The Cultivated Species of Primula.* Berkeley: University of California Press, 1948.

Blunt, Wilfrid. *Tulipomania.* Harmondsworth, Middlesex (Eng.): Penguin Books, 1950.

Cannart d'Hamale, Frédéric. *Monographie Historique et Litteraire des Lis.* Malines: Ryckmanc-van Deuren, 1870.

Dykes, W. R. *A Handbook of Garden Irises.* London: M. Hopkinson, 1924.

———— *Notes on Tulip Species.* London: H. Jenkins, 1930.

Ellacombe, H. N. *The Plant-Lore and Garden-Craft of Shakespeare.* London: Satchell & Co., 1884.

Elwes, Henry John. *A Monograph of the Genus* Lilium. London, 1880.

Fox, Helen M. *Garden Cinderellas.* New York: Macmillan, 1928.

Gardener, "Mayster" John. "On a Fifteenth Century Treatise on Gardening." *Archaeologia, or Miscellaneous Tracts Relating to Antiquity.* Vol. LIV. Published by the Society of Antiquaries of London, 1894. Communicated by the Hon. Alicia M. Tyssen-Amherst.

Hall, Sir A. Daniel. *The Genus* Tulipa. London: Royal Horticultural Society, 1940.

[Hanmer, Sir Thomas.] *The Garden Book of Sir Thomas Hanmer.* London: G. Howe, 1933.

Harding, Mrs. Edward. *The Book of the Peony.* Philadelphia: J. B. Lippincott Co., 1917.

Hedrick, U. P. *A History of Horticulture in America to 1860.* New York: Oxford Univ. Press, 1950.

Hill, Sir John. *Eden: or, A Compleat Body of Gardening.* London, 1757.

Bibliography

Hogg, Thomas. *A Practical Treatise on the Culture of the Carnation, Pink, Auricula, Polyanthus, Ranunculus, Tulip, Hyacinth, Rose and Other Flowers*. London: Whittaker & Co., 1839.

Jacob, Rev. Joseph. *Tulips*. New York: F. A. Stokes, 1912.

Jekyll, Gertrude. *Lilies for English Gardens*. London: "Country Life." 1903.

Kent, Elizabeth. *Flora Domestica; or, The Portable Flower-Garden*. London, 1823.

[L'Ecluse, Charles de.] *A treatise on Tulips*, by Carolus Clusius. Translated and annotated by W. Van Dijk. Haarlem: Printed for the Associated Bulb Growers of Holland, 1951.

MacNeil, Alan and Esther. *Garden Lilies*. New York: Oxford Univ. Press, 1946.

MacWatt, John. *The Primulas of Europe*. New York: Scribner, 1923.

Marshall, W. E. *Consider the Lilies*. New York: W. E. Marshall & Co., 1927.

Miller, Philip. *The Gardeners Dictionary*. 7th ed. London, 1759.

Ramsbottom, J. *A Book of Roses*. Harmondsworth, Middlesex (Eng.) : Penguin Books, 1939.

Rockley, Alicia M., Baroness Cecil. *A History of Gardening in England*. New York: E. P. Dutton & Co., 1910.

Shepherd, Roy E. *History of the Rose*. New York: Macmillan, 1954.

Singleton, Esther. *The Shakespeare Garden*. New York: H. F. Payson, 1931.

Sitwell, Sacheverell. *Old Fashioned Flowers*. New York: Scribner, 1939.

Stager, Walter. *Tall Bearded Iris*. Sterling, Ill., 1922.

Taylor, Geoffrey. *The Victorian Flower Garden*. London: Skeffington, 1952.

Bibliography

Taylor, George M. *British Garden Flowers*. London: Collins, 1946.

———— *Old Fashioned Flowers*. London, 1946.

Wheelwright, Edith Grey. *The Physick Garden; Medicinal Plants and their History*. Boston: Houghton Mifflin Co., 1935.

Woodcock, Hubert B., and Stern, William Thomas. *Lilies of the World*. New York: Scribner, 1950.

Wright, Richardson. *The Story of Gardening*. New York: Dodd, Mead, 1934.

MISCELLANEOUS

Abrams, Meyer Howard. *The Milk of Paradise*. Cambridge, Mass.: Harvard Univ. Press, 1934.

Bartholomaeus Anglicus. *De proprietatibus rerum*. English Trans. by John of Trevisa, first pub. in Basle about 1470. Printed in London by Wynken de Worde, 1495 (?).

Burton, Robert. *The Anatomy of Melancholy*. London: G. Bell & Sons, 1926–1927.

Collis, Maurice. *Foreign Mud*. London: Faber & Faber, 1946; New York: Knopf, 1947.

Daubeny, Charles. *Lectures on Roman Husbandry*. Oxford: J. Wright, 1857.

De Quincey, Thomas. *The Confessions of an English Opium-Eater*. New York: E. P. Dutton, 1930.

Hawks, Ellison. *Pioneers of Plant Study*. New York and Toronto: Macmillan, 1928.

Hedrick, U. P. *Sturtevant's Notes on Edible Plants* (Ed. by U. P. H.). Albany, N. Y.: J. B. Lyon Co., 1919.

Peattie, Donald Culross. *Green Laurels*. New York: Simon & Schuster, 1936.

Bibliography

Pliny, *The Natural History of.* Trans. by John Bostock and
H. T. Riley. London: H. G. Bohn, 1855–1857.
Singer, Charles. *From Magic to Science.* New York: Boni &
Liveright, 1928.
Thompson, R. Campbell. *A Dictionary of Assyrian Botany.*
London: British Academy, 1949.